Contemporary Poetry

C000060680

smoke
STACK
BOOKS

For Miles and Kit, and their global brothers and sisters.

I need to speak about living room
where the land is not bullied and beaten into
a tombstone
I need to speak about living room
where the talk will take place in my language
I need to speak about living room
where my children will grow without horror.

June Jordan

The artist must elect to fight for Freedom or for Slavery.
I have made my choice.

Paul Robeson

SEEDS OF FIRE:
Contemporary Poetry from the *Other* USA

Edited by Jon Andersen

Published 2008
by

**STACK
BOOKS**

Smokestack Books
PO Box 408, Middlesbrough TS5 6WA
e-mail : info@smokestack-books.co.uk
www.smokestack-books.co.uk

Seeds of Fire:
Contemporary Poetry from the *Other* USA

Copyright remains with the authors
Introduction copyright Jon Andersen, 2007
Cover art: *Temporary Sanity*, by Mike Alewitz
Mural at the Roosevelt School,
New Brunswick, NJ, 1994 (Detail)
Original mural: approx 9' x 12'
Used by permission of the artist

Author photograph by Bob Smith

Printed by
EPW Print & Design Ltd

ISBN 0-9554028-2-4
New ISBN 978-0-9554028-2-1
Smokestack Books
gratefully acknowledges the support of
Middlesbrough Borough Council
and Arts Council North East

Smokestack Books is a member of
Independent Northern Publishers
www.northernpublishers.co.uk
and is represented by Inpress Ltd
www.inpressbooks.co.uk

Contents

Poetry

Like many other good things
Should be taken in small amounts
So keep this wonderful volume
In the car, so when you are
Stuck in traffic -
Or in the bathroom
When you are sitting
Or buy an extra copy
for the waiting room
of your favourite doctor's office
and it will be one more
of a hundred million reasons
there is still a world here
for our children's children

Pete Seeger

Introduction

Here, in the early years of the 21st century, we find ourselves trapped in a spiral of Total War, genocides, ecological catastrophes, murderous corporate policies, and staggering wealth propped up by staggering mass misery.

Americans are stereotyped, not undeservedly: we wear super-sized, star-spangled shades while crashing around in behemoth vehicles, totally incapable of comprehending or admitting our culpability in the planetary mess. Still, in recent years an increasing number of U.S. citizens have begun the work of sabotaging our patriotic force field and reaching out to the world. Two recent internationalist-minded role models for social action have been particularly audacious and inspiring. A young woman from Olympia, Washington named Rachel Corrie was crushed to death by an Israeli army bulldozer in March 2003 as she stood her ground, hoping to stop the destruction of another Palestinian home in Gaza. Efforts to crush her story in the U. S. have been only partly successful; Corrie quickly disappeared from mainstream media outlets, but her legacy has grown, as has awareness of Israeli crimes against humanity. Another brave woman, Cindy Sheehan, mother of a slain US soldier, continues to mince no words in her condemnation of an illegal war perpetrated and perpetuated by Democrats and Republicans alike. Unlike the political class she confronts, the only promise she's broken is that she would go away.

I have assembled this collection with the firm conviction that small acts count - even the act of writing (or reading) a poem. We must no longer abide the notion that poetry should limit itself to the creation of pleasant illusions or the exploration of isolated pain. The poems here suggest other ways of writing, other ways of *being*. While they display a range of poetic strategies and focal points, all, on some level, urge us on in exposing and resisting the full-spectrum dominance of US imperialism and global capitalism. After all, the best poems do not merely move us, but help *us* to move. And move we must.

Jon Andersen
Storrs, Connecticut, USA
July 2007

Fourth of July, 2002

Maysoun and Zuhair's flagless house
offers an oasis after the longest parade
through our small town.
At dinner Zuhair recalls his days as an Iraqi schoolboy
finding 150 varieties of dates. Maysoun says,
remember the names of just 15. He smiles,
closes his eyes, sweet words roll off his tongue:
Zehdi, Berhi, Braim, Teberzal, Ashresi.
Mudjul is really mujdul.
Everyone gets it wrong here. It means braided.
If you look at the mujdul, you will see it is braided.
I learn that there were 15 million date palms,
more trees than people in all Iraq—
until the war with Iran. Today they say
life is back to normal. Children
who don't get enough milk die.
Their Armenian guest looks into my eyes
with the tenderness of a lover:
 Arabs are a hospitable people--
you could go into any house and they would feed you.

Denise Abercrombie

Psalm for Distribution

Lord,
On 8th Street
Between 6th Avenue and Broadway
In Greenwich Village
There are enough shoe stores
With enough shoes
To make me wonder
Where there are shoeless people
On the earth.
Lord,
You have to fire the Angel
in charge of distribution.

Jack Agüeros

If I Live

Maybe someday I'll sit
creaky on the creaky porch
dispensing wisdom and warnings
no one understands -
my grandfather voice full of iron and irony
quoting Orwell's Benjamin:

'None of you has ever seen a dead donkey.'

Maybe I'll give in, give up
take up prayer and reruns.

But I'd rather stay impetuous and injured
than inured – better to screw decorum
than to have decorum screw me:

sit on my hands when my fists should be pumping the air?

No - even stooped and grey I'll keep sluffing off
their sprung nets and blindsides.
I'll keep saying that this is wrong,

it's wrong, it's practical and wrong,
it makes perfect economic sense and it's wrong
it's wrong, it's the law and the invisible hand,
it's brand new, cutting edge, scientifically feasible,
it's hot, it's the American way and it's blood-bath
wrong, it's beautiful and genocidal, it's hilarious
and bloated and wrong as an underwater corpse,
it's patriotic and wrong, it's wrong I'll yell
until they could just go ahead and kick themselves
                to death
for counting Grampa out
for making him this dangerous.

Jon Andersen

Bamboo Bridge

We cross the bridge, quietly.
The bathing girl does not see us
till we've stopped and gaped like fools.
There are no catcalls, whoops,
none of the things that soldiers do;
the most stupid of us is silent, rapt.
She might be fourteen or twenty,
sunk thigh deep in the green water,
her woman's pelt a glistening corkscrew,
a wonder, a wonder she is; I forgot.
For a moment we all hold the same thought,
that there is life in life and war is shit.
For a song we'd all go to the mountains,
eat pineapples, drink goat's milk,
find a girl like this, who cares
her teeth are stained with betel nut,
her hands as hard as feet.
If I can live another month it's over,
and so we think a single thought,
a bell's resonance.
And then she turns and sees us there,
sinks in the water, eyes full of hate;
the trance broken.
We move into the village on the other side.

Doug Anderson

Torturer's Apprentice

Almost a man now,
he used to shudder
when the old man
slipped hatpin under fingernail
but now he's got
the master's calm,
the seducer's whiskey drift
to ply his subject
to give up his neighbour, tease
from him how many,
where and when.
Next month he'll have his first,
no more dabbing the old man's brow
with a cool towel,
no more sopping up the blood,
spraying air-freshener
to mask the lingering stink
of fear and anguish.
They've saved a little nun
for him, some dear thing
who still believes
that deep down people
are good.
We don't have to do this, Sister,
he'll say,
like a doctor, like a priest,
like he who giveth more
than you ever wanted.
Tell me
what I want to know
and I'll send you to God
with a single bullet in the nape.
You do not want
to finish this poem.
You do not want
to know who writes the check.
You do not want to know the fugitive self

you've sent down there,
where people do those things.
Where people do those things.

     Doug Anderson

Hole

One morning they dig up the sidewalk and leave
No sign of the truck
only the large
dark shadow digging and digging
piling up sludge with a hand shovel
beside the only tree
Two o'clock I come by
and he's slumbering in the grass beside rat holes
Three and he's stretched across a jagged stone wall
folded hands tucked beneath one ear
a beautiful young boy smiling
not the heavy large shadow who can't breathe
Four-thirty and the August heat
takes one down here
He's pulled up an elbow joint
some three feet round
At seven I head home for the night
pass the fresh gravel mound
a soft footprint near the manhole
like the 'x' *abuelo* would place beside his name
all the years he couldn't write

Naomi Ayala

Vocabulary Test

Question 1: What is a statue?
But my fifth-grade students have never seen a statue.
The principal refuses to spend allotted monies for field trips —
Too many discipline problems, she says,
Here between two tough city housing projects.
These children need to focus on testing, she says.
Testing is what will give them future success.
One girl answers, 'A statue is something people build or buy.'
She recalls a vague reference in a textbook.
A boy answers, 'A statue is a big thing you can
Climb up in the head of,'
His uncle once went in the
Statue of Liberty, he remembers hearing once.
Most leave the answer blank.
They have never seen a statue. This is a test.
They are afraid of wrong answers.
Tests show how bad they are at
Everything in advance of trying for the first time.
Question 2: What is the arrow pointing to in this picture?
It is pointing to a suburban lawn.
The correct answer in the teacher's guide is 'lawn.'
But my students do not live in houses with lawns in front of
             them.
They are crammed into brick boxes
Barely big enough for their beds,
And there is grass for sale outside the elevator,
But not even a whole lawn of contraband grass.
There are patches of dying grass in the park,
But the park is too dangerous, even in the middle
Of the day, to go roll
Around on the green, and a barefoot walk
Would shoot used hypodermic needles in their toes.
Only one student, a prophet, answers:
'Other kids have this, maybe. We don't have this. This test is
             not fair.'

Anne Babson

Got Any Change?

Instead of this street with its wasted brothers Asleep on the
        corners So
the crackjackers Have to step over them with the cuss out
        laugh

Of the soon to be wasted Themselves.

Instead of this street

In a city, where aint nothin Pretty, but the people

Who keep on standing & really laughing &

actually underneath our night make love to each other even if they
        fight

A city ruled by a Negro

Ghoul, a sepia Lieutenant Nazi with license to fool, a Looney
        Tunes
coon, so skilled

At deception, everything he thinks Is a lie, and he has had his

Snoring altered to resemble Casual remarks

We are in New Ark, the BrickCity, Like I sd

Where only the people Are pretty

& they have a hell of a

time being that

Ruled by his dishonour, the May Whore Who has crowned

Hese'f Emperor, His Majesty The Rat.

Ghost Brain

In a rubber brown

'Black Man' costume Like TB spit.

He sick, always laughing

To cover the fact he has no face.

& Like post Dallas JFK look for his brain aint even a trace

So we have climbed the ladder to this, where white folks Seem to
recede to the margins of our pain, and their

Black substitutes are prostitutes and clinically insane.

We are being taught about classes and class struggle

& the people of whatever colour are not what they look like

but exactly how they act, a cold fact

We are in a city ruled by a mad nigger punk a Mobutu, Abacha

Backward petty bourgeois Heels and Scum

Who serve imperialism & Corporate rule,

Who hate Black People Any poor people

They are well made tools
We must overthrow

The negro asst. beasts Loathsome things

For whom evil is sexual release

Are they puppets? Ask them...

They'll tell you they aint no such thing They're just very
        very smart,
you know, They get to help the rulers pull their strings.

Negroes like Dull Jimmy, from the most backward

Sector of the black petty bourgeoisie, a millionaire slum
        lord on a
first name basis with international murderers and thieves.

When he leaves office, they'll find a lawn in the suburbs,
        where he
can stand a traitorous spook, grinning in stone.
        Immortalized by our
enemies as permanently useful

        Amiri Baraka

To Dance With Uranium

Uranium islands shadow the side of the hill.
There is no hill unworthy of our love.
There is no hill that is not home to someone.

If I were not dancing with uranium, would you dance with me?
You could dance with me wearing forks and spoons.

My dance tells of fields and streets and homes
no one can live in.
My dance tells of rivers flowing in five directions.
Uranium gives me this power to dance
without ever tiring.

What has a hole in the side of a word
got to do with what the word says?
What has the word 'uranium'
got to do with uranium?
How can a word ever take us
to the place where the word ends its conjuring?

At last, uranium will embrace you
just as you have invited it to.
At last, you will know what it is to dance
long after your body has stopped dancing.

This is not magic.
This is a dance you already know the steps to.

I draw a circle on the ground
so everything I say will be contained and not harm you.
One day the circle will break.
This is not magic.
It is the dance with uranium that awaits you.

John Bradley

The 'SHU': Special Housing Unit

'there was an old woman
she lived in a shoe'
   what did she do?

9/11   *no prisoner may speak to you*
        you may not speak to any prisoner
9/12   overheard voices
        there are terrorists here
         who are the terrorists?
        silence, everyone behind her door listens
9/14   a legal call
        small relief: it's political -- Washington --
         not something i did
9/17   no more calls
        no visits
        no mail
         until further notice

incommunicado
i hang from a winding string
   winding in this cocoon
i breathe deep
   the air isn't good here

(from outside the walls Susan yells
   you are not alone)
i breathe deeper

Sunday i get a radio: KPFA lifeline
   Sikhs dead, detainees disappeared
   political prisoners buried deeper
      incommunicado

i remember another September 11: Chile '73
   more than 3,000 dead
   tortured assassinated disappeared
      a CIA-supported coup

(the WTC bombers not-yet-born)
   many people there still mourn
let us mourn all the dead
and the soon-to-die

i worry about the prisoners
isolation sucks at the spirit
i am furious: inferred association
held hostage in place of men
   with u.s. weapons and CIA training
      an infernal joke
the puppet masters laugh

i laugh to stay sane
before i explode in irony's flame

we are hostages
   to blood-thirsty oil men
   ready to splatter deserts
      with daisy-cutters
their collateral damage
   dead mothers and children
   dead mother earth
      dead daisies

(hasn't this happened before?
      u.s. cavalry and smallpox blankets
      special forces and blanket bombing)

(Susan is back
   she taps on the wall: *you are not alone*)

i walk around the edges
   how many walk on edges?
      what edges do the Palestinians walk?

cold radiates whitewashed
   walls press against my edges
      suspend animation
      no butterflies to break out
      no silken thread to weave sweet dreams

panic rises in my throat
   thick white choking cold
so cold
      i swing hope on a thread
a transparent sliver it crashes
against the cinderblocks
     i drop
frozen chrysalis
cold into a coffin box

Marilyn Buck

Faneuil Hall

We come to Faneuil Hall,
where legendary meetings
were planned by U.S. revolutionaries
against the infamous British government.
Sam Adams spoke here,
our guide tells us,
and Hancock and Revere,
and one evening it was decided
to write the Articles
of Confederation.
We come to Faneuil Hall,
wide eyed, like refugees
from some greater disaster,
or like pilgrims
cast upon the beach,
searching for something,
a seed of fire
perhaps, or a glint
on the walnut tabletops
from our own
dubious future.
The question of slavery was tabled
for a future generation
and Paine spoke of a need for struggle
against the new lords
of America.
We come to Faneuil Hall,
pit stop on the long road,
wreckage of monopoly capital
littered all around us,
gaze up and wonder
at the gilded ceiling.
Troops opened fire
on the Whiskey Boys.
Paine moved to France.
Manifest Destiny up for grabs,
Hamilton landed the treasury.

Two centuries later
Faneuil Hall is still a political centre.
Community organizations meet here,
such as the Red Cross.
And to this day,
says our tour guide,
with a twinkle in his eye,
true to this tradition,Faneuil Hall is open for anyone
to hold public meetings --
as long as one doesn't
advocate the overthrow
of the U.S. government.

Christopher Butters

The Spark

He sits back in the chair as he reads
Kim's essay and calls it that swear word *reformist*.
Worlds collide as the Marxist guy
I uphold calls the woman I love
a reformist.
The clock ticks.
BAM.
BOOM.
SILENCE.
I could run out the door,
I could move like Ken to Minneapolis,
I could ditch the personal life,
I could shelve the politics,
but there must be a reason why Kim and I
have worked with each other
these years. There must be something
in this universe working itself out
through the chemistry of our minds and bodies.
My deepest instincts got me this far,
past the blur of schools, the black hole of
rock and roll, the haze over the White House,
the feeling something is rotten
in the state of Denmark,
my identification with the workers movement
after the debacle of the Vietnam War,
the long and winding road to where we are
this evening.
My deepest instincts are all I have
if I am to ever get
to where the children play with rabbits
in the sumac.
At the party she circulated amid
the usual transitional figures,
talking Johnny Rotten and the decade that failed,
but later that night after everyone left
in the porch behind the summer house
our bodies seemed to fit.

We have lived together ever since,
her Marge Piercy and my Karl Marx
hopelessly mixed together
in the bookshelf on East 6th Street
towards some unfathomable future synthesis.
Oh,
she is my apple blossom,
she is my bell that tolls,
she is my mocking bird
that howls it like it is,
she is my bridge over troubled water.
If our love grows and grows,
unlike some other flashes in the pan
I have become enamoured with,
I will be the happiest man on earth.
If she goes away
I will survive,
though it will be
a catastrophe.
Last night as the subway train lurched
to yet another halt
and the man on the garbled loudspeaker
announced we would be moving shortly,
a single spark could have ignited
the pent-up rage against the mayor,
the governor, the bankers
who take taxis.
A single spark.
The frazzled nerves.
The deadend jobs.
The gutted services.
The loops of rage.
The Blacks and Latinos exchanging glances
with all the casualness
of the very foundations of the earth shifting
or the first flutterings of a new coalition.
Then, just as suddenly as the train lurched
to a halt, the lights and power switched off,
it was so still you could hear a pin drop,
the silence and the darkness and the strange cameraderie,

the lights and power snapped back on again,
the motorman thrust the throttle forward,
and we began to move,
almost as if it were nothing,
we began to move,
through the ancient tunnel
towards the distant lights of Borough Hall
and of Carroll Street and of Fourth Avenue.
'Funny how quickly things can change,'
I thought later on,
sitting on my bed
in the dark.
The workers gazed down
from the world of their poster.
Outside the window the moon shone
through the branch of the gingko tree.
A single spark.
I sat and ate a stick of celery
and wondered what
everything meant.
Tonight, bounding
up the stairs in her purple sweatsuit
from the martial arts class,
Kim kissed me and she tasted like vitamins.

Christopher Butters

Global Inequalities

Chairperson of the board
is not digging for roots
in the shadows
There's no dying-of-hunger stare
              in the eyes of
Chief executive officer of petroleum
Somebody else is sinking into
spring freeze of the soil
Somebody else is evaporating
in dry wind of the famine
there's no severe drought of funding services
No military contractor is sitting
        in heat of a disappearing lake
No river is drying up
in kidneys of
        a minister of defence
Undersecretary of interior
        is not writing distress signals
              on toilet walls
Do you see refugee camp cooped up
              in head of
Vice president of municipal bonds
There's no food shortage
          in belly of
          a minister of agriculture
Chief economic advisors are
          addicted to diet pills
Banking committee members are
          suffering from obesity
Somebody else is sucking on dehydrated nipples
Somebody else is filling up on fly specks
The Bishops are not
          forcing themselves to eat bark
The security exchange commission members
              are sick from
          too many chocolate chip cookies

The treasury secretary
                    is not going around in circles
                              looking for grain
There's no desert growing in nose of
                    Supreme commander of justice
It's somebody else without weight
without blood without land
without a cloud cover of water on the face
It's somebody else
Always somebody else

Jayne Cortez

What's Your Take

If a two-headed goat pisses its
long piss of death for your
conversion into a free trade zone
If napalm is being buried in the ground
between tuner of concert pianos and
the pioneer of mathematical analysis
If the corporate terminology settles in
          your mouth like a sweatshop
If a hyena shows you how to eat yourself up
& the blowflies blow your way
& you become like shredded flesh on teeth of the IMF
          Watch out
You are in the globalization economic domination process
          Now what's your take
If the world's most potent drink comes from
juice of a festering sore called
institutionalized brutality
If the most extravagant treaty of abuse
sits like an occupying force on
broken body of an abandoned child
& if the political strategy is to be
          both covert & overt
at the same time   on the same level
& if intimidation becomes a patriotic
          theme song called Intimidation
& responsibility remains a potty-training session
for all those holding their tee tees & wee wees
& if a newborn baby comes out looking like
          2 pounds of soggy grapes
after a nuclear reactor meltdown
& if you find yourself radioactively depleted
invaded   bombed out   borderless   dislocated
delinked
          Watch out
You're in the globalization economic domination process
          Now what's your take

Jayne Cortez

The Sound of It

When my mother gave my father a back rub
in their bedroom, we had to turn up the TV
and behave. We offered to give him
back rubs. He claimed it wasn't the same.

I got engaged when I was nineteen. $300 ring
from the mall jeweller. When she went on vacation
with her family, I kept a pair of her panties
under the front seat of my car.

After we broke up, I could still talk her into a back rub
now and then, shamelessly invoking history
like some pompous prime minister. She disappeared
with an old friend of mine - not old enough, yeah....

My back gets a little sore just thinking about it.
My mother has steel rods in her back now.
She can't bend at the waist. They sleep
in separate rooms so they don't keep

each other up. I sold the ring for $50. The jeweller
said he was giving me a deal. That I'd paid for the setting,
not the gold. They'd melt it down, reuse the diamond.

My mother stored condoms in her jewellery box.
Once I unrolled them and called them 'finger gloves.'
I filled them with water at the sink. My mother
didn't say a word. She was cooking dinner.

It all melts down again, even the steel in my mother's
back. We are all still alive somewhere, metal detectors
going off as we step through our lives. I wish
they could still escape into that tiny room,

one bed squeaking. When I'm having back trouble,
the doctor tells me *backs are funny*, as if that explained
everything. *Rank your pain on a scale of one to ten.*

That girl is in her forties now, like me.
She had beautiful breasts, though I'm not sure
I ever told her so. They're called massages now -

perhaps that sounds more soothing. From behind,
I saw my parents hold hands last year, my mother
leaning against her cane with her other hand.
They were walking down a path toward a waterfall.

The sound of it drowned out everything.

Jim Daniels

Time, Temperature

for James Baldwin

1967, Detroit. My grandfather watches
tracer bullets zing past
his window. The National Guard's taken over
Lillibridge School on the corner.

    He remembers the strike at Packard
        when they promoted blacks,
        then the riots in `43,
        how the crowds gathered on Belle Isle
        just down the road, all the bloodshed
        just down the road.

On the phone with my father, he is saying *niggers*
and my father is saying *Dad* he is saying
Dad stay in the house, stay away from the window.

    My grandfather has his theories
      why they can't take the cold
      can't skate can't swim
      why they can't park their cars
      why grape's their favourite flavour
    why if you get bit by one with purple lips
    it will kill you.

My father shakes his head into thick air
saying *stay away, stay away*.
A drop of sweat hits the dirty kitchen floor.
Dad. *Dad*. My father's long sigh.
*

Eenie, meanie miney moe
catch a nigger by the toe
our toes wedged in a tight circle
to see who'd be It. My mother
wouldn't let us say *nigger*.

She said say *froggy*.
We said *froggy*. The other kids said
froggy?

She washed my mouth with soap.
Where did you hear that word?
I heard it everywhere. *Where?*
*

1967. 11, I climbed on the garage
with my father's camera. In the streaked photos
flocks of helicopters blotch the sky, nothing
like birds. I held on to the rough shingles
as the spinning blades roared above me.
Helicopters spilled guardsmen
onto the armoury lawn on 8 Mile Road,
the border between Detroit and Warren.

We lived on that edge. Sirens
wailed their crazy tune, no Motown Sound,
nothing we could dance to.

Fear of heights seemed more real
than what I heard on the radio, than rumours
panting on the street: *They're at Belmont.*
They're at Farwell Field.
They're crossing 8 Mile.

Getting up was easy. I needed help
getting down, my feet dangling in air,
the camera somersaulting down onto the grass.
*

8 Mile Road. 6 lanes wide. The long barbed
shout, pale slab, sizzling fuse.

I didn't know a black person til I was 19.
I could have almost shouted from my porch.
*

Nigger pile. Riding nigger.
Nigger pile on Tony. Nigger beard.
Nigger stompers. Nigger-rigged.
Nigger-lipped. Niggered up. Nigger pillows.
How far you have to chase that nigger
to get that shirt? A fight, a fight
a nigger and a white.

Should I explain the terms, include an index
and glossary? Do we all possess
such footnotes, filed, hidden, backward,
in code, watermarks revealed by light?

Plenty of words for hate around here.
Like Eskimos with snow, we have
our subtle distinctions.

No one can trace
all the secret white tunnels
or break the white code.
Invisible, white on white.
Squint and hope for the best.
*

1970. Roger Edwards, our new history teacher,
gave us roles to play: KKK members,
Black Panthers. I was Huey Newton.
I said *honky* and *pig* a lot.
I wore a black beret. We dressed in black,
took toy guns to class.

I learned a little about the burning fuse -
Bobby Seale, H. Rap Brown, Stokeley Carmichael.
If this town don't come around...
We knew our town hadn't, and how it burned.
Huey Newton walking into our class
would have turned us all to tin soldiers,
to brittle glass.

Roger taught us what he could
till the nuns fired him.
He played records by Lightning Hopkins,
Coltrane, such strangeness we wanted to like
because he liked it. He let us swear in class,
but he made us swear
not to say *nigger*.
*

Our fathers worked with their fathers
in factories in Detroit, Warren,
brought home their hate in greasy lunch pails:
better watch out for that nigger.
That's a nigger department.
Don't help that nigger
lazy nigger.

It spilled across the dinner tables,
through the muddy alleys,
across the concrete playgrounds,
into the schools, and we learned
our lessons well.
*

1974. Black students
from Pershing High two miles away
visited Fitzgerald, my school.
We asked them questions
in a room crowded with teachers
who prompted us in whispers.
So foreign even those translators couldn't help.
Stilted as a high-school play.
Someone took pictures for the yearbook.

They filled our halls with a flavour
foreign and pungent. Some new kind of cooking
I wasn't sure about.
The next day in class we sat glum
while a perky teacher preached brotherhood.
We knew better. *They only brought*
the nice ones, somebody said.
*

1975. I worked in a liquor store
where we didn't cash checks for blacks
but sold them booze and cigarettes.

A man held a gun to my head
where's your hiding place
where's your fuckin' hiding place?
I said we don't have a hiding place
he said motherfucker, everybody
got a hiding place
I said we took it to the bank
he said *I'm gonna kill you motherfucker*
where's your hiding place?

His gun brushed my temple.
We looked each other in the eye: no recognition.
He grabbed money from the register,
took off down 8 Mile. I reached down
and fingered the cigarette carton
filled with checks and twenties.
The boss called the cops.
Fingerprints on a can of Colt 45
and no clues or suspects.
Colt 45, I said, *figures*.
I flipped through the mug shot pages:
Some nigger, I said.
*

Carl the gun collector
handed out rifles to the neighbours
in '67 *just in case just in case*
they cross 8 Mile. *To protect*
our families and homes, he said.
The right to bear arms.
My father did not take one.

In 1974 under the threat of bussing
neighbours took pledges
put signs in their windows:
I will not send my kids.

I will keep my kids home.
My mother took no sign.

The Supreme Court ruled against
cross-district bussing.
Neighbours smiled archly
no thanks to you, as if my mother
was a scab in this union town.
*

My grandparents both got mugged
on their street. My grandmother bent
into a sad turtle in her chair,
dazed and afraid, black circles
deep under her eyes in the house
her parents built.

We ate early when they came over
so they could be home before dark.
The golden rule: home before dark.

My grandfather would not move,
spraying his hose on the fire
in the abandoned house next door,
buying up the vacant lots around him
ten bucks a piece.

They watched their one good television
in a living room lined with three broken ones
so they won't know which one to take.

9000 vacant lots in their old neighbourhood,
another 1000 homes empty and boarded up.

*There's only three things
wrong with blacks*, he said.
They lie, they steal, and they kill.
He did say *blacks*.
*

My grandfather loaded up his old Ford
with old baked goods from Sanders,
bruised fruit and vegetables, distributed
to the poor for Father Connors, the priest
from the church across the street.
St. Rose, razed now, just another vacant lot.

He fixed bikes for the black kids
on his street. Kids. Kids
were kids, the contradictions
rattling around his head,
as if he had separate brains
for theory and practice,
separate hearts.

Old man. All things harden inside him.
No way to explain generations
of prejudice, poverty and hunger,
bad schools and no hope, and hate,
no way to explain it.

In Detroit, it has always been a matter
of taking sides. *They*
drove us out of Detroit, he says.
*

My old neighbourhood in Warren
red-lined. Too close to 8 Mile.
Blacks moving in. Property values
plunging. *Shoulda sold years ago*,
a realtor said.

Old neighbours move out, refining their excuses.
Two streets over, a black family lines the curb
with boulders to keep cars off their lawn.
*

A black guy on the assembly line
offered to break my machine for me
accidentally. I nodded.

We stood together, not smiling
just breathing and waiting

waiting and resting
resting and sighing
sighing and nodding.

The nod. It's too easy
to say *That's the kind
of cooperation we need.
That's the kind of cooperation we need.*
*

Dogs growl. Women peek out curtains.
A black man is delivering circulars
on a hot August afternoon in 1968
surrounded by the echo of his own steps.
He is coming up our walk.
My mother opens the door, offers him iced tea.
I sit on the stoop, staring.
My mother leans against the bricks.
I can hear his throat swallowing
the cold tea. Little
is said and what is said
is said about the heat.
Thank you, he says. *Back to work.*

Hope your mom washed that glass good.
Something I will hear from time
to time. Not too loud or
too mean, but I will hear it.
*

1980. In the department store,
those foam packing chips that last forever
poured from an overhead funnel
into gift boxes full of vases, clocks, books,
ceramic dogs, martini glasses, china, silver.
To cushion and protect.

Kim's dark skin
surrounded by the white, white foam.
We worked in that blizzard together.
We leaned across the table toward each other
in the basement under the store
where all the black people worked,
along with me and another white kid.

We felt like robots down there,
filling and sealing. Till our eyes locked
in the hard stare of mannequins.
We ate lunch together
in the lounge. People talked.
It only took me a year to ask her out.
Dixie scowled. *What are you doing?*
This is Detroit you're talking about.

We went to a movie in my part of town
out for coffee in her part.
I can't remember what we saw
because I held her hand in the dark
and we were alone there just like
two white kids, or two black kids.

All night the stares bit into us
like tiny bugs we couldn't see.
Walking to the car, I squeezed
her hand into a fist.
I guess you have to be rich
to get away with it, she said
and maybe she was right.

Our own sizzling skins could not
our own good fire could not blend
or overwhelm or distract or soothe enough.
We were not rich enough or fast enough, fat enough
or thick-and-thin enough. We could not slam
our car doors loud enough to break the long stare.

At work the next day
the foam rained down between us.
It lay in heaps.
I couldn't look at her.
I grabbed two handfuls and squeezed:
nothing can destroy them.
*

I said *Some nigger robbed the store*
the white cops said *What else is new?*
The board tilts, and all the balls
roll into the same hole.

I felt bad, but I said it anyway.
My shrunken head, tiny eyes
sewn shut. There is no
immunization, no shot, no cure,
no pill, no magic, no saint,
no argument, no prophet,
no potion, no confession,
no gift, no miracle, no fucking miracle.

No.
*

Last summer, the dog next door
scared away two black kids
trying to break into my basement.
I saw them running away. A week later
the same two kids cased out a house
down the street. I stood at the door
watching, sweating, heart jumping.

I stepped out toward them. They said
You keep following us you gonna get hurt.
I said *I'm only trying to protect my property.*
They said *Listen man, you wanna get hurt?*

No, I don't want to get hurt.
Yes, I have property now,
an old house in this mixed neighbourhood.

Maybe I was afraid because they were black.
Maybe they were angry because I was white.
I tried to talk calmly but I know enough
about being stoned to know
they were stoned on something.

Everybody stoned on something -
stoned on history and hate.
Everybody got a hiding place.
*

Pressed flat to the shingles
a little afraid of the height
as the helicopters pass
a little afraid of the noise and sirens
a little afraid of blacks
and rumours and everything I don't understand:
why burn, why here?
*

1990. Waiting for the light at 8 Mile and I-75
I see a naked black man lunge between cars,
two cops chasing him, his feet slapping
hot cement in the silence of engines idling July heat
two cops chasing him down the road
between Detroit and Warren
between two hard places
and he is naked and soft and running
till the cops wrestle him to the ground
scraping his knees and chin.
I pass by as he lies there getting cuffed.
As he lies there.

He looks a little dazed. The cops lift him
by the cuffs and he stands, his arms
tight behind him. He looks a little stoned
a little stoned on something.
The cuffs cut into his wrists
but he barely flinches.
Even naked, he barely flinches.
Maybe his story is the story I want to tell.
But I do not know his story.

I do not know what he has done.
I am telling you everything I know.
*

Carl took his guns back
but they are there someplace.
I know Carl. His nose twitches
with the gunpowder of his own hate.

They are someplace.
*

I am trying to be naive.
It has come down to this.
Naive enough to keep from being rolled
into another bitter pill.

An open fire hydrant in hot August
after an afternoon game at Tiger Stadium.
I am walking toward my car.
A young black kid, maybe 6, is dancing
in his underwear in the cool spray
he is holding his wrists up toward the sky
as if to say *take me, take me like this*,
and I am so hot I join him
dancing too in my cut-offs and t-shirt

and I raise my arms above my head
thinking *yes, I would like to be taken like this*
and we dance under the same sun
and there is room enough for both of us
in the spray on Rosa Parks Boulevard
in Detroit in Michigan in America saying
take me take me under one big sun
that will take us, take us all,
in its own good time.

Jim Daniels

Over There

for Olga Cabral

Again, I return from the other world.

Sometimes you can see it from here,
through the blue doors of the sky....

Over there,
on the other side of this page,
are roofs for all to make love under,
and fires for all to share.
Every hand is guaranteed a wheel,
every restlessness a road.
And you are all there with me in that far country -
laughter and ladders in the harvest orchards,
a light enkindled on the shores of our skin,
and the long streets of poverty have ended,
like a poet's arguments,
in the sea.

Again, I return from the other world,
with my hands full of wind.

But I have seen the giant morning of that country,
brothers and sisters under the skin
of the sky, have breathed its free peace.
And I want us to arise
and go now,
together,
leaving our chains in the sea,
laughing on our way to that place
we have hunted since the first money drew blood.

Sometimes you can see it from here,
in the darkest angry eyes.

Robert Edwards

Stand

in memory of Rachel Corrie

How much courage does it take to stand
in front of a U.S. made bulldozer driven
by an Israeli soldier toward a Palestinian
doctor's house? As the blade is lowered,
as the treads grind and crunch over bricks
and stones, how much courage does it take
to plant your feet like an olive tree
at ground zero, to put the smoke of your flesh
against a hurricane of steel and say: *No.*
No more houses. No more.
How much courage does it take to hide
behind law and order, to drive a bulldozer
over an unarmed woman while joking soldiers
with machine guns guard your back, look on?
Who is tough enough to join hands and sing,
drowned out by tanks and helicopters? Who
believes in peace enough to speak against a gun,
to pick up a bullhorn against a bulldozer and stand
in the crosshairs of the combat zone, armed
only with hope? One by one, someone
always has the will of millions to hold out
an empty, trembling hand and say: *Stop...*
What kind of boot camp do you have to pass
to follow orders into murder, to back over
the woman you've just crushed into the sand,
to make sure the job is done? Brave soldier -
is this what heroes are made from in your army?
Leaping out of the television trenches
of the public relations machine come the generals,
splattered with medals of blood,
and trotting to heel: the spin doctors,
licking lies off their lips, with the courage to stand
in front of microphones, to say: We deeply regret
the death of Rachel Corrie, but
she jumped, she tripped, she fell, it was an accident,

so regrettable. We are investigating, but
why was this her fight? What was she doing there?
An accident. So regrettable. Like all
the regrettable accidents shot in the back
in self-defence or run over by bulldozers.
Who can stand to witness broken people sob
among the rubble and do nothing? *Whose fight*
       is this not?
The man who drove that bulldozer, the men
who guarded him, the man who gave the order,
the men who designed and built the lies
about her murder, the men who told the lies
to the dumb sponge of the Press, and those
who knew they were lies and said nothing:
cowards. Who, among the olive drab uniforms
of any army has the courage to take off
tanks, bulldozers, helicopters, armour plating,
Kevlar, Plexiglas, and laws, lay down their guns
and grenades, toss their helmet and stand
chin up in the ruins to look stone-faced survivors
in the eyes, ready to die for the right to oppress?
Pin your medals to the dust and stand
aside, at the foot of her grave, in the ocean
of her shadow, to study real courage under fire.
On March 16, 2003, Rachel Corrie stood
her ground, everyone's ground -- toweringly
defenceless, and a soldier driving a bulldozer
ran over her and killed her because she was
in the way. She was a 23 year old college student
from Olympia, Washington, who left the rain
and cedars for the desert and olives of Rafah, Israel.
She was a good kid.
She stood with the victims and died in their shoes.
She was braver than armies.

Robert Edwards

Alabanza: In Praise of Local 100

*for the 43 members of Hotel Employees and Restaurant
Employees Local 100, working at the Windows on the World
restaurant, who lost their lives in the attack on the World
Trade Centre*

Alabanza. Praise the cook with a shaven head
and a tattoo on his right shoulder that said *Oye,*
a blue-eyed Puerto Rican with people from Fajardo,
the harbour of pirates centuries ago.
Praise the lighthouse in Fajardo, candle
glimmering white to worship the dark saint of the sea.
Alabanza. Praise the cook's yellow Pirates cap
worn in the name of Roberto Clemente, his plane
that flamed into the ocean loaded with cans for Nicaragua,
for all the mouths chewing the ash of earthquakes.
Alabanza. Praise the kitchen radio, dial clicked
even before the dial on the oven, so that music and Spanish
rose before bread. Praise the bread. *Alabanza.*

Praise Manhattan from a hundred and seven flights up,
like Atlantis glimpsed through the windows of an ancient
             aquarium.
Praise the great windows where immigrants from the kitchen
could squint and almost see their world, hear the chant of
             nations:
Ecuador, México, Republica Dominicana,
Haiti, Yemen, Ghana, Bangladesh.
Alabanza. Praise the kitchen in the morning,
where the gas burned blue on every stove
and exhaust fans fired their diminutive propellers,
hands cracked eggs with quick thumbs
or sliced open cartons to build an altar of cans.
Alabanza. Praise the busboy's music, the chime-chime
of his dishes and silverware in the tub.

Alabanza. Praise the dish-dog, the dishwasher
who worked that morning because another dishwasher

could not stop coughing, or because he needed overtime
to pile the sacks of rice and beans for a family
floating away on some Caribbean island plagued by frogs.
Alabanza. Praise the waitress who heard the radio in the
>> kitchen
and sang to herself about a man gone. *Alabanza.*

After the thunder wilder than thunder,
after the shudder deep in the glass of the great windows,
after the radio stopped singing like a tree full of terrified
>> frogs,
after night burst the dam of day and flooded the kitchen,
for a time the stoves glowed in darkness, like the lighthouse
>> in Fajardo,
like a cook's soul. Soul I say, even if the dead cannot tell us
about the bristles of God's beard because God has no face,
soul I say, to name the smoke-beings flung in constellations
across the night sky of this city and cities to come.
Alabanza I say, even if God has no face.

Alabanza. When the war began, from Manhattan and Kabul
two constellations of smoke rose and drifted to each other,
mingling in icy air, and one said with an Afghan tongue:
Teach me to dance. We have no music here.
And the other said with a Spanish tongue:
I will teach you. Music is all we have.

>> *Martín Espada*

Federico's Ghost

The story is
that whole families of fruitpickers
still crept between the furrows
of the field at dusk,
when for reasons of whiskey or whatever
the cropduster plane sprayed anyway,
floating a pesticide drizzle
over the pickers
who thrashed like dark birds
in a glistening white net,
except for Federico,
a skinny boy who stood apart
in his own green row,
and, knowing the pilot
would not understand in Spanish
that he was the son of a whore,
instead jerked his arm
and thrust an obscene finger.

The pilot understood.
He circled the plane and sprayed again,
watching a fine gauze of poison
drift over the brown bodies
that cowered and scurried on the ground,
and aiming for Federico,
leaving the skin beneath his shirt
wet and blistered,
but still pumping his finger at the sky.

After Federico died,
rumours at the labour camp
told of tomatoes picked and smashed at night,
growers muttering of vandal children
or communists in camp,
first threatening to call Immigration,
then promising every Sunday off
if only the smashing of tomatoes would stop.

Still tomatoes were picked and squashed
in the dark,
and the old women in camp
said it was Frederico,
labouring after sundown
to cool the burns on his arms,
flinging tomatoes
at the cropduster
that hummed like a mosquito
lost in his ear
and kept his soul awake.

Martín Espada

General Pinochet at the Bookstore

Santiago, Chile, July 2004

The general's limo parked at the corner of San Diego street
and his bodyguards escorted him to the bookstore
called La Oportunidad, so he could browse
for rare works of history.

There were no bloody fingerprints left on the pages.
No books turned to ash at his touch.
He did not track the soil of mass graves on his shoes,
nor did his eyes glow red with a demon's heat.

Worse: His hands were scrubbed, and his eyes were blue,
and the dementia that raged in his head like a demon,
making the general's trial impossible, had disappeared.

Desaparecido: like thousands dead but not dead,
as the crowd reminded the general,
gathered outside the bookstore to jeer
when he scurried away with his bodyguards
so much smaller in person.

> *Martín Espada*

Revolutionary Spanish Lesson

Whenever my name
is mispronounced,
I want to buy a toy pistol,
put on dark sunglasses,
push my beret to an angle,
comb my beard to a point,
hijack a busload
of Republican tourists
from Wisconsin,
force them to chant
anti-American slogans
in Spanish,
and wait
for the bilingual SWAT team
to helicopter overhead,
begging me
to be reasonable

Martín Espada

Heading for Manhattan by Train

Elevated above Queens mist gathers
in the tree-line. Fifty years from now
this could be where the confusion dissipated and
the revolution knew itself - sky line beyond the river
hidden from view but flowing.
      I am a subway rider
in a green winter coat and navy blue pants
about to lead my comrade commuters in song

Savour the commuting activity
Propel the day like hives
The tunnel our fluid destiny
The track our iron sides

You'd be surprised how many people know this song.
You'll be surprised.

     Ed Friedman

Mao and Matisse

Matisse was no hedonist. He articulated ideas with pleasure.
Same with Mao, only he had a Long March.
Since he couldn't afford new fruit each day for his still-life
Matisse painted in a studio with no heat and the windows open.
The point being what?
Two legends of the 20th century
having almost nothing to do with each other.
One can shape a revolution for several billion people that in a
million tangible ways each day makes life better. Or you can
paint paintings, some good, some bad and some great, that
when people see them they'll remember that life is terrific to
look at and re-invent in each moment with magnificent shape
and colour. Wouldn't Mao have loved an Henri Matisse there in
his headquarters as he planned the final assault on Chiang
Kaishek's reactionary regime? Wouldn't Henri Matisse have
revelled in the discipline of the People's Liberation Army?
Probably not. Unless of course I was there to explain it to them.
'Mao? Henri? Isn't this an inspired moment of history?'

Ed Friedman

Arroz Poetica

I got news yesterday
from a friend of mine
that all people against the war should
send a bag of rice to George Bush,
& on the bag we should write,
'If your enemies are hungry, feed them.'

But to be perfectly clear,
my enemies are not hungry.
They are not standing in lines
for food, or stretching rations,
or waiting at the airports
to claim the pieces
of the bodies of their dead.
My enemies ride jets to parties.
They are not tied up in pens
in Guantanamo Bay. They are not
young children throwing rocks. My enemies eat
meats & vegetables at tables
in white houses where candles blaze, cast
shadows of crosses, & flowers.
They wear ball gowns & suits & rings
to talk of war in neat & folded languages
that will not stain their formal dinner clothes
or tousle their hair. They use words like 'casualties'
to speak of murder. They are not stripped down to skin
& made to stand barefoot in the cold or hot.
They do not lose their children to this war.
They do not lose their houses & their streets. They do not
come home to find their lamps broken.
They do not ever come home to find their families murdered
or disappeared or guns put at their faces.
Their children are not made to walk
a field of mines, exploding.

This is no wedding.
This is no feast.
I will not send George Bush rice, worked for rice
from my own kitchen
where it sits in a glass jar & I am transfixed
by the thousands of beautiful pieces
like a watcher at some homemade & dry
aquarium of grains, while the radio calls out
the local names of 2,000
US soldiers counted dead since March.
&, we all know it, there will always be more than
what's been counted. They will not say the names
of an Iraqi family trying to pass a checkpoint
in an old white van. A teenager caught out on some road
after curfew. The radio will go on, shouting
the names &, I promise you,
they will not call your name, Hassna
Ali Sabah, age 30, killed by a missile in Al-Bassra, or you,
Ibrahim Al-Yussuf, or the sons of Sa'id Shahish
on a farm outside of Baghdad, or Ibrahim, age 12,
as if your blood were any less red, as if the skins
that melted were any less skin, & the bones
that broke were any less bone,
as if your eradication were any less absolute, any less
eradication from this earth where you were
not a president or a military soldier.
& you will not ever walk home
again, or smell your mother's hair again,
or shake the date palm tree
or smell the sea
or hear the people singing at your wedding
or become old
or dream or breathe, or even pray or whistle,
& your tongue will be all gone or useless
& it will not ever say again or ask a question,
you, who were birthed once, & given milk,
& given names that mean: she is born at night,
happy, favourite daughter,
morning, heart, father of
a multitude.

Your name, I will have noticed
on a list collected by an Iraqi census of the dead,
because your name is the name of my own brother,
because your name is the Tigrinya word for 'tomorrow,'
because all my life I have wanted a farm,
because my students are 12, because I remember
when my sisters were 12. & I will not
have ever seen your eyes, & you will not
have ever seen my eyes
or the eyes of the ones who dropped the missiles,
or the eyes of the ones who ordered the missiles,
& the missiles have no eyes. You had no chance,
the way they fell on avenues & farms
& clocks & schoolchildren. There was no place for you
& so you burned. A bag of rice will not bring you back.
A poem cannot bring you. & although it is my promise here
to try to open every one of my windows, I cannot
imagine the intimacy with which
a life leaves its body, even then,
in detonation, when the skull is burst,
& the body's country of indivisible organs
flames into the everything. & even in
that quick departure as the life rushes on,
headlong or backwards, there must, must
be some singing as the hand waves 'be well'
to its other hand, goodbye;
& the ear belongs to the field now.
& we cannot separate the roof from the heart
from the trees that were there, standing.
& so it is, when I say 'night,'
it is your name I am calling,
when I say 'field,'
your thousand, thousand names,
your million names.

Aracelis Girmay

Ode to the Watermelon

It is June.

At El TaContento near 17th,
the cook slices clean
through the belly of a watermelon,
       Sandía, día santo!
& honey bees
grown in glistening temples
dance away from their sugary hives,
ants, in lines,
beetles, toward your red,
(if you are east, they are going east)
over & over,
toward your worldly luscious,
blushed fruit freckled with seeds.

Roadside, my obtuse pleasure,
under strings of lights,
a printed skirt, in grocery barrels,
above park grasses on Sunday afternoon
to the moan & dolorous moan
of swings.

Ripe conjugationer of water & sun,
your opening calls
even the birds to land.
& in Palestine,
where it is a crime to wave
the flag of Palestine in Palestine,
watermelon halves are raised
against Israeli troops
for the red, black, white, green
of Palestine. Forever,

I love you your colour hemmed
by rind. The blaring juke & wet of it.
Black seeds star red immense
as poppy fields,

white to outsing jasmine.
Again, all that green.

Sandía, día santo,
summer's holy earthly,
bandera of the ground,
language of fields,
even under a blade you swing
your quiet scent
in the pendulum of any gale.
Men bow their heads, open-mouthed,
to coax the sugar
from beneath your workdress.
Women lift you
to their teeth.
Sandía, día santo,
yours is a sweetness
to outlast slaughter:
Tongues will lose themselves inside you,
scattering seeds. All over,
the land will hum
with your wild,
raucous blooming.

Aracelis Girmay

Ride

Barrio Obrero, San Juan, Puerto Rico

I take the B9 from Viejo San Juan
through Santurce, down
into Barrio Obrero of doo-rags, cornrows,
brown skin, white skin.
Wide women scrub the counters
of bars & restaurants. Palo Viejo,
botellas de ron, shine diamond
in the park.

A little boy says *'Parmiso, Mrs., pero tu tiene la hora?'*

I think I hear him say *Let's take over the bus.*
I think I hear him say *Let's ride it into Banco Popular.*
Let's fill our bags, & build proper houses
with radios & speakers in all the rooms,
fans, mattresses, books,
refrigerators full of refrigerated foods.
For every car let's build a printing press,
libraries, gardens, schools
for all the people.

     Aracelis Girmay

Paying the Bills

By her tail 49 has dragged my dad
from the barn to the farmhouse porch.
He rests a minute, stands, dust
of the gravel drive rising
from the gulleys cut by his heels.
She is not stupid; she knows the smell
of slaughter on that trailer. In seconds
she'll kick at his ribs and sprint again,
yank him over the volted fence, away
through the corn to the chicken coop.
Who is more stubborn, more animal?
She in an hour will climb the ramp
in her heaviness, beaten, he in a year
will running, bucking, be hauled
to the suburb, the factory, torn
by his heels from his earth.
But for now, each other's simple danger, they
go tensing, Homeric, bound
in their clash to the dust they rile—
as if such strife could undo
their fortunes, could settle their debts
in the books of men.

Amy Groshek

Ipomoea Purpurea

The farmers revile the glorious flower
whose noxious vine reduces crop yield.
The resolute blossoms prosper

beyond the scientists' active favours
meant to rid the world of such discord -
the farmers so revile these glorious flowers.

I don't envy the researchers' herbicidal pressure,
though it's kept them in labs for a decade.
The resolute blossoms prosper

while the pertinent vegetables of farm labour
prove stunningly fragile in the fragile field.
The farmers revile the glorious flowers -

for others, the wild Ipomoea purpurea,
is not the strangler weed.
Although fundamental blossoms do prosper.

Who mourns the dying or the dead -
the fate of the proletarian seed?
I too curse the glorious flower
where parasitic vines rise in prayer.

Kimiko Hahn

from Blue Monody:
Blues for Thomas McGrath

And now the winds return,
blowing in from the sea,
driving summer steadily away,
south toward tall palms
we dreamed of when we were children
shivering in snows
that never ended.

And now these winds return
with frozen hands and laughter,
tormenting mountains,
twisting trees until you think
that like any human heart
they cannot bend farther
and will surely break.

I've kept my heart in my hands
through all these storms and seasons.
I've held it tight.
When the great trees bend
and their groans are almost human,
I've looked up more than once
from the desk where I invent a life,
looked up stunned
when they cried out,
thinking it a friend
arrived for comfort in the cold,
or my own harsh voice
grown suddenly old and fearful,
the fitful cry of a man whose name
was never counted among the names
of the innocent
and now must face the winter.

I've held my heart
in my hands and pushed
my breath across it
to blow the snow away.

Travelling, travelling, I've learned
a few exotic names
and places where great deaths occurred,
where the lonely
are buried in their trenches,
in mass graves which couldn't
under all that earth, disguise
the misery carved
into ordinary faces.

The winds continue to grieve
although the dead ask nothing
from us now. And nothing
is what we gave: I've held tight
to this heart I could not break
like an egg to eat.
The wounds, the wounds I bore
were not my own,
but this hunger is all mine.
These trees, defeated by the wind,
endure: they cling to the earth
and won't let go
despite sea-winds drumming blows

      *

Down in the bay, the old wharf
slowly crumbles,
grey wood bleached almost white,
huge timbers ruptured.
Homer thought a field of lovely asphodels
would mark the homelands
of the dead, but we know
differently, having seen
those faces rising from the sea
a thousand times or more,
their own chewed hearts
rotting in their hands, each
marching slowly inland
with his broken oar.

No matter how far inland
we may stray,
we can't escape the sea.
Each heart longs to be
Odysseus, to bear its wounds
forthrightly,
long enough not to survive,
but to embrace,
if only once again,
Penelope. Here
on a gnarled coast, winds play
cruel jokes, twisting trees
into almost human forms
reminding us of nothing
so much as our own brutality.

Cold September winds blow in from the stormy sea.
I've got my heart in my hands again.

If you pass by, do not think that I
am not afraid.
Winds will drive me down beneath the waves,
under ravaged trees I cannot save.
They are neither laurel nor myrtle;
nor am I
a Milton;
nor you
a Lycidas,
nor dead.

Here is the wreckage of a heart:
take it from my hands.
No one understands
the winds or the sea. We mourn because
we are alive. I give you this monody.

Sam Hamill

No

Yes that was me you saw shaking with bravery, with a
government issued rifle on my back. I'm sorry I could not
greet you as you deserved, my relative.

They were not my tears. I have a reservoir inside. They will
be cried by my sons, my daughters if I can't learn how to turn
tears to stone.

Yes, that was me standing in the back door of the house in the
alley, with fresh corn and bread for the neighbours.

I did not foresee the flood of blood. How they would forget
our friendship, would return to kill me and the babies.

Yes, that was me whirling on the dance floor. We made such a
racket with all that joy. I loved the whole world in that silly music.

I did not realize the terrible dance in the staccato of bullets.

Yes. I smelled the burning grease of corpses. And like a fool
I expected our words might rise up and jam the artillery in the
hands of dictators.

We had to keep going. We sang our grief to clean the air of
turbulent spirits.

Yes, I did see the terrible black clouds as I cooked dinner.
And the messages of the dying spelled there in the ashy sunset.
Every one addressed: 'mother'.

There was nothing about it in the news. Everything was the
same. Unemployment was up. Another queen crowned with
flowers. Then there were the sports scores.

Yes, the distance was great between your country and mine.
Yet our children played in the path between our houses.

No. We had no quarrel with each other.

Joy Harjo

A Story of Ash

All that was left was a box of grey crumbs.
A little box
such as one might use for pencils
or to save old letters.
Such a small box to hold the remains of a man.
On the day of the funeral,
they strapped the box to his bicycle
and it marched right with us
through the streets
Then, after the speeches, prayers, and song,
there was a quiet time
when those who loved him most closely
took the box of ash
and spooned the granules of cinder
into the places he most favoured,
the park, the alley, the garden,
and the yard of the homeless shelter.
And I imagine that,
among those who most closely loved him,
one had a thought
to place a pinch of cinder on her tongue.
What a power that might give!
But ash is bitter.
I do not think she did so.
They scattered the ash
into the grass of each place,
and it drifted down to the hardened earth
to rest among the broken glass
dried blood
bones of moles
lost buttons
fragments of torn letters
the roots of the grass
and the hidden bones of the uncasketed poor.

Michael Henson

Haiti

One day in the future these sounds are seeds of,
there will be a moment when not even the monkeys chirp in the
trees,
when burros will hold their brays,
when the coconut-milky clouds will not stir in the sky,
when the thatchwork of huts will not be gossiping
and there is no breeze or sweat between your body and your rags.
One day when that moment lived for years, for centuries, is here
and everything is still
like death
or zombie bread holding its breath,
a drum will begin sounding
and then another and another, multiplying,
and the voices of the simidors will be heard in every field.
And the backs, those backs with everything written on them,
which have bent like nails hammered into the wooden cross
of the land for ages,
will plunge their arms into the ground
and pull out the weapons they've planted.
For the drums aren't an invitation to a voodoo ceremony.
The voices of the simidors are singing another song.
The lambis are growling lions of Africa.
And it isn't the cranium of a horse hung on the wooden cross
braided with limes;
it isn't a wooden cross at all that's planted in the good earth
of new Haiti.

On the night of that day the taste of a mango will be
a rapturous fireworks bursting and dying into
the ecstasy of the simple truth in our mouths.
Our acres will sleep with their arms round each other.
The child free from terror and death will bound with
the boundless, and the maize amaze the sky upon waking
for as long as humanity is.

Jack Hirschman

Human Interlude

for Terry Garvin

She was standing against
        the wall near
the Tevere Hotel holding
        a plastic cup
as it began to rain.

I dug for a coin, walked
        up to her
and dropped it in.
        It fell to the bottom
of an orange drink.

I blushed, looked into her
        ravaged eyes and skin
                and hair prematurely
greying, and said
I was sorry, I'd thought

she needed some bread.
        'I do,' she said
and smiled, 'I was
        just having a little
                drink.'

And we stood there
        laughing together
as we watched the raindrops fall
        on the orange lake
above the drowning money.

Jack Hirschman

Youknowwomsayin

How many sons and daughters
of all the hundreds of men and women in Congress
are fighting in Iraq? Two.
Well, it's a volunteer army
and the men and women in Congress, what with
deals and private investments,
are pretty much all of them millionaires. Youknowomsayin.
Their kids don't have to take
a military wash because they're dirtied up
with racist slurs, riddled with fear of jail,
hounded by poverty, like the 20 per cent
of African-Americans in the armed forces
(African-Americans represent only
12 per cent of the population),
or the heavy per cent of Latinos
and poor whites as well, taking orders,
doing a job on a country half of whose people
are children 15 years old and younger.
Youknowomsayin.
And I'm supposed to feel patriotic
and embrace this push for planetary domination
on the part of that junta of deaths-heads
that daily floats its moral abominations
on the channels of our despair?
Nuclear fear's brought God back from the dead,
and Holy Wars look each other in their lies,
while children here and children there
are ravaged to the roots of their still possibly
innocent smiles.
In their little heads, in their doorways and beds,
they wish they may, they wish they might
bury you, you killer squirt,
for all the children that you've hurt,
and they'll throw happy dirt on your corpse,
Mr. President. Youknowomsayin!

Jack Hirschman

A Jew in New York

Like everybody else, I wasn't a Jew
Until I came to New York. In Portland, OR,
The other day, a young Latina asked me
If I were Jewyorican. Papa and Bubby
Came from Ukraine, landed in Brooklyn,
Settled in Harlan, KY, and named my father
Benjamin Franklin. My mother, the offspring
Of a coalminer, married Ben, the only Jew
In town. He didn't last. Ma remarried.
In kindergarten, in Cincinnati, instead
Of moving to the afternoon session the second

Semester, I stayed in Morning and changed my name.
This is the year 5755. In Chinese it is Year
Of the Dog. I just learned that the time between
Rosh Hashanah (Jewish New Year) and Yom Kippur
(Day of Atonement) are the Days of Awe. Moody
And grey, with dashes of absolute clarity, I love
These days. Cleansing summer's sweat from the streets
Of New York, I always think of the year beginning in
September. 'That's when school starts.' A holdover
from Youth. This year, for the first time, woo,
It's the real New Year, and I am a real Jew.
A real Jew, and a real coalminer's son, too.

Bob Holman

Leena

One day, there was a girl named Leena
she journeyed to the outskirts of her medina
the sun shined to squint her eyes
she watched floating clouds
and the mountains that gave rise
as she walked she paid no attention
to her footsteps' direction
reflecting
on the soaring birds
their wings moved in forms like the Arabic words
that she studied forever
suddenly a bird dropped a feather
to descend from heaven
Leena was age eleven
like the feather she was also very thin
she ran to catch it, every step in connection
to the feather's motion
it was a blessing
without expecting, she tripped and fell in
a bushel of barbed wiring
she felt the stings and the pain burn like a fire in
a drop of blood fell from her thigh
soaked in the ground
she began to cry
not because of her bruises and cuts
she was trying to figure out where the feather was
the birds flocked
and the rocks sat there and thought
about the hope Leena's single drop of blood brought
She's a Palestinian
her blood says to them
reminding the earth
that one day soon it would be free again
Israel needs to take a look in a mirror
they're doing wrong and it can't get any clearer
They started this by moving Palestinian homes
as the descendants of the former residents

fight with stones
against tanks in refugee camps
Let me shed light on the situation like a lamp
In case you didn't know the Palestinian fate is pending
Israel was founded on Ethnic Cleansing
or Transfer as their leaders like to call it
a sanitized term for these alcoholic
drunk on power like degenerates who run FOX
we need to uprise to send the fools to detox
we need to show the time they stole from our clocks
all the hours on the land was taken by an Israeli man
Israel was founded on taking land
In 1948 they had a master plan
called Dalet, they moved as a hand
to remove Arabs like they were just peas in a can
If you don't understand the Palestinians, at least recognize
this
what we suffered was a major injustice

Iron Sheik

Exile's Return

December, 1919. When Emma Goldman
was deported for 'hysterically' agitating for peace,
did she see this as the ultimate irony?
From now on her life's in reverse.
She exits the Court for Ellis Island,
the *Buford* chugs down the East
River like a tired-out worker,
past Our Lady of Exiles.
Steams toward Long Island Sound
and the nauseous Atlantic, onto Mother
Russia and to Lenin's dull rhetoric.
What did she do to provoke
the Eagle and the Bear?
In truth, she'll miss 'her America'
as much as her womanizing lovers,
in spite of the Bosses, Warmongers,
hard work beyond belief.
Only in death will they allow
her back in the *Imperium*.
She's buried in Chicago near the 'legally'
lynched Haymarket Anarchists.

Maggie Jaffe

Poverty Sucks

'We have the right
not to know about the poor,'
my student wrote
after I showed the class
photos of people working,
specifically a Haitian cane-cutter,
propped up on his scythe, dead
asleep on his feet.
This particular cane-cutter
earns 5 *gourdes* for 10 hours,
(approximately one dollar a day).
With luck he'll live to be 54:
in Haiti the sun is boss
as well as the bosses.
My student vacations in the Bahamas,
sips his *Cuba Libre*,
eyes the girls, tans, doesn't see
the sweating Blacks.
Has never seen anyone sweat
at work: not on TV, in videos, in movies.
I should give him no more than a '**D**'
(as in **d**ollars **d**isseminate **d**eath)
but he still wouldn't **get** it:
that a man can be so broke
he falls asleep on his feet.

Maggie Jaffe

The Homeless

At a Jewish wedding
the groom smashes a wine glass
under his heel
not as I once thought to signify
the hymen shattered at a stroke
but to recall
amid merrymaking
the destruction of the Temple
and centuries of the Diaspora
ending at barbed wire.

As I paint my house,
focused on the wood grain
under each horizontal
stroke, I see refugees
lining documentary footage;
the camera pans quickly
but the faces are endless, alike,
dark; on the horizon
the glare of flames, famine.

This stroke of luck
I learned as a wartime child:
to be born here
and in a small slip of time
while children just like me
were gassed and burned
out of less lucky houses.
I called my left fist Hagar
and tortured it to cry.

I know my house both temporary
and well chosen: in the fireplace
only logs burn.
Once we were slaves in Egypt
my grandfather said,
which meant suffering for others,
subdued rejoicing.

Joan Joffe Hall

The Monster's Belly

for Ernesto Cardenal

In the epic drought of my growing years,
I practiced leaping under my desk
to survive the rain of Cuban bombs.
I learned to kneel on a splintered floor
and with the carnal fervour
of a body aching from boredom and tortured knees,
to pray to God that the Communists
wouldn't come, and make us stop praying.

Now, Father, Ernesto, I find you were there all along
with the monks at the Gethsemani, Kentucky.
I could have walked there
in my blunt shoes, could have visited you
and your laughing Lord who made the best rain fall
on beans and rice. What a difference
to have known this Lord, or at least to know
he shared the same small sky with mine, who promised only
that the horned and headed monster
would come out of the sea
for the purpose of ending the world.
In your dark shirt smelling of leaves,
I would empty out the ache of my natural childhood
to find some greater love than the end of the world.

But the roads I knew were lost at the edge of town
in willow forests of apprehension. You and I
were no closer than the living and the dead
who share a cemetery on a Sunday afternoon.
Father Ernesto, you were a citizen of the domain
of your profound desire to kill the monster,
and I was already in its belly.

Barbara Kingsolver

A Song for the Santee

'On the day after Christmas 1862, 38 Santee warriors were brought to a specially built gallows and hanged simultaneously. "As the platform fell," reported an eyewitness, "There was one not loud, but prolonged cheer from the soldiery and citizens." The death penalty had been sustained by President Lincoln.'
(Benjamin Capps, *The Indians*)

Jesus
my sweet saviour Jesus
I
was a good
brown-skinned
Minnesota
farmer
who wore
a suit
to church.
I
was ready
to take
America
for my wife
until I saw
the false pride
of the home hearth
and the dull warmth
of lamplight
when she bent
toward the hanging tree
and made purple
tongued
fruits
of my people.

Adrian C. Louis

Another Day in the English Dept.
(or Meet me at Medicine Tail Coulee)

for Steve Pacheco

'Let Bacchus' sons be not dismayed
But join with me each jovial blade
Come, drink and sing and lend your aid
To help me with the chorus.'
(From *Garry Owen*, unofficial marching song of Custer's 7th)

There's this supremely blond kid from Fargo, North Dakota in
class who tells my two Indian students that their poems whine
too much! I'm just barely going through the motions of
metaphor and rhyme, but when he says that, I twitch and
wonder if an iceberg of Haight Street acid has broken loose
from some ancient mooring and is now coursing my veins. I
secretly pinch my thigh and remind myself that I am indeed in
Morlock, Minnesota. Then the white kid says, 'you Indians
should be thankful you weren't all massacred.' Damn! This
(Stick a needle in my eye!) is what he says: You Indians
should be thankful you weren't all massacred!' I'm breathless
because he's not using one iota of irony. I call a ten-minute
recess and retreat to the nearest exit to smoke a smoke....

If this were a poem I could contrive some witty comeuppance
where at the conclusion of this tale I slap an ounce of sense
into the junior storm trooper. An ending where truth and
justice triumphs is so immaculately American, but my life is
not a poem, and this is only a brief bookmark in the trudging
tale of a middle-aged half-breed.

After class, I'm filled with guilt, shame, and impotence, so I
take the young *Dakotapi* out and buy them some Grain Belt
beers at the Legion bar. There is silence until the third round
arrives. Then I shake my head and tell them that this is a very
strange and screwed-up *wasicu* town. They say, 'Ayyyy.' I tell
them I am sorry that they had to endure this, but they know I

know they know and all the rest of this horseshit nation
knows: *The white man is still in deep psychic turmoil for
stealing our land and calling themselves Christians at the
same time.* They nod their heads and drink. One of the
young Skins says, 'Hey, we should be thankful we weren't
... all massacred!' and we howl deep NDN laughs and
ignore the golden poison glazing on our souls. We drink and
talk until closing time when the full moon night brightens
our once-dying eyes.

Adrian C. Louis

fillmo'e street woman

she is a dark woman
treading water
in a life of hard choices.
wrong decisions
limited alternatives
stockpens are embedded
in her eyes and mouth.

once she knew she was beautiful.

if you look closely
you can still feel
the edges of the fire that burned
in her eyes, on her skin
in the way her back arched
across fillmo'e street corners.

she wore her nails
sculpted in red
in those days
when that street
when this street
was ours

she sat on a barstool
snapped her fingers
and hunched her shoulders
as smoke rose between
a bandstand and counter
and the scene
got hot and sultry
and the music
pressed out the doors
and down the street.

further down
she slid in at jacks

had another cigarette lit,
flashed her teeth, laughed
as the club spun tight
shoulder to shoulder
thick smoke and blaring saxophone.

then she checked in with minnie,
bought a pitcher of beer and half-way
listened to some crazy poets
chant a continent of promises
with congo drum and shakere
punctuating the rhythms
and a flute solo
bursting out over
the tastiest of love poems

maybe, maybe
she slipped into connies
for some curried goat and coconut bread
or sweated spices next door
as leonard pulled another
sweet potato pie
out the oven and poured
his brown-red biting sauce
over smoking tender ribs
telling stories
as she savoured another mouthful
then, when the street was ours.

she can see those days.
she knows them.
she remembers before, before
imported cheese
before brandy filled truffles
before double lattes
hand-made paper cards.

she sits on the iron rimmed
privately owned bench

to rest her feet
and take the pinch
out of her back.
she holds the bitter in her mouth
sometimes spits it out at passer-by,
with steel in her stare,
there on that bench
on that corner
on that block
on that street
that was ours, that was hers
that was taken, that we let go
that is lost, that was fillmo'e
when the streets held the people
and the musicians had names
and the rhythm was blues,
and the downbeat was jazz
and the colour
was black and fierce
like her.

devorah major

political poem

what makes a poem revolutionary
does it violently refuse the page
construct a chaos of grammar
that denies metaphor or defeats meter
is it armed and ready for prolonged struggle
is it loud and insistent assaulting your senses
full of gun powder and iron pellets
is it unavailable for canonization
despite an early death as martyr
or does it instead
find guerrilla survival
hidden
underground
exploding in unexpected places
appearing once again   just
when you thought it dead

devorah major

Elm Street, October 1977

Up the sidewalks we went together mornings
under the elms, along picket fences
from our temporary too-expensive
rented quarters: first grade, third grade

children of divorce. I met with their teachers,
pushing my weight of loss before me
like a bus I wasn't licensed to drive:
a pound a day it was taking. Hallowe'en

I walked the charcoal streets between them,
so small I wore a costume, too.
Real women opened their doors onto foyers,

music, flowers, - homes that petalled
out from them like safe places -
and lavished us with what we could not
buy. Door after door like their father's

I took them away from, the light following
just to the foot of the stairs. A hundred
times that night I took their hands
and drew them with me back into the darkness.

Linda McCarriston

Le Coursier de Jeanne d'Arc

You know that they burned her horse
before her. Though it is not recorded,
you know that they burned her Percheron
first, before her eyes, because you

know that story, so old that story,
the routine story, carried to its
extreme, of the cruelty that can make
of what a woman hears a *silence*,

that can make of what a woman sees
a *lie*. She had no son for them to burn,
for them to take from her in the world
not of her making and put to its pyre,

so they layered a greater one in front of
where she was staked to her own -
as you have seen her pictured sometimes,
her eyes raised to the sky. But they were

not raised. This is yet one of their lies.
They were not closed. Though her hands
were bound behind her, and her feet were
bound deep in what would become fire,

she watched. Of greenwood stakes
head-high and thicker than a man's waist
they laced the narrow corral that would not
burn until flesh had burned, until

bone was burning, and laid it thick
with tinder-fatted wicks and sulphur,
kindling and logs - and ran a ramp
up to its height from where the grey horse

waited, his dapples making of his flesh
a living metal, layers of life
through which the light shone out
in places as it seems to through the flesh

of certain fish, a light she knew
as purest, coming, like that, from within.
Not flinching, not praying, she looked
the last time on the body she knew

better than the flesh of any man, or child,
or woman, having long since left the lap
of her mother - the chest with its
perfect plates of muscles, the neck

with its perfect, prow-like curve,
the hindquarters' - pistons - powerful cleft
pennoned with the silk of his tail.
Having ridden as they did together

- those places, that hard, that long -
their eyes found easiest that day
the way to each other, their bodies
wedded in a sacrament unmediated

by man. With fire they drove him
up the ramp and off into the pyre
and tossed the flame in with him.
This was the last chance they gave her

to recant her world, in which their power
came not from God. Unmoved, the Men
of God began watching him burn, and better,
watching her watch him burn, hearing

the long mad godlike trumpet of his terror,
his crashing in the wood, the groan
of stakes that held, the silverback hide,
the pricked ears catching first

like driest bark, and the eyes.
And she knew, by this agony, that she
might choose to live still, if she would
but make her sign on the parchment

they would lay before her, which now
would include this new truth: that it
did not happen, this death in the circle,
the rearing, plunging, raging, the splendid

armour-coloured head raise one last time
above the flames before they took him
- like any game untended on the spit - into
their yellow-green, their blackening red.

Linda McCarriston

Public Poem in the First Person

Myself, the poet, is musing
on the spiritual. Not religion, opium
of the people, spirituality
opium of the elite. Trying
I keep trying to break my mind

so it will match my heart.
'My mind's not right' Lowell
told us, and Sexton, and Plath put her mind
we know where. Poetry, I will
stand forever outside your door

in the winter square, outside
your edifice, cathedral or prison,
and never go in again, I will
stand as Keats stood with his
paper sword by the door of his
dying mother, if as I am

I am unwelcome. My mind's not
not right. Shall I come in?

Linda McCarriston

To Judge Faolain, Dead Long Enough: A Summons

Your honour, when my mother stood
before you, with her routine
domestic plea, after weeks
of waiting for speech to return
to her body, with her homemade
forties hairdo, her face purple still
under pancake, her jaw off just a little,
her holy of holies healing,
her breasts wrung, her heart
the bursting heart of someone
snagged among rocks deep
in a sharkpool - no, not 'someone,'

but a woman there, snagged
with her babies, by them,
in one of hope's pedestrian
brutal turns - when, in the tones
of parlours overlooking the harbour,
you admonished that, for the sake
of the family, the wife
must take the husband back to her bed,
what you willed not to see before you
was a woman risen clean to the surface,
a woman who, with one arm flailing,
held up with the other her actual

burdens of flesh. When you clamped
to her leg the chain of justice,
you ferried us back down to the law,
the black ice eye, the maw, the mako
that circle the kitchen table nightly.
What did you make of the words
she told you, not to have heard her,
not to have seen her there? Almost-
forgivable ignorance, you were not
the fist, the boot, or the blade,

but the jaded, corrective ear and eye
at the limits of her world. Now

I will you to see her as she was, to ride
your own words back into light: I call
your spirit home again, divesting you
of robe and bench, the fine white hand
and half-lit Irish eye. Tonight, put on
a body in the trailer down the road
where your father, when he can't
get it up, makes love to your mother
with a rifle. Let your name be
Eva-Mary. Let your hour of birth
be dawn. Let your life be long
and common, and your flesh endure.

Linda McCarriston

the blood of Colorado miners

the blood of Colorado miners
machinegunned down by Rockefeller's cops in 1914
forms abstract expressionist smears on canvasses hung
on the boardroom walls of Chase Manhattan Bank

Sarah Menefee

human star

we're all subjected to their *good work*:

the poor tormenting the poor

for power's sake

it's an old familiar scene down in power's

underbelly: *this is what we do*

with all the subjected humiliated

and dead

innocence gagged inside the lyncher's hood

she was lounging against a corpse with long fingers

and a gaping mouth: sadist death

a joke

smoking a cigarette

hoods? torture? how ridiculous! said

sneering Rumsfeld

before we saw

what a brave young soldier

slipped under a door

black executioner's hood pulled over the sweet sun

above the head of sneering Rumsfeld

is the human garbed as a black star

in cloak and hood:

his fine-drawn feet below

a pyramid of bodies

human star tethered there

by electrocution's wires

if you fall through this night

you will bring down

the whole rotten prisonhouse

bury the devourers in the suffering earth

in the holes they explode in her breast

human suffering star!

shame? it's naked brutal power's shame

as though these beautiful cocks and backs could be a shame

to any but the obscene

where the powerless with blood on their tongues

humiliate their own

in master's name

that's how it's always done

and here and there are mothers' sons unlimbed

left poor and legless

to a life of pain: here and there

the poor boys show

their stumps:

the long nightmare

again

Sarah Menefee

Looking For Omar

I'm in the school bathroom
washing my hands without
soap but I'm still washing my hands.
I turn the water off
and look for a paper towel
but paper towels have been gone
since the first day of school
and it's June now.

I start to leave the bathroom
with my wet hands but then
the big boys come in talking
loud and cussing like they
rap stars or have new sneakers.

I hear the one named Pinto
talking about how someone
should get Omar after school
since he's the only Muslim they know.

Pinto talks with an accent
like he's new in the neighbourhood too.

I don't have to ask him
what he's talking about
since everybody is talking
about the Towers and how they
ain't there no more.

My momma said it's like
a woman losing both
breasts to cancer and my daddy
was talking at the dinner table
about how senseless violence is
and Mrs. Gardner next door lost
two tall boys to drive-bys

Bullets flying into
both boys' heads
making them crumble too.

Everybody around here is
filled with fear and craziness
and now Pinto and the big boys
thinking about doing something bad.

I stare at my wet hands
dripping water on my shoes
and wonder if I should run
and tell Omar or just run.

I feel like I'm trapped
in the middle of one of those

Bible stories but it ain't
Sunday.

I hear my Momma's voice
saying

*Boy, always remember to wash
your hands but always remember
you can't wash your hands from
everything.*

E. Ethelbert Miller

from Capitalization

Capitalize the first word
of every sentence, whether or not
it is a complete sentence.
Capitalize the first word of every line
of poetry. **I started work**
on an assembly line
at the huge Westinghouse plant
in East Pittsburgh when I was sixteen.
The Work was dull and repetitive.
From 1954 to 1962,
Ronald Reagan served as host
of the television program, 'G.E. Theatre.'
In some modern English poetry forms,
only the first word of the first line
is capitalized, and sometimes
even this is written lower-case.
Six times a year he acted in the dramas
(once starring in a two-part program
as an FBI agent who infiltrates
Communist-front organizations).
We tried to make the time go
by talking to each other.
Capitalize *father* and *mother*
when used in address, but do not
capitalize such nouns
when a possessive pronoun
is used with them.
The remainder of the year
Reagan toured G.E. factories,
speaking to employees and local civic groups on,
as he put it in his autobiography,
'the attempted takeover of the [electrical] industry
by Communists' and 'the swiftly rising tide
of collectivism that threatens to inundate
what remains of our free economy.'
Sometimes I would fantasize,
making believe I was somewhere other

**than at that long bench
with the never-ending noise,
the whining of machines.**
*

**In spite of those tough times,
there was a feeling of solidarity.
If a family was put out of their house,
people would gather there to stop the eviction.**
*As the 'host,' he occupied a more defensible position.
It was Reagan who ended each show
with the famous slogan,
'Here at General Electric,
progress is our most important product.'*
**When gas and electricity were shut off,
unemployed workers would go around
and turn them back on.**
Do not capitalize the following
when they stand alone: judge, justice
Capitalize President
Capitalize Vice President
Capitalize Senator, Congressman
Capitalize Speaker
Capitalize Governor, Mayor, Cardinal
*That 'here' was located at some imaginary point
between General Electric itself and your living room.
But unlike more recent TV pitchmen,
such as Lee Iacocca and Frank Perdue,
Reagan was never burdened
with the pretence that he was himself
part of the actual production.
He never purported to know anything
about building cars, plucking chickens,
or designing light bulbs.*
**They fought for surplus food, then flour
oleo and dry milk were distributed.**
Capitalize all Government titles
when referring to definite persons
in high positions or to their positions,
and all titles of honour or nobility
when referring to specific persons.

On the contrary, our host was someone like us—
a typical consumer of the sponsor's products.
There were kidney beans and canned meat, too.
Not gourmet, but it was something to eat.

Mark Nowak

Bobcats

This world provides the poetry.
We just assemble its arrival,
us bobcat mutt girls intent on unravelling
our impatient prognoses travelling us town to town.
And my hair sort of looks like a lion's and your mouth is
shaped like a roar
and we have never been invested in the state of unruly,
I guess it's that tameness has always seemed boring to us.
But, we are in a mean armwrestling match with our passion,
our elbows slipping off the table as she's cradling our palms.
She looks us square in the face, says this is not about brute
strength, girls,
this is just about holding on.
So, we are holding on, you and me, we are flying past the
past lives of pastures
where walmarts now sit, autocrats snuffing out fields of
breath
and stuffing them dull with steel rows of plastic shit.
And even the highways are adopted these days,
and we have been adopted by them.
We are road-weary sophisticates, we are truck-stop
debutantes,
we are bobcat mutt girls.
We got an atlas as a lover in her backless attire, we got a
gas-guzzler chauffeur,
and she is steering us spent towards our next check-in desk,
she is ducking her head just barely clearing,
you open sleepy eyes, tell me that's how you're feeling.
So, here we are again. Another round of tacky pictures of
boats and lamps shedding thin,
paper-shrouded soaps and floral-bound beds itching our skin.
Yes, here we are again, spewing paroxysms at another motel
television,
at the commander-in-chief of collateral damage,
at the bodies buried beneath this perverse double-speak.
Yes, here we are again, awaking to another today of the
USA, shoved underneath our motel door.

And the air conditioner gasps, as the past masks incognito as
the present on that front page.
She's in a police protection program, she's afraid to be seen,
she knows too much about the bombings, it's her recurrent
bad dream.
And it's an epidemic now, this moral amnesia, a good people
coming down with a bad case of evil.
And sometimes this violence breaks us, baby,
we go scattering like pool balls after each direct hit,
blame scrambling frantically towards one another's pockets.
But we are in a meaner arm-wrestling match with this
country, our elbows slipping off the table as she's cradling
our palms.
She looks us square in the face, says this is just about blind
faith girls, this is just about signing on.
But we are not signing on, you and me,
so we forfeit, stamp our biceps proudly anti-patriotic,
see we reject the premise of your entire border concept.
And we are moving onward, America, here is to another
town well-spent.
And here's to inspiring the counter-clockwise uprising of
two bobcat mutt girls.
And how they chose to live.

Alix Olson

Here

Here I am in the garden laughing
an old woman with heavy breasts
and a nicely mapped face
how did this happen
well that's who I wanted to be
at last   a woman
in the old style   sitting
stout thighs apart under
a big skirt   grandchild sitting
on   off my lap   a pleasant
summer perspiration
that's my old man across the yard
he's talking to the meter reader
he's telling him the world's sad story
how electricity is oil or uranium
and so forth   I tell my grandson
run over to your grandpa   ask him
to sit beside me for a minute   I
am suddenly exhausted by my desire
to kiss his sweet explaining lips

Grace Paley

What it Was Like

If you want to know what
it was like, I'll tell you
what my tío told me.
There was a truck driver,
Antonio, who could handle a
rig as easily in reverse as
anybody else straight ahead.

Too bad he's a Mexican was
what my tío said the
Anglos had to say
about that.

And thus the moral:

Where do you begin if
you begin with if
you're too good
it's too bad?

Leroy V. Quintana

Doctrine

Except occasionally, the Church provides a set of rules.
Simple or complex, austere or glittering,
if we believe and tithe, our future is secure.
If not in this life, in the next or the one beyond.

Belief: an investment in eternity. More often than not
a priest will guide us home. And he in turn responds
to a higher priest (the priests almost always men).
Different rules judging us than govern them.

All my movements for social change
have their origins in science:
scientific socialism, the economics
of surplus value,
those who work reaping the benefits
of their labour, those who need
receiving what they need.

Leader, chairperson, *comandante*
become president: these too,
despite our courage and commitment,
are likely to be male.

Religious or revolutionary: when the questions
are answered and faith settles in
for the duration,
power raises its muscled arm
and curiosity curls foetus-like
beneath a thick blanket of ice.
Great battalions of every sex and hue
march in identical direction.

After Dad died, we sailed the islands,
waded with white-tipped shark,
watched nursing sea lion cubs
on yellow beaches. Blue-footed boobies
nested at our feet.

The giant tortoise moved from sea
to highlands and back to sea, implacable.
A tuft of scrawny feathers on a pelican's nape.

I reminded myself then, energy never dies.

Margaret Randall

The Unburied, The Missing

for Otilia Vargas, compañera

come back to me now. Roque, months older than I
when we started out, forever forty.
Doris María, who would not become a teen.
The plane that took her falls from the sky,
falls again each time I turn my eyes to hers:
round in their fear of fire. Nothing will happen next.
María Otilia Vargas, seventy-five-year-old retired teacher,
widow of Osvaldo Pérez, mother of
Dagoberto, Aldo, Carlos, Iván, Mireya and Patricia,
the first gunned down in a fire-fight against the dictator,
next two extinguished in that long war's torture cells
and the twins still missing, 'disappeared'
in that language of Chilean pain. Only Patricia
lives, one year unravelling into the next,
accompanying her mother's purpose
in sweet madness. Together they study each release
on a list published all these years too late.
Their beloved names aren't there,
yet the mother continues to tempt them
with rice pudding,
shelter their bodies from the night air,
cradle them against her hopeful breast.
Otilia, condemned
to live these years her children could not have.
Even Patricia has lost count: the sister and brothers
torn from her childhood murmur in her ear.
The missing will only come back to eat with us
when we set a table
served with the food of change.

Margaret Randall

113

The Apology

The Café serves late breakfast, lunch, and tea.
It's open every day from ten to three.
       TODAY THE CAFÉ IS CLOSED.
       Sorry for the inconvenience

The things the museum keeps of historic note
are there for you to value by modern vote.
       TEMPORARILY CLOSED FOR
       REFURBISHMENT.
       Sorry for the inconvenience

There's a hole in the lane because they're digging again
to repair last year's relaid water mains.
       ROAD CLOSED. LOCAL ACCESS ONLY.
       Sorry for the inconvenience

In Baghdad girls—well-dressed, still alive—
run down the steps where mortar shells killed five.
       SCHOOL CLOSED UNTIL FURTHER NOTICE.
       Sorry for the inconvenience

The fighting raged through the night. As the sun rose
over the desert, the dead, and the half-burned town,
       it turned out all the streets were closed.
       Sorry for the inconvenience

Warm weather melts the polar ice; great storms
toss containers on the sea; fish swarm, not bees;
       farms are gone, mortgages, foreclosed.
       Sorry for the inconvenience

When The Cat sets out tomorrow I bet there'll be
a new sign floating on the sea:
       EARTH FOREVER CLOSED
       Sorry for the inconvenience

       FD Reeve

The Blue Cat Blues

The river rose, done took my house,
the Devil made off with my jack;
sail or swim like a fish -
how'll I ever get it back?

Chorus: No way today
to wash the blackness from the sea;
no way, no way
to take the blueness out of me.

The levee's broke, no more canal,
the Gulf has swallowed up town hall;
no place safe, no dry land -
Satan's won the Power Ball.

Chorus: No way today
to wash the blackness from the sea;
no way, no way
to take the blueness out of me.

My girl ran off where livin's free,
FEMA got the best of me;
whites drove out, blacks swam in -
gone, long gone racial harmony.

Chorus: No way today
to wash the blackness from the sea;
no way, no way
to take the blueness out of me.

Lower Ninth was drowned, our town,
lost my parrot and my pup;
jack all gone, no help coming -
no one here to build the levees up.

Chorus: No way today
to wash the blackness from the sea;
no way, no way
to take the blueness out of me.

FD Reeve

Delivered Clean

for Jack Foley

You've got to separate what they signify from what
they are   distinguish
their claimed intentions from the stuff coming
out from their hands and heads   The professor of cultural
dynamics
taught us this   They're disasters   in absentia
really   when supposedly working
Look at the record:
lost their minds wrote bad checks and smoked in bed
and if they were men were bad with women and if they were
women
picked men like that or would go with women
and talked too much and burnt the toast and abused all
known substances   Anyone who says
they were generous to a fault putting change
in whoever's cup if they had it on them   always room for
the friend
with no place to sleep   refused to make what they made
in the image of the going thing
cooked up stew that could keep you alive with
gizzards and onions and splashes of raw
red wine   were
loyal where they loved and wouldn't name names
should remember   said the professor of cultural
dynamics   what
messes they made

The building will be delivered vacant
of street actors   so-called artists in residence
fast-order cooks on minimum wage
who dreamed up a life where space was cheap
muralists doubling as rabble-rousers
cross-dressing pavement poets
delivered clean
of those who harbour feral cats illegals illicit ideas

selling their blood to buy old vinyls
living at night and sleeping by day
with huge green plants in their windows
and huge eyes painted on their doors.

2002

Adrienne Rich

Underdogs

Chorus : This is for my folkers who got bills overdue
this is for my folkers, umm check 1-2
this is for my folkers never lived like a hog
me and you toe-to-toe, I got love for the underdog

I raise this glass for the ones who die meaningless
and the newborns who get fed intravenously
somebody's mama caught a job and a welfare fraud case
when she breathe she swear it feel like plastic wrap around
       her face
lights turned off this is the third month the rent is late
thoughts of bein' homeless, cryin' till you hyperventilate
despair permeates the air and sets in you hair
the kids play with that one toy they learned how to share
comin' home don't ever seem to be a celebration
bills stay piled up the coffee table like they decoration
heapin' spoons o' peanut butter, big ass glass o' water
make the hunger subside, save the real food for your daughter
you feel like swingin' haymakers at a movin' truck
you feel like laughing so it seems like you don't give a f -
you feel like getting' so high, you'll smoke the whole damn crop
you feel like cryin' but you think you might never stop
homes with no heat stiffen your bones like arthritis
if this was fiction it'd be easier to write this
some folks wanna front like they so above you
They'd tear this motherfucker up if they really loved you

Chorus

There's certain tricks of the trade to try to halt your defeat
like takin' tupperwear to an all you can eat
returnin' new for new sayin' you lost your receipt
and writin' 4 figure checks when yo accounts deplete
then all your problems pile up about a mile up
thinkin' bout a patnah you can dial up
to help you out this vile stuff
whole family sleepin' on the futon
while you clippin' coupons
eatin' salad tryin' to get full off the croutons
crosstown the situation is identical

somebody gettin' strangled by the system and its tentacles
misconceptions raised questions to be solved
lotta D-boys is broke
lotta homeless got jobs
you can make 8 bones an hour to you pass out
and still be ass out
most pyramid schemes don't let you cash out
they say this generation made the harmony break
but crime rise consistent wit the poverty rate
you take the worker from jobs
you gon' have murders in mobs
a gang of preachers screamin' sermons
over murmurs and sobs
sayin' pray for a change from the lord above you
they'd tear this muthafucker up if they really loved you

Chorus

You like this song cuz it's relatable, it's you in a rhyme
we go to stores that only let us in 2 at a time
we live in places where it cost to get your check cashed
arguments about money usually drown out the tech blasts
work 6 days a week, can't sleep Saturday though
muscles tremblin' like a pager when the batteries low
and you just don't know where the years went
although every long shift feel like a year spent
and you could write your resume but it wouldn't even mention
all the life lessons learned during six years of detention
and how you learned the police was just some handicappers
on the ground next to broken glass and candywrappers
now don't accept my collects on the phone
just hit me at the house so I know I ain't alone
and we could chop it up about this messed up system
homies that's been killed, how we always gon' miss 'em
it's almost impossible survivin' on this fraction
sip a 40 to your brain for the chemical reaction
you gatta hustle cuz they tryn' a push and shove you
I'll tear this muthafucker - up since I really love you

Chorus

Boots Riley

Carrying My Tools

Any good craftsman carries his tools.
Years ago, they were always at the ready.
In the car. In a knapsack.
Claw hammers, crisscrossed heads,
32 ouncers. Wrenches in all sizes,
sometimes with oil caked on the teeth.
Screwdrivers, with multicoloured
plastic handles
(what needed screwing got screwed).
I had specialty types: Allen wrenches,
torpedo levels, taps and dies.
A trusty tape measure. Maybe a chalk line.
Millwrights also carried dial indicators,
micrometers - the precision kind.
They were cherished like a fine car,
a bottle of rare wine, or a moment of truth.
I believed that anyone could survive
without friends, without the comfort of blankets
or even a main squeeze
(for a short while anyway).
But without tools...now there was hard times.
Without tools, what kind of person could I be?
The tools were my ticket to new places.
I often met other travellers, their tools in tow,
and I'd say, 'Go ahead, take my stereo and TV.
Take my car. Take my toys of leisure.
Just leave the tools.'
Nowadays, I don't haul these mechanical implements.
But I still make sure to carry the tools
of my trade: Words and ideas,
the kind no one can take away.
So there may not be any work today,
but when there is, I'll be ready.
I got my tools.

Luis J. Rodrgiguez

The Shoes

holocausts of them
genocides of them
massacres of them

or one pair you recognize
left in her closet
the heels worn crooked
the way she would walk
all her life

or one alone, alone, blown
off the child's foot
off the old woman's foot
off the man's foot

lying on its side
in a pool of blood

Richard Schaaf

What If

When Dr. Martin Luther King's
papers were to be sold
at auction
to the highest bidder,
liberals and Democrats
in the black city
without shadows
of Washington, DC
protested:

What gets us is this:
Dr. King belonged to all of us!
What if a Saudi
or an Iraqi
or a Palestinian
or a Mexican
buys them!

What then?

Richard Schaaf

Arc

'The arc of the universe is long, but it bends toward justice.'
(Martin Luther King)

Like a dowsing rod reaching for water
the arc of the universe
bends toward justice -

but what if there is none?

nothing in the scheme of things
as far as we
in our lifetime see
bends, surely, toward justice

what may we do then
to bend
the arc of justice
back down to earth?

it won't be with speeches,
no one needs to strain, daydreaming
after words the wind blows through

attend instead
to the coming and going
of those who are better off
with justice, than without -

all the colours, shapes, customs
being done-to unto death
but don't dwell on that,
don't cling to debris

let the slop and flow
of whatever feels like feeling
carry you along
as on a great wave cresting
an unfathomed sea of nameless peoples

who are bound to arrive somewhere

when you yourself arrive
cast up on the shore
imagine you've happened on
a folktale, or a fairytale,
the way peasants once did
in stories of yore

imagine you're a prince
or long lost princess
cast as a peasant, a noble
foundling from the sea,
the sea of peasants
storming the wicked lord's castle
saving everyone saving
the beauty of the bending universe
from the wrack and ruin
of the lord's stupidity,
his arrogance, his greed,
the dazzling panoply of his dementia
cutting words off
from the truth of the matter

imagine for that matter
Washington DC now
right now
is such a regime, its
lords ravage the countryside

imagine living this
imagine

seeing what other peasants see
feeling what they feel
having nothing left to prove
nothing more to discover
nowhere else to go

when you torch the manor house
ransack the cold cellar
tear down the whole rotten structure
imagine that

      James Scully

DU Blues

DU
death row

wind blow

continents countries cities
flags
wind don't know
which way wind blow

whip up sandstorm
go wherever,
4 plus billion years
it got
to go forever

number the years
of forever

eat sleep fuck
uranium forever

X ray ever hour
the hours of a life
gone catch up forever

o swindled innocence of breath

o life condemned to kill
the life it come to save
save to rob it blind
gone wait alone together

DU DU DU
death row

wind blow

James Scully

Listening to Coltrane

listening to Coltrane, hearing
the original people

who abide us, sometimes
kill us

as always
we are killing them -

he blows through all
the abiding and killing

blows the send-off
we got on leaving the cosmos
the beauty of its harmony
behind us, blows

there is never any end,
there are always new sounds
to imagine,
new feelings to get at

squawking
brass, reeds, battered skin
steel wires *there is*

always the need to keep
purifying
these feelings and sounds

honking out over
            our cosmic exile

the bent strains of the original people
their long shadows riding shotgun on his wing

to give the best of what we are

            James Scully

Qana

where the wedding was
where water turned to wine
where the best was saved
for last

shsh they're trying to sleep
in the dark wood
of dreamless dreaming -
coughing farting snoring sighing
turning over

where the wedding was
the rolling storm
that is not a storm
flies over

it doesn't feel much
to drop a bomb -
a slight bump
under the wing

the thing is done -

their deaths
like little yapping dogs
rush out
into the nerve-endings of the universe

the bodies stay put,
impossibly still

so it was said in school
Macbeth doth murder sleep -
with so much life to kill
there's no room for sleep

in Qana
where the wedding was
those who sleep, die

the future of sleep
is buried alive

in Qana where the wedding was
the murdered in their sleep
wake just long enough to die
to become the woods
where the wedding was...

they are on the move now,
which is impossible

these impossible dead
growing out of their deaths
into an army of trees

James Scully

There is No Truth to the Rumour

There is no truth to the rumour
the Constitution's
a goddamned piece of paper

it's not vegetable, but animal
dressed as parchment--

invented in Pergamon
in not yet Turkey
3rd century BCE
when the papyrus ran out

Ionian Greeks called sheets of it
diphtherai, or 'skins'

by the time of Herodotus
writing on skins was common

Assyrians and Babylonians
in what for now is called Iraq
were already writing on skins

writing and rewriting
past traces of earlier writing
on recycled skins
they'd scrubbed and scoured

they wrote what they believed
mattered
on something meant to last

rabbinic books weren't books
but scrolls of parchment, as
were, later, early Islamic texts

great civilizations as living cultures
writing themselves on skin

writing rewriting
laws, histories, religions, all
on cured skin: split
sheepskin, goatskin, cowhide,
horsehide, squirrel and rabbit

aborted calf foetuses
hairless through and through
as is the skin of angels
would be reserved
for especially precious stuff

yet regardless of grade, without exception,
skin being mostly collagen,
the water in ink or paint
would melt it slightly
creating a raised bed for the writing

like welts on a body
showing what's been done to it

even today, to write on parchment
or colour it
the tiniest bit watery
is to bring all this doing up

each writing a rewriting
overwriting the life of skin

so if its breath is gone, its muscles
having lost all sense of purpose
bereft of heart and liver, still
in the heat and humidity
of human and meteorological exertion
it buckles, shifts, sweats and squirms

uplifting a little,
like from a death bed,
giving lie to the rumour
the Constitution is a piece of paper
damned or not

because, even dead, it will let us know
this was a living matter
that was being painted up, written off on
chewed by dogs and lied over

James Scully

Invasion of the Body Snatchers

A lot of building and violence. The wars.
You tortured each other.

You thought you understood
what money meant, what money
wanted, but you never imagined.

The things done for the sake of country.
For the sake of *race*.
Labour.
The carefully broken wheel of class.

You all had been so energetic and determined –
so plump with what we named 'Freedom'

The jobs were everywhere.

When the televisions first came on
you were ready to sit down and watch.
You must have been almost praying

for someone to save you, to send
the worries away. We gave you
religion. There wasn't any big
hurry, but by the time

there were 3 stations and colour
it seemed like you really wanted it

our way   to see and believe, to
laugh, laugh, laugh, to become
a faithful shopper –
another day   another dollar:

That's a pretty simple prayer.

And gosh, look how bright it stays out there!
All the friends want *cable* now.

Shouldn't everyday be as Saturday as this -

the sun so blonde it's making everybody blind.

Do you ever catch yourself wondering
what they're thinking - *other people*,
how they keep coming to work so calm?

Some   you used to know. Some
were just like you. Remember:

those soaring conversations? Your hands
open to the speed of words,

as though you could actually
hold them: your ideals -

the will to do *Good*, to claw
evil's clean-cut company face, the
we shall overcome   and all that.

Well, you needed to be born again so   you were.

Sometime between civil rights and *Oprah*,
somewhere between Vietnam and *Desert Storm*.

remember how Baghdad lit up that first time -
all the 'sorties,' and here, the yellow ribbons -

weren't you almost feeling   kind of glad?

You think all this has something to do with *Republicans*?

Look at your watch,
how those thin hands move you around:

it's like you're floating, like you're

not really here now.

You think there's something strange in the water?
You think there's some new germ in the air?

Think fewer trees   just mean   fewer birds?

I guess we'll see.

Tim Seibles

Ladder

But look! The churches keep opening
their mouths   like trout left to dry in the grass.

And the corporations don't fall down - see
how they run:

the blue suits, the black robes, and their President
whose brain is a bug rolling dung.

Of course, there's blood on the money.

The vampires have always
walked among us.

But so have the trees!

The great stalker called *commerce*
and the Earth's primordial solo
continue to be the windows

through which we arrive - one by one - naked,
splashing like birdless birds into the air,
almost blind, begging to be fed.

Why? To become *this*?
These workaday trolls scared of our newspapers,
revved up ready to buy bigger alarms?

Look how the world rolls around the sun's gold belly,
how the ocean is so much stranger than its word.

Isn't everybody still 3/5ths water?
How lonely   does a truth have to be

before we bring its blues to our lips?

What we do not sing, what we drown in
not saying -

is already music. And still, we keep
turning from the sound

like two-legged animals all buttoned and zipped
unwilling to recognize this tall ladder of bones
to which we cling briefly with our small teeth.

And because we do not see well into the future
because we are busy taking as much as we can get because
money has infected these days with its prolific germ,

what surrounds us looks like forever
but it is not -

just as today's wind
with its grim whistle and bruise
is only the weather for a little while,

on past the dying edge   of the usual
what they said   could never be

begins

Tim Seibles

Night Flight

'After awhile everything is a metaphor for everything.'
(Mark Cox)

By the feel of things, this dark
must be rough. The jet strides
and scuffs the air the way someone
might walk a crowded row
in a movie theatre - here
and there bumping a knee,
stubbing a toe - and I regret that
we weren't given a moment
before take-off to shake hands,
trade names, maybe pray
like members of an expedition
travelling a territory both visible
and not visible, both deadly
and kind. The kid to my left

is in the 'Navy Police.' Though,
with his baby-face, he'd do better
in a powder-blue tuxedo enlisting
a purple corsage for the prom.
Across the aisle a businessman
taps his brass ring on the tray,
and when the wings shudder

his wife just keeps her eyes closed,
and the redhead who needlepoints
never even glances at the gigantic
blackness - which must be
exactly what the pilots see, what
a bug sees when something
hungry suddenly swallows it whole.

We could easily be lost in the great
gulf of the ultimate toad,
but only a bug-eyed child is crying.

We could be a single mile
from the side of a mountain
that would make us the *extra*
to read all about, and I just want
somebody to tell me how
to keep on living these hours
completely blind to what's ahead.

And I am black; the wig-wearing
woman is white, the navy kid
is Filipino - and we're way, way
above America, riding a machine
none of us can explain, believing
the future has reserved a seat
for us, so why *aren't* we a little
more willing to see each other
in light of all the nighttime
that surrounds us?

I spend a lot of darkness
trying not to give up
on being human, listening
to the engines of powerful things
moving us around: the war
makers, the iron maiden
of capital, the fundamentalists
sharpening their one crooked
stick, television - the imperceptible
swarm filling the air,
and how can I *not* say
this jet is like the world?
All umpteen-trillion tons of impossible Earth
zooming along
near the speed of sound,
carrying so many people
thinking about something else.

Tim Seible

Skinhead

They call me skinhead, and I got my own beauty.
It is knife-scrawled across my back in sore, jagged letters,
it's in the way my eyes snap away from the obvious.
I sit in my dim matchbox,
on the edge of a bed tousled with my ragged smell,
slide razors across my hair,
count how many ways
I can bring blood closer to the surface of my skin.
These are the duties of the righteous,
the ways of the anointed.
The face that moves in my mirror is huge and pockmarked,
scraped pink and brilliant, apple-cheeked,
I am filled with my own spit.
Two years ago, a machine that slices leather
sucked in my hand and held it,
whacking off three fingers at the root.
I didn't feel nothing till I looked down
and saw one of them on the floor
next to my boot heel,
and I ain't worked since then.
I sit here and watch niggers take over my TV set,
walking like kings up and down the sidewalks in my head,
walking like their fat black mamas *named* them freedom.
My shoulders tell me that ain't right.
So I move out into the sun
where my beauty makes them lower their heads,
or into the night
with a lead pipe up my sleeve,
a razor tucked in my boot.
I was born to make things right.
It's easy now to move my big body into shadows,
to move from a place where there was nothing
into the stark circle of a streetlight,
the pipe raised up high over my head.
It's a kick to watch their eyes get big,
round and gleaming like cartoon jungle boys,
right in that second when they know

the pipe's gonna come down, and I got this thing
I like to say, listen to this, I like to say
'Hey, nigger, Abe Lincoln's been dead a long time.'
I get hard listening to their skin burst.
I was born to make things right.
Then this newspaper guy comes around,
seems I was a little sloppy kicking some fag's ass
and he opened his hole and screamed about it.
This reporter finds me curled up in my bed,
those TV flashes licking my face clean.
Same ol' shit.
Ain't got no job, the coloureds and spics got 'em all.
Why ain't I working? Look at my hand, asshole.
No, I ain't part of no organized group,
I'm just a white boy who loves his race,
fighting for a pure country.
Sometimes it's just me. Sometimes three. Sometimes 30.
AIDS will take care of the faggots,
then it's gon' be white on black in the streets.
Then there'll be three million.
I tell him that. So he writes it up
and I come off looking like some kind of freak,
like I'm Hitler himself. I ain't that lucky,
but I got my own beauty.
It is in my steel-toed boots,
in the hard corners of my shaved head.
I look in the mirror and hold up my mangled hand,
only the baby finger left, sticking straight up,
I know it's the wrong goddamned finger,
but fuck you all anyway.
I'm riding the top rung of the perfect race,
my face scraped pink and brilliant.
I'm your baby, America, your boy,
drunk on my own spit, I am goddamned fuckin' beautiful.
And I was born
and raised
right here.

Patricia Smith

S.Z. Home from Vietnam

He uses his Zippo without the wrist-flicking flourish
the rest of us still admire and he's already begun
the first of the hundred great novels every intelligent
person is expected to have read. He's suspicious

of those who are against the war: they come from
well-to-do families and care only about themselves;
and yet, the people he grew up with, people like him,
people like us, seem so eager to send him off to die.

He talks about the lives society has reserved for him,
lives no one ever wishes for or dreams of. When he
says he wants someone to expect great things of him,
we don't know what he means. We see him on the library

steps reading and smoking: the books look as if they're
on fire. He says reading is his insurance against ever
getting caught again with his dick exposed and with
no other option than waiting for someone to shoot it off.

John Surowiecki

Baghdad

When they declare 'precision bombing'
get ready for the bodies of women and children in the
streets,
get ready to watch the limp child tossed into the back of the
wagon,
the black bullets of his open eyes fixed on your heart.

O surgical strike, pre-emptive action,
landslides of buildings, huge holes to nowhere,
the dark mouth frozen in a monstrous O.

In the press room the handsome general
publicly regrets the occasional collateral damage
from behind his polished podium
under the bright TV lights.

In the hospital a black-eyed girl waves the stump of her arm;
all around are bandages bigger than limbs.
Get ready in a century where we suffer
the little children to come and suffer for us.

There is nothing we will not do to one another.
and no word we will not use to deny it.

Alexander Taylor

Because

for Lyn Frazier's students

Because we listened to the madness coursing in our blood,
Because we snapped the hollow words of fathers
               like chicken bones,
Because we left our mothers crying with strange smiles
               on their lips,
Because visions fractured our irises and etched flaming
               images into our skulls,
Because hope drove us like rain through dry grasslands
               covered with bones,
Because we could see blue mountains shining in the distance
               like the face of a lover,
Because *nada* and *dada* floated seawards on the muddy river,
               which we crossed, singing,
Because every blow made us stronger, and the four spirits
               kept us from the killing one,
or luck, because many of the bravest *have* died,
Because we never fed on the carcass of history in the tomb
               of academe or believed our teachers,
Because always we listened to the struggling voices inside us,
that greased the wheels of the caravan
and made us weep at the old cripple in the doorway
               and the young mother
clutching her child, pale, with nowhere to go,
Because spirit made us laugh at
the 'reasons' that this should be,
proclaimed by strange economists
with the hearts of dead birds,
Because we know the road is long
and we can only go singing and dancing and fighting part way
Because in our hearts there is a tiger
               stirring and stretching in the glorious sun
and because everything we carry is really ours and will go
               with us forever.

Alexander Taylor

Carry the Stone

Hidden in the beauties of Babylon
A civilized behavioural notoriety
The more evil the empire
The more paranoid the society

Building to the new world order
We're expected to carry the stone
Emperors and the feeding class
Human being, being used up fast

The miners keep on mining
Intelligence is the mother lode
Imagination as an energy source
In this predators way of dining

Defining how and what we think
As we're led to the way to believe
Conditioned reaction we call thought
Our reality rides in how we perceive

In the ways of being lost and alone
Who runs from their doubt and fear
In the mask of everything's normal
Who's not feeling or seeing too clear

Could be we're being programmed
In a way our spirit bleeds
All over our lives, our lives
Become fuel for predator needs

Building to the new world order
We're expected to carry the stone
Emperors and the feeding class
Human being, being used up fast

Hidden in the beauties of Babylon
A civilized behavioural notoriety
The more evil the empire
The more paranoid the society

John Trudell

He Will Make Steel Sing

Told
to go to the back of the factory onto the engine lathe
he has never seen
or run the machinist stands
before all of the lathe's handles and set screws and speed
settings and chucks
that could leave him helpless
and without a job in this factory where he has only worked
for a month.
He forces the panic
over all the things he doesn't understand about this machine
back down
inside himself
and spends 10 minutes searching for the power button and
finds it
and punches it and hears the engine start humming
as 20 years of machinist experience tells him to stay calm
calm as the lion
on the African grass where it has belonged
for millions of years
calm as the stars
that return each night like there is nowhere else they could
ever have been
calm
as reason
that invented fire and time and gravity
as he moves to the silvery smooth handles in front of the
lathe's shiny tool steel ways
and with fingers tries each one
this way and that and this way and that for half an hour
until he throws the one
that starts the chuck spinning smoothly at 600 rpm
and suddenly he knows
that it will all fall into place
as surely as each moment will pass
each
handle each set screw each cutting tool will one by one

sooner or later make sense
and he will be able to go on feeding his family
because he will lean over this machine and turn wrenches
and throw its handles
cutting
      steel part
after steel part after steel part more and more smoothly until
they sing
proving
once again that it isn't the machine
that made man but man
who made
the machine.

Fred Voss

The Apostate

I've listened to you
the apostles
of American power, who assign
me enemies, who hire
the agile-minded to design
instruments of annihilation
who've issued, in my lifetime,
commands to let the blood
of eight million
dark-skinned people.
I've lived in granite mountains
laboured long beneath the sky.
There's nothing left in me
for you to employ.
I've turned away
from your voices,
your murderous schemes. Out here
on Starvation Ridge
I feed sticks into a fire
and let your flames
dance in my eyes.

Rob Whitbeck

Working Late

Squared in his spot on line six,
he chalks a number
on the board, locks the chuck.
Fronds curl against his hands
and arms. He keeps nodding off,
even though the roof kicks with rain
and wind turns
on itself in the empty truck docks.

Each piece he lifts
is heavier than the last.
He cleans the finished ones
in the oil soup.
He turns the heat off, sips black coffee,
remembers the guy on graveyard
fell asleep for a moment and woke
to his finger lying on the cement.

Don Winter

The Mill-Race

Four-fifty. The palings of Trinity Church
Burying Ground, a few inches above the earth,
are sunk in green light. The low stones
like pale books knocked sideways. The bus so close to the curb
the brush-drops of ebony paint stand out wetly, the sunlight
seethes with vibrations, the sidewalks
on Whitehall shudder with subterranean tremors. Overhead,
      faint flickers

crackle down the window-paths: limpid telegraphy of the
late afternoon July thunderstorm unfurling over Manhattan.
Its set and luminous velocity, long stalks of stormlight, and then
      the first drops
strike their light civic stripes on the pavement.
Between the palings, oat-panicles sift a few bright
grains to the stonecourse. Above it, at shoulder height
a side door is flung open, fire-exits; streaming from lobbies

come girls and women, white girls in shadowy-striped rayon
      skirts, plastic ear-hoops,
black girls in gauzy-toned nylons, ripples of cornrows and plaits,
one girl with shocked-back ash hair, lightened eyebrows;
one face from Easter Island, mauve and granitic;
thigh on thigh, waist by waist; the elbow's curlicue and the
fingers'; elbow-
      work, heal-work,
are suddenly absorbed in the corduroyed black rubber stair
      of the bus. Humid
sighs, settling, each face tilts up to the windows'
shadowless yards of mercuric green plate glass. An

interspace then, like the slowing of some rural
water mill, a creaking and dipping pause
of black-splintered paddles, the irregularly
dappled off-lighting - bottle-green - the lucid slim sluice
falling back in a stream from the plank edge. It won't take us
altogether, we say, the mill-race - it won't churn us up altogether.

We'll keep a glib stretch of leisure water, like our self's self
       - to reflect the sky.
But we won't (says the bus rider now to herself). Nothing's
left over, really, from labour. They've taken it all for the mill-
race.

In close-ups now, you can see it in every face,
despite the roped rain light pouring down the bus-windows -
it's the strain of gravity itself, of life hours cut off and offered
to the voice that says 'Give me this day our
life, that is LABOUR, and I'll give you back
one day, then another. For mine are the terms.'
It's gravity, spilling in capillaries, cheek-tissue trembling,
despite the make-up, the monograms, the mass-market
        designer scarves,

the army of signs disowning the workplace and longing for
        night...
But even as the rain slackens, labour
lengthens itself along Broadway. The night signs
come on, that wit has set up to draw money: O'DONNELL'S,
BEIRUT CAFE, YONAH'S KNISH ... People dart out from
awnings. The old man at the kiosk starts his late shift, whipping
off rainstreaked lucite sheets from his stacks of late-market
newsprint.

If there is leisure, bus-riders, it's not for you,
not between here and uptown or here and the Bronx.
Outside Marine Midland, the black sea of unmarked
        corporate hire-cars
waits for the belated office lights, the long rainy run to the
        exurbs;
and perhaps on a converted barn roof in Connecticut
leisure may silver the shingles, somewhere the densely packed
labour-mines that run a half mile down from the sky
to the Battery rise, metamorphic, in water-gardens,
lichened windows where the lamp lights Thucydides or Gibbon.

It's not a water-mill really, labour. It's like the nocturnal
paper-mill pulverizing, crushing each fibre of rag into atoms,

or the workhouse tread-mill, smooth lipped, that wore down
a London of
            doxies and sharps,
or the flour-mill, faërique, that raised the cathedrals and
wore out hosts of dust-
            demons,
but it's mostly the miller's curse-gift, forgotten of God yet
still grinding, the salt-
mill, that makes the sea, salt.

            Anne Winters

Supermax

The guards hate their mothers;
They who got no love in childhood.

Only anger breeds
Like Norway rats
Inside a city of stone and steel.

The prisoner asks simply
Not to be beaten or maced.

In the isolation cell
Not a spider to kiss
Or a neighbour's hand to touch.

A naked light bulb sponges up
Healing dreams.

Six officers -
An infestation of dark green toads -
Pile on the naked man;
Excrete all over him.

Their penises still hard
When they go off shift -
Return home to beat their wives
And kick the boys for being 'pussies.'

Such men as these
Contracted to civilize Iraq.

William Witherup

Praise Song for a Dead Girl

For a girl of mixed race found strangled to death and stuffed into a duffle bag behind Carrow's Restaurant, Castro Valley, California, on May 1, 2003

On International Workers' Holiday, workers at Carrow's|
        Restaurant
found you, strangled and stuffed into a duffle bag, dumped
behind the restaurant. On this May Day, as millions
of working people celebrated the world over, you gave
your last breath. You were 13, maybe 15, or 17, of mixed
        race.
Part Black, part white, part Asian, part Latina,
part Native American, or all of the above,
no one will ever know. No one has claimed you.
no mother or father, no uncle or aunt, not even
a loving grandmother, a teacher, a next-door neighbour.
What did you do, dear sister, except try to live, to study
Algebra, U.S. History, or even Computer Science,
to swim or play tennis, to while away hours
listening to Eminem, Cristina Aguilera, Nelly.
Perhaps you loved to dance, played jigsaw puzzles,
babysat, tried pot, waited on tables, peddled
hand-made necklaces of rhinestone
on Market Street in San Francisco.
Perhaps you ran away from home to escape abuse,
arriving in California, to lose yourself, to find
a new identity.
Now a man, a gardener with a teenaged daughter,
has come forth to honour you, to bury you. An anonymous
        donor
is paying for your burial clothes. And at your memorial
services this hot July, your newfound friends will say
farewell to you, a girl with no name, who simply lived
until a pair of enraged hands decided your demise.
This praise song is for you, a girl
who must have laughed, cried and fought, home
at last amid the care and love of strangers and workers.

Nellie Wong

The Snowy Owl

Excitement along the beach,
a snowy owl,
rare here
so far from its Arctic home,
found perched on the church roof
but when seen
(it had been roused by crows)
was fixed like a white kite
among the green branches of a spruce tree,
perfectly visible from a distance
and up close, the details:
swivel-necked and gimlet-eyed,
mechanical as a toy clock,
a yearling with barred body,
white facedisk,
hook nose and a soft ruff of white feathers.
Almost immobile,
half-comatose in daylight -
the night's bloody work over,
the raptors scream muzzled,
the great wingspan
collapsed to its side,
as it sat watchful,
planning to survive
as species after species
fades away.

Marilyn Zuckerman

Notes on the Contributors

Denise Abercrombie's one woman shows of monologues, poems and songs include *Something Like Sex* and *The Most Dangerous Animal in the World*. Her poetry has appeared in numerous journals, including *The Blue Collar Review, Connecticut Review, The Lumberyard,* and *Minnesota Review.* She is co-founder of Connecticut's Stage Left Ensemble. She has been a public high school English teacher for over 20 years.

Jack Agüeros was born in 1934 in East Harlem, New York City. A community activist who has written extensively on issues of immigration, his work deals with the complexities of the Puerto Rican experience in America. His books of poems include *Lord, Is This a Psalm?*, *Sonnets from the Puerto Rican* and *Correspondence Between the Stonehaulers* (all Hanging Loose Press). He has translated *Song of the Simple Truth: The Complete Poems of Julia de Burgos* and *Come, Come My Boiling Blood: The Complete Poems of José Martí* (both for Curbstone Press). He lives in New York.

Jon Andersen is the author of *Stomp and Sing* (Curbstone 2005) and is a member of the English Department at Quinebaug Valley Community College in Connecticut.

Doug Anderson is currently working on a memoir about his experience as Corpsman in the Vietnam War. His most recent book of poems is *Blues for Unemployed Secret Police* (Curbstone Press). He lives in Connecticut.

Naomi Ayala is the author of two books of poetry: *Wild Animals on the Moon* and *This Side of Early*. She has been featured on *Poetry Daily*, and her poems and book reviews have appeared in such publications as *Ploughshares, MARGIN: Exploring Modern Magical Realism, Saheb Ghalam Daily* (Afghanistan), *Feminist Teacher* and *The Washington Post*. She lives in Washington D.C.

Anne Babson has won numerous awards in the United States for her work, including The *Columbia* Prize, an International Merit Award from *Atlanta Review*, and has twice been nominated for a Pushcart Prize. She wrote the libretto for composer Su-Lian Tan's opera, *Upbringing*, about the traditional cultural constraints on Chinese women. Her spoken word poetry is included on the urban gospel CD *The Cornerstone*. She lives in New York.

Amiri Baraka is the author of over 40 books of essays, poems, drama, and music history and criticism, a poet icon and revolutionary political activist who has recited poetry and lectured on cultural and political issues extensively in the USA, the Caribbean, Africa, and Europe.

John Bradley is the author of *Terrestrial Music* (Curbstone Press), and *War on Words* (BlazeVOX). He teaches at Northern Illinois University.

Marilyn Buck began her anti-racist activism as a teenager in Texas, where she was involved in protests against the war in Vietnam. In 1973 she was convicted of purchasing two boxes of handgun ammunition and was given a ten year sentence. After serving four years in Federal prison in Alderson, West Virginia, she was granted a furlough and did not return. The following eight years she lived underground. In 1985, she was recaptured and convicted of conspiracy for the successful escape of Assata Shakur from her New Jersey prison. In 1988 she was given another ten years for 'conspiracy to protest and alter government policies' (the invasion of Grenada, intervention in Central America) 'through use of violence' against government and military property.

Christopher Butters's books include *The Propaganda of a Seed* (Cardinal Press) and *Americas* (Vietnam Generation) and *The Algebra of Doing It* (Partisan Press). A former poetry editor of *Political Affairs: A Journal of Marxist Thought*, he works as a court reporter at Brooklyn Criminal Court in New York City.

Jayne Cortez is the author of ten books of poems. She has performed her poetry with music on nine recordings and presented her work at universities, museums and festivals in Africa, Asia, Europe, South America, the Caribbean and the United States. Her poems have been translated into many languages. She lives in New York.

Jim Daniels's most recent books are *Revolt of the Crash-test Dummies* (Eastern Washington University Press), *In Line for the Exterminator* (Wayne State University Press) and *Mr Pleasant* (Michigan State University Press). He lives in Pittsburgh.

Robert Edwards is the author of *Radio Venceremos, Fragments From A Graffitied Wall, The Death of Communism* and *American Sounds*. He is the editor of Pemmican, an online magazine of poetry, and lives with his family in Seattle.

Martín Espada is a former tenant-lawyer. He has published fourteen books as a poet, editor and translator, including *Alabanza: New and Selected Poems* (Norton) and *The Republic of Poetry* (Norton) which received the Paterson Award for Sustained Literary Achievement and was a finalist for the Pulitzer Prize. He has received numerous awards and fellowships, including an American Book Award, the Robert Creeley Award, the PEN/Revson Fellowship and a Guggenheim Foundation Fellowship. He teaches in the Department of English at the University of Massachusetts-Amherst.

Ed Friedman is the former Artistic Director of the Poetry Project at St. Mark's Church in New York City. He is the author of nine books, including *Mao and Matisse* (Hanging Loose Press).

Aracelis Girmay writes poetry, fiction and criticism. Her books include a children's art book, *Changing, Changing* (George Braziller) and a collection of poems *Teeth* (Curbstone). She lives in Brooklyn.

Amy Groshek grew up in rural Wisconsin. She holds a BS in Botany, and an MFA from the University of Alaska Anchorage. She works as a writer and instructional designer. She lives in Madison, Wisconsin.

Kimiko Hahn has received an American Book Award and a Lila Wallace-Reader's Digest Award. She lives in New York City and teaches at Queen's College/City University of New York.

Sam Hamill has published more than forty books, including translations from Chinese, Japanese, Greek and Latin. Recent books include *Almost Paradise: Selected Poems & Translations; Avocations: Essays on Poetry; Measured by Stone* (recent poems). He is Director of Poets Against War. He lives in Washington State.

Joy Harjo's most recent book is *How We Became Human: New and Selected Poems*. Renowned for her performances, she has recorded three CDs of her music and poetry.

Michael Henson's most recent work is *Crow Call* (West End Press), a collection of poems written in response to the killing of the homeless activist Buddy Gray. He is also author of *The Tao of Longing* (Dos Madres Press) and two works of fiction. He lives in Cincinnati.

Jack Hirschman is currently poet laureate of the City of San Francisco. His book *The Arcanes* - written over thirty years - was recently published (in English) by Multimedia Edizioni in Italy.

Bob Holman's latest collection of poems, a collaboration with Chuck Close, *A Couple of Ways of Doing Something*, was exhibited at the Peggy Guggenheim Museum during the Venice Biennale. The TV series he produced for PBS, *The United States of Poetry*, won the INPUT, International Public Television Award. He founded Mouth Almighty/Mercury Records, a spoken word label, and ran the poetry slams at the Nuyorican Poets Café from 1988-1996. He is Visiting Professor of Writing at Columbia School of the Arts, Founder/ Proprietor of the Bowery Poetry Club.

Iron Sheik (Will Youmans) is a hip-hop poet. His first album, *Camel Clutch* was released in 2003.

Maggie Jaffe is the author of several books, including *The Prison* (Cedar Hill Publications), *1492 : What is it Like to be Discovered?* (Monthly Review Press) and *How the West was One* (Burning Cities Press). She lives in San Diego, home of the world-famous zoo and numerous military installations.

Joan Joffe Hall grew up in New York City, studied at Vassar and Stanford, and taught English, Women's Studies, film, and creative writing for many years at the University of Connecticut. She has published many stories, three full-length volumes of poetry, a fiction collection, and over a dozen chapbooks.

Barbara Kingsolver is the author of *The Bean Trees, The Poisonwood Bible*, and many other works. Kingsolver established the Bellweather Prize - an award for a first novel that 'exemplifies outstanding literary quality and a commitment to literature as a tool for social change.' She lives with her family on a farm in southern Virginia.

Adrian C. Louis teaches in the Minnesota State University system. His most recent book, *Logorrhea* (Northwestern University Press), was a finalist for the 2006 Los Angeles Times Book Prize.

Linda McCarriston teaches at the University of Alaska Anchorage. Her second book, *Eva-Mary* (Triquarterly) won the Terrence Des Pres Prize and was a finalist for the National Book Award.

devorah major is a poet, novelist and spoken word artist. She was San Francisco's Poet Laureate from 2002-2006. Her most recent poetry books are *where river meets ocean* and *with more than tongue*. She has published two novels and wrote the text for *Trade Routes*, a symphony with poetry composed by Guillermo Galindo, which premiered November 2005 under Maestro Michael Morgan and the Oakland East Bay Symphony Orchestra.

E. Ethelbert Miller is a literary activist. He is the board chair of the Institute for Policy Studies (IPS) and the author of *How We Sleep On The Nights We Don't Make Love* (Curbstone Press, 2004).

Sarah Menefee is a poet and poor people's rights activist in San Francisco. Her recent books include *Human Star* (Factory School) and *The Box* (Azul Editions). She is a founding member of The League of Revolutionaries for a New America.

Mark Nowak is the author of *Revenants* and *Shut Up Shut Down* (afterword by Amiri Baraka) and co-editor (with Diane Glancy) of *Visit Teepee Town: Native Writings after the Detours*, all from Coffee House Press. He is currently facilitating poetry dialogues between autoworkers at the St. Paul Ford assembly plant (slated for closing in June 2008 as part of Ford's 'Way Forward' plan) and Ford workers at plants in Port Elizabeth and Pretoria, South Africa.

Alix Olson is an internationally-known folk poet and progressive queer artist-activist. Since winning the 1998 National Poetry Slam with her New York City team and the 1999 OutWrite LGBT Slam, Alix has co-authored *Burning Down the House* (Soft Skull Press), published two books of poetry, released two spoken word CDs and made an award-winning documentary-film. She lives in Massachusetts

Grace Paley used to describe herself as a 'militant pacifist and cooperative anarchist'. Although she was best known for her award-winning fiction, she wrote poetry almost exclusively since the 1980s. A long-time resident of Vermont, in 2003 was named the Vermont State Poet. She died in 2007.

Leroy Quintana is the author of six books of poetry and twice winner of an American Book Award from the Before Columbus Foundation. He served in Vietnam during 1967-68, where he kept a notebook that became the source for many of his poems. He lives in California.

Margaret Randall is a writer, photographer and activist. Among her recent poetry collections are *Where They Left You for Dead / Halfway Home* (Edgework Books) *Into Another Time: Grand Canyon Reflections* (West End Books) and *Stones Witness* (University of Arizona Press). Other recent titles include *When I Look into the Mirror and See You: Women, Terror and Resistance* (Rutgers University Press) and *Narrative of Power: Essays for an Endangered Century* (Common Courage Press 2004). After working for many years in Latin America she now lives in New Mexico.

FD Reeve is an award-winning poet, novelist, short story writer, critic and translator, and is professor of letters emeritus at Wesleyan University. He is the author of *Robert Frost in Russia* (Zephyr Press), *The Return of the Blue Cat* (Other Press) and *The Blue Cat Walks the Earth* (Azul Editions), among many other works.

Adrienne Rich is one of America's most distinguished poets. She continues to be a tireless champion and practitioner of radically aware poetry.

Boots Riley is co-founder, along with Pam the DJ Funktress, of The Coup - a raptivist hip hop group. Growing up in the Oakland, California area he became active in the Progressive Labor Party and was president of the International Committee Against Racism (INCAR).

Luis J. Rodriguez was active in the Chicago Poetry Slam scene for many years and was part of the first US Slam Poetry tour to Europe in 1993. He is founder-editor of Tia Chucha Press and creative director of Tia Chucha's Bookstore & Cultural Center in Los Angeles. His most recent book is *My Nature is Hunger: New & Selected Poems* (Curbstone Press/Rattle Edition).

Richard Schaaf's books include *Revolutionary at Home, Roque Dalton: Poems* (translation), and most recently, *The Shoes*. He is the founder and editor of Azul Edtions, specializing in poetry, prose, essays, literary and art criticism, speeches, broadsides, and manifestoes that heighten the consciousness of their readers and accompany them in their struggles for economic, political and social justice.

James Scully's books include *Santiago Poems, Donatello's Version* and *Line Break: Poetry As Social Practice* (all Curbstone Press) and a translation of *Aeschylus' Prometheus Bound* (with C.J. Herington, OUP). He lives in San Francisco.

Tim Seibles was born and raised in Philadelphia. A former high school English teacher, he is the author of six books of poetry, including, most recently, *Buffalo Head Solos* (Cleveland University Press). He teaches at Old Dominion University.

Patricia Smith is the author of four books of poetry, including *Teahouse of the Almighty*, a 2005 National Poetry Series selection and winner of the 2007 Paterson Poetry Prize. She is a Pushcart Prize winner, a Cave Canem faculty member and a four-time individual champion of the National Poetry Slam. She lives in New York.

John Surowieki is the author of *The Hat City after Men Stopped Wearing Hats* (The Word Works, 2007), which won the 2006 Washington Prize, *Watching Cartoons Before Attending a Funeral* (White Pine Press, 2003) and five chapbooks.

Alexander 'Sandy' Taylor was the author of five books of poems, including *Dreaming at The Gates of Fury* (Azul Editions 2006). He was co-founder, along with his wife Judy Doyle, of Curbstone Press, where he was an editor for over thirty years. Sandy was an international force in the recognition and promotion of underserved, high-quality, engaged literature. He died in 2007.

John Trudell grew up in and around the Santee Sioux reservation. A Vietnam Veteran, he participated in the occupation of Alcatraz Island by Indians of All Tribes. After the occupation ended, he became a leader in the American Indian Movement until 1979 when his family was killed in a fire of unknown origin. Trudell emerged from this horrific tragedy to become one of the most powerful spoken word poets of our time.

Fred Voss has worked as a machinist and poet for many years. He lives in Long Beach, California.

Rob Whitbeck is a farmer and timber-thinner living in eastern Oregon. He has published two collections, *Oregon Sojourn* and *The Taproot Confessions*, with Pygmy Forest Press.

Don Winter is co-editor of the journal of literature and art *Fight These Bastards*. His poetry has been published in hundreds of magazines, including *New York Quarterly* and *Southern Poetry Review*, and several chapbooks, notably *Things About to Disappear, On the Line, and Beware the Madmen*. He lives in Michigan.

William Witherup is an essayist, playwright, poet and director of the Gene Debs Labor Ensemble, a radical theatre troupe. His works include *Men at Work* (Ahsahta Press, 1989), *Black Ash, Orange Fire : Collected Poems 1959-85* (Floating Island Publishers, 1986) and *Down Wind, Down River: New and Selected Poems* (University of New Mexico Press, 2000). He lives in Seattle, Washington.

Anne Winters is the author of the award winning *Key to the City* and, most recently, *The Displaced of Capital*. She teaches at the University of Illinois in Chicago.

Nellie Wong is the author of three books of poetry. She is a revolutionary feminist activist with Radical Women and the Freedom Socialist Party. She lives in San Francisco.

Marilyn Zuckerman has published four books of poetry: *Personal Effects* (Alice James Books), *Monday Morning Movie* (Street Editions), *Poems of the Sixth Decade* (Garden Street Press), and *Amerika/America* (Cedar Hill Publications). She has also received a PEN Syndicated Fiction Award and an Allen Ginsberg Poetry Award. She lives in Seattle.

Acknowledgements

Many individuals were of great assistance to me in this endeavour, especially Mike Alewitz, Bob Edwards, Martín Espada, Al Markowitz, Linda McCarriston, Alison Meyers, Richard Schaaf, Jantje Talkien, and Alexander Taylor. The deep critiques and advice of Denise Abercrombie, Jim Coleman, Andy Croft, and Jim and Arlene Scully were essential. Any weaknesses or errors are, of course, my own, and are likely the result of my having ignored their counsel.

Jack Agüeros
'Psalm for the Angel of Distribution' appeared in *Lord, Is This a Psalm?* (Hanging Loose Press: Brooklyn, New York). Copyright Jack Agüeros, 2002. Used by permission of Jack Agüeros and Hanging Loose Press.

Doug Anderson
'Bamboo Bridge' appeared in *The Moon Reflected Fire* (Alice James Books: Cambridge Massachusetts). Copyright Doug Anderson, 1994. Used by permission of Doug Anderson.
'The Torturer's Apprenctice' appeared in *Blues for Unemployed Secret Police* (Curbstone Press: Willimantic, Connecticut). Copyright Doug Anderson, 1998. Used by permission of Doug Anderson and Curbstone Press.

Naomi Ayala
'Hole' appeared in the journal *Ploughshares* (Spring 2005). Copyright 2005 Naomi Ayala. Used by permission of Naomi Ayala.

Anne Babson
'Vocabulary Test' appeared in *The Minnesota Review*, no 65-66, Spring, 2006. Copyright 2006 by Anne Babson. Used by permission of Anne Babson.

Amiri Baraka
'Got Any Change?' appeared in *XCP: Cross-Cultural Poetics*, no. 15-16, 2006, College of St. Catherine: Minneapolis, Minnesota. Amiri Baraka, 2006. Used by permission of Amiri Baraka.

John Bradley
'To Dance With Uranium' appeared in *Terrestrial Music*
(Curbstone Press: Willimantic, Connecticut). Copyright John
Bradley, 2006.

Marilyn Buck
'The "SHU": Special Housing Unit' is excerpted from the long
poem "incommunicado" and appears on
www.theprisonactivist.org. Used by permission of Marilyn
Buck.

Christopher Butters
'Faneuil Hall' and 'The Spark' appeared in *Pemmican* Summer
2007. Copyright 2007 Christopher Butters. Used by permission
of Christopher Butters.

Jayne Cortez
'Global Inequalities' and 'What's Your Take' appeared in *Jazz
Fan Looks Back* (Hanging Loose Press: Brooklyn, New York).
Copyright 1992 by Jayne Cortez. Used by permission of Jayne
Cortez and Hanging Loose Press. These poems also appeared in
Present/ Tense: Poets in the World, edited by Mark Pawlak.
Hanging Loose Press, 2004.

Jim Daniels
'Show and Tell' and 'Time, Temperature' appeared in *Show and
Tell: New and Selected Poems* (The University of Wisconsin
Press: Madison, Wisconsin). Copyright Jim Daniels, 2003. Used
by permission of Jim Daniels.

Robert Edwards
'Over There' appeared in *American Sounds* (Partisan Press:
Norfolk, VA). Copyright Robert Edwards, 2003. Used by
permission of Robert Edwards and Partisan Press. 'Stand'
appeared in *Pemmican*, Summer 2007. Used by permission of
Robert Edwards.

Martín Espada
'Alabanza,' 'Federico's Ghost,' and 'Revolutionary Spanish
Lesson' appeared in *Alabanza: New and Selected Poems 1982 -
2002* (W.W. Norton & Company: New York). Copyright Martín

Espada, 2003. Used by permission of Martín Espada. 'Federico's Ghost' and 'Revolutionary Spanish Lesson' also appeared in *Rebellion is the Circle of a Lover's Hand* (Curbstone Press: Willimantic, Connecticut, 1990). 'General Pinochet at the Bookstore' appeared in *The Republic of Poetry* (W.W. Norton & Company: New York). Copyright Martín Espada, 2006. Used by permission of Martín Espada.

Ed Friedman
'Mao and Matisse' and 'Heading for Manhattan by Train' appeared in *Mao and Matisse* (Hanging Loose Press: Brooklyn, New York). Copyright Ed Friedman, 1995.

Aracelis Girmay
'Arroz Poetica,' 'Ode to the Watermelon,' and 'Ride' appeared in *Teeth* (Curbstone Press: Willimantic, Connecticut). Copyright Aracelis Girmay, 2007. Used by permission of Aracelis Girmay and Curbstone Press.

Joy Harjo
'No' appeared in *How We Became Human: New and Selected Poems* (W.W. Norton & Company: New York). Copyright Joy Harjo, 2004. Used by permission of Joy Harjo.

Jack Hirschman
'Haiti' and 'Human Interlude' appeared in *The Endless Threshold* (Curbstone Press: Willimantic, Connecticut) and in *Front Lines: New and Selected Poems* (City Lights Books: San Francisco). Copyright Jack Hirschman, 2002. 'Youknowwomsayin' appeared in *Street Spirit: Justice News and Homeless Blues in the Bay Area*, 2005. Used by permission of Jack Hirschman.

Bob Holman
'A Jew in New York' appears by permission of Bob Holman.

Iron Sheik
'Leena' appeared on the album *Camel Clutch*. Copyright 2003 by Iron Sheik. Used by permission of Iron Sheik.

Maggie Jaffe

'Exile's Return' and 'Poverty Sucks' appeared in *How the West Was One* (Viet Nam Generation and Burning Cities Press: Tuscon, Arizona). Copyright 1997 by Maggie Jaffe. Used by permission of Maggie Jaffe. Exile's Return' also appeared in *The Prisons* (Cedar Hill Publications: Mena, Arkansas). Copyright by Maggie Jaffe 2001.

Kimiko Hahn

'Ipomea Purperea' appears courtesy of Kimiko Hahn. Copyright Kimiko Hahn 2007.

Joan Joffe Hall

'The Homeless' appeared in *In Angled Light: Selected Poems* (Antrim House: Simsbury, Connecticut). Copyright Joan Joffe Hall, 2005. Used by permission of Joan Joffe Hall.

Sam Hamill

'Blue Monody: Blues for Thomas McGrath' appeared in *Almost Paradise: New and Selected Poems and Translations* (Shambala Publications: Boston, Massachusetts). Copyright Sam Hamill, 2005. Used by permission of Sam Hamill.

Michael Henson

'A Story of Ash' appeared in *Crow Call* (West End Press: Albuquerque, New Mexico). Copyright Michael Henson, 2007. Used by permission of Michael Henson and West End Press.

June Jordan

Excerpt from 'Moving Towards Home'. Copyright 2006 June M. Jordan Literary Estate; used by permission.

Barbara Kingsolver

'The Monster's Belly' appeared in *Another America/ Otra America* (Seal Press: Seattle, Washington). Copyright 1992 by Barbara Kingsolver. Used by permission of Barbara Kingsolver.

Adrian C. Louis

'Another Day in the English Department or Meet Me at Medicine Tail Coulee' appeared in *Evil Corn* (Ellis Press:

Granite Falls, Minnesota). Copyright Adrian C. Louis, 2004.
Used by permission of Adrian C. Louis. 'A Song for the
Santee' appeared in *Among the Dog Eaters* (West End Press:
Albuquerque, New Mexico). Copyright Adrian C. Louis, 1994.
Used by permission of Adrian C. Louis.

devorah major

'fillmo'e street woman' appeared in *Street Smarts* (Curbstone
Press: Willimantic, Connecticut). Copyright devorah major,
1997. Used by permission of devorah major and Curbstone
Press. 'political poem' appeared in *Where River Meets Ocean*
(City Lights Books: San Francisco). Copyright devorah major,
2003. Used by permission of devorah major.

Linda McCarriston

'Elm Street: October 1977' and *'Le Coursier de Jeanne D'Arc'*
appeared in *Little River: New and Selected Poems* (Salmon
Publisher, Ltd.: Cliffs of Moher, Co. Clare, Ireland). Copyright
2000 by Linda McCarriston. 'To Judge Faolain, Dead Long
Enough, A Summons' appeared in *Eva-Mary* (Another Chicago
Press: Chicago). Copyright Linda McCarriston, 1991. Used by
permission of Linda McCarriston.

Sarah Menefee

'The blood of Colorado miners' appeared in *i'm not
thousandfurs* (Curbstone Press: Willimantic, Connecticut).
Copyright Sarah Menefee. Used by permission of Sarah
Menefee and Curbstone Press. 'human star' appeared in *Human
Star* (Factory School, Heretical Texts). Copyright 2005 Sarah
Menefee. Used by permission of Sarah Menefee.

E. Ethelbert Miller

'Looking for Omar' appeared in *How We Sleep on the Nights
We Don't Make Love* (Curbstone Press: Willimantic,
Connecticut). Copyright E. Ethelbert Miller, 2004.

Mark Nowak

Sections 1 and 3 from 'Capitalization' appeared in *Shut Up/
Shut Down* (Coffee House Press: Minneapolis, Minnesota).
Copyright Mark Nowak, 2004. Used by permission of Mark
Nowak.

Alix Olson
'Bobcats' appeared on www.alixolson.com. Copyright Alix
Olson, 2004. Used by permission of Alix Olson.

Grace Paley
'Here' appeared in *Begin Again: New and Collected Poems*
(Farrar, Straus and Giroux: New York). Copyright Grace Paley
2000. Used by permission of Grace Paley.

Leroy V. Quintana
'What it Was Like' appeared in *The Great Whirl of Exile*
(Curbstone Press: Willimantic, Connecticut). Copyright Leroy
V. Quintana, 1999. Used by permission of Leroy V. Quintana
and Curbstone Press.

Margaret Randall
'Doctrine' and 'The Unburied, The Missing' appeared in *Where
They Left You For Dead/ Halfway Home* (EdgeWork Books:
Boulder, Colorado). Copyright Margaret Randall, 2002. Used
by permission of Margaret Randall.

F.D. Reeve
'The Apology' and 'The Blue Cat Blues' appeared in *The Blue
Cat Walks the Earth* (Azul Editions: Washington, D.C.).
Copyright F.D. Reeve, 2007. Used by permission of F.D. Reeve
and Azul Editions.

Adrienne Rich
'Delivered Clean' appeared in *The School Among the Ruins:
Poems 2000-2004* (W.W. Norton & Company: New York and
London). Copyright 2004 Adrienne Rich. Used by permission
of Adrienne Rich and W.W. Norton & Company.

Boots Riley
'Underdogs' appeared on The Coup's *Steal This Album*
(Dogday Records, 1998). Copyright Boots Riley, 1998. Used by
permission of Boots Riley.

Luis J. Rodriguez.
'Carrying My Tools' appeared in *My Nature is Hunger: New*

and Selected Poems (Curbstone Press: Willimantic, Connecticut). Copyright Luis J. Rodriguez, 2006.

Richard Schaaf
'The Shoes' appeared in *The Shoes* (privately printed chapbook). Copyright Richard Schaaf, 2007 and used by permission.

James Scully
'Arc,' 'DU Blues,' 'Listening to Coltrane,' 'Qana,' and 'There is No Truth to the Rumor' appeared in *Donatello's Version* (Curbstone Press: Willimantic, Connecticut). Copyright 2007 by James Scully. Used by permission of James Scully and Curbstone Press. 'Qana' also appeared in *We Begin Here: Poems for Palestine and Lebanon* (Olive Branch Press/ Interlink Publishing: Northampton, Massachusetts).

Tim Seibles
'Invasion of the Body Snatchers,' 'Ladder,' and 'Night Flight' appeared in *Buffalo Head Solos* (Cleveland State University Press: Cleveland). Copyright Tim Seibles, 2004. Used by permission of Tim Seibles and Cleveland State University Press.

Patricia Smith
'Skinhead' appeared in *Big Towns, Big Talk* (Zoland Books: Hanover, New Hampshire). Copyright 2002 by Patricia Smith. 'Skinhead' also appeared in AGNI. Used by permission of Patricia Smith.

John Surowiecki
'S.Z. Home from Vietnam' appeared in *The Hat City After Men Stopped Wearing Hats* (The Word Works: Washington, D.C.). Copyright John Surowiecki, 2007. Used by permission of John Surowiecki.

Alexander Taylor
'Because' appeared in *Dreaming at the Gates of Fury: New and Selected Poems* (Azul Editions: Washington, D.C.). Copyright Alexander Taylor 2004. 'Because' also appeared in *Connecticut Review*. 'Baghdad' appeared in *Reaching into Darkness: This War and The Other* (Glad Day Books: Thetford, VT). Copyright 2007 Alexander Taylor.

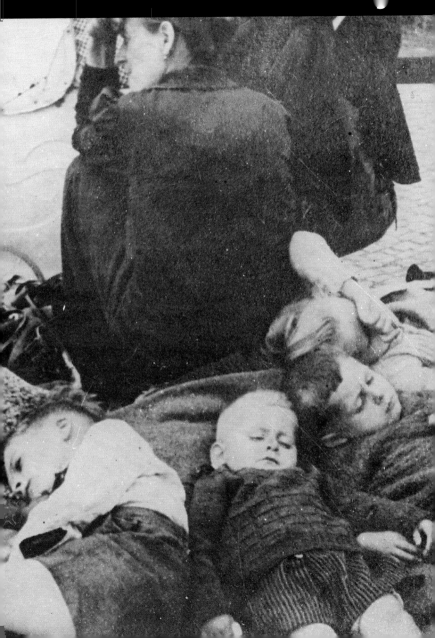

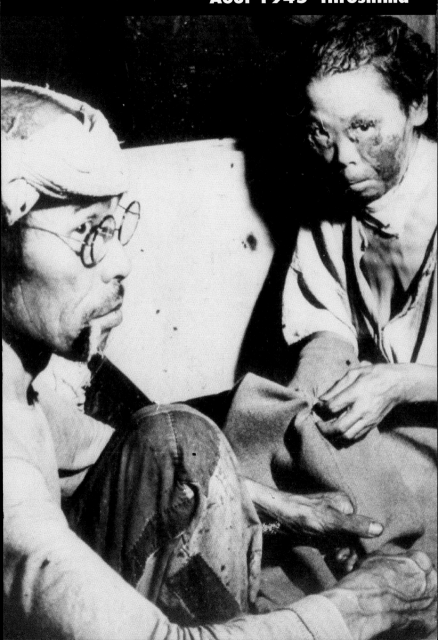

Anthony Kemp est né à Londres en 1939. Après plusieurs années de service en Allemagne dans la RAF, il entreprend des études d'histoire moderne à l'université d'Oxford. Il devient alors lecteur spécialisé dans l'histoire du IIIe Reich et les origines de la Seconde Guerre mondiale. En 1980, il entre à *Television South* comme conseiller, producteur et directeur de programmes documentaires. Il vit aujourd'hui en Charente où il combine ses carrières d'écrivain, de journaliste et de producteur de télévision indépendant.

Il est l'auteur de dix-huit ouvrages, essentiellement sur divers aspects de la guerre et de l'histoire contemporaine. Il collabore régulièrement avec le Mémorial de Caen et a été nommé citoyen d'honneur de Thionville pour son *Histoire de la campagne de Lorraine* en 1994. Il est également l'auteur du *6 juin 1944, la bataille de Normandie* dans la collection Découvertes Gallimard.

Tous droits de traduction et d'adaptation réservés pour tous pays
© Gallimard 1995

Dépôt légal : avril 1995
Numéro d'édition : 71637
ISBN : 2-07-053320-4
Imprimé en Italie

1939-1945
LE MONDE EN GUERRE

Anthony Kemp
Traduit par Pierre-M. Reyss

DÉCOUVERTES GALLIMARD
HISTOIRE

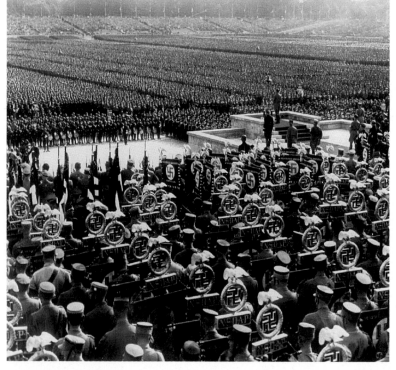

A u cours de l'été 1936, des milliers de militants nazis sont rassemblés sur la pelouse du stade de Nuremberg, spécialement édifié pour cette cérémonie; ils y acclament un discours triomphaliste de leur *Führer*, Adolf Hitler, et assistent à la grandiose parade de l'armée allemande. Au printemps, ces mêmes troupes ont réoccupé la rive gauche du Rhin, la Rhénanie, décrétée zone démilitarisée par le traité de Versailles en 1919.

CHAPITRE PREMIER
PRÉLUDE À LA GUERRE

L'année 1936 est cruciale pour les dictatures. Les milliers de fidèles de Hitler paradent à Nuremberg (à gauche). Mussolini, son allié italien, utilisant massivement son aviation et les gaz de combat en Abyssinie, remporte des succès sans gloire. Les deux despotes finissent par se croire invincibles.

L'irrésistible ascension des dictateurs

A la fin de la Première Guerre mondiale, les chefs d'Etat et de gouvernement s'étaient réunis à Versailles pour définir les moyens d'empêcher, de façon définitive, toute tentative d'agression de l'Allemagne et d'instituer une paix durable. Saignés à blanc par les effroyables pertes provoquées par le conflit, les Européens veulent écarter pour toujours le spectre de la guerre et croient y être parvenus. Cependant, en Allemagne, la peur du communisme et le ressentiment

Dès 1924, les membres du parti national-socialiste se lancent dans une propagande effrénée dans toute l'Allemagne (ici à Berlin).

éprouvé contre la sévérité des diktats du traité, s'ajoutant aux effets désastreux de la crise économique de 1929, engendrent un fort courant nationaliste qui se traduit par la constitution de partis politiques extrémistes, notamment le parti national-socialiste dont Adolf Hitler prend la tête. En Italie, le parti fasciste conduit par Benito Mussolini a déjà

Des membres des Jeunesses hitlériennes (*Hitler Jugend*) défilent au son des tambours. Le parti nazi repose sur une idéologie omniprésente, destinée à encadrer, à brider tout un peuple et à le soumettre à la volonté de son *Führer*. Mélange pernicieux de nationalisme exacerbé et de mysticisme typiquement teuton, le nazisme exalte l'âme germanique et les tentatives de s'y soustraire sont impitoyablement réprimées.

L'Italien Benito Mussolini (1883-1945) est nommé Premier ministre en 1922 et, en 1928, il se proclame «Duce», chef du parti unique d'un Etat fasciste. N'ayant pas le magnétisme de Hitler, il fait plus penser à un bouffon qu'à l'empereur romain qu'il s'efforce d'imiter.

accédé au pouvoir, en 1922, de même que, un peu plus tard, l'Espagne, la Hongrie et la Roumanie ont vu s'installer à leur tête un dictateur. L'entre-deux-guerres voit éclore de nombreuses manifestations, parfois violentes, d'idéologies politiques diamétralement opposées : le communisme d'inspiration soviétique et la dictature fasciste. Entre ces deux extrêmes, les régimes démocratiques, en France et en Grande-Bretagne, toutes deux ruinées par la guerre, n'ont ni la volonté ni les moyens d'assurer leur suprématie.

Du caporal autrichien au maître de l'Allemagne : Adolf Hitler

Hitler naît en Autriche en 1889. Enfant illégitime d'un douanier, il a mené, avant 1914, une vie assez misérable. Il s'engage dans un régiment d'infanterie bavaroise et, au cours de la bataille des Flandres, est décoré de la Croix de fer. Démobilisé, il fréquente assidûment les cercles d'extrême droite de Munich où ses talents d'orateur et de démagogue le conduisent à la tête d'un groupuscule qui donne naissance au parti nazi. En 1923, une tentative avortée de coup d'Etat lui vaut treize mois de prison pendant lesquels il élabore, en un livre confus intitulé *Mein Kampf* («Mon combat»), ses théories visant à l'élimination des Juifs et des communistes ainsi qu'à la constitution d'un «espace vital» en faveur du peuple allemand en Europe de l'Est. A la fin des années 1920, il mène campagne à travers tout le pays,

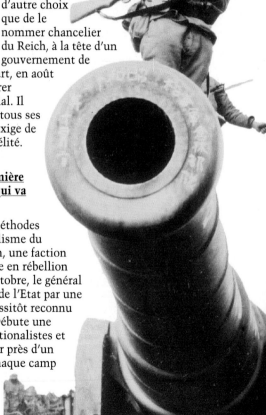

Les exactions des Japonais en Chine furent parmi les plus terribles de la guerre.

rassemble un nombre sans cesse croissant de fidèles et de sympathisants, si bien qu'aux élections de janvier 1933 les nazis constituent le parti le plus important avec 37 % des voix. Le vieux président Hindenburg n'a d'autre choix que de le nommer chancelier du Reich, à la tête d'un gouvernement de coalition, et lorsqu'il meurt, en août 1934, Hitler se voit conférer un pouvoir quasi dictatorial. Il élimine l'un après l'autre tous ses adversaires politiques et exige de l'armée un serment de fidélité. Il est le *Führer*.

La guerre d'Espagne : première cristallisation du conflit qui va embraser l'Europe

En 1936, contestant les méthodes socialistes et l'anticléricalisme du gouvernement républicain, une faction d'officiers supérieurs entre en rébellion contre le régime. Le 1er octobre, le général Franco est proclamé chef de l'Etat par une junte militaire et il est aussitôt reconnu par Hitler et Mussolini. Débute une guerre atroce opposant nationalistes et républicains, qui va coûter près d'un million de morts, et où chaque camp trouve des alliés à l'extérieur. Les «volontaires» allemands et italiens se battent aux côtés de Franco. Pour sa part, l'Union soviétique apporte son concours aux républicains sous la bannière desquels des milliers de jeunes Européens de gauche s'enrôlent. Au début, les républicains connaissent quelques succès, mais la puissance allemande donne à leurs adversaires la victoire finale. Après le désengagement de l'URSS, Barcelone en janvier 1939 et Madrid fin mars tombent aux mains de Franco.

Le Japon à la conquête du continent chinois

A peu près à la même époque mais à l'autre bout du monde, le destin du monde asiatique se joue. En 1931, l'armée japonaise entre en Mandchourie et s'empare de la ville de Moukden. Cette offensive, décidée par l'état-major sans l'aval du gouvernement civil de Tokyo, marque le point de départ de la prise progressive du pouvoir par les militaires, qui exigent une extension de la sphère d'influence nippone en Chine et déclenchent en juillet 1937 une guerre ouverte. Les envahisseurs prennent Shanghai et Nankin, exerçant sur la population civile une atroce répression. La résistance chinoise est dirigée par un général du Kouo-min-tang («parti du peuple»), Tchang Kaï-chek, avec l'aide des révolutionnaires communistes de Mao Tsé-toung. Tchang établit son quartier général à Chung-King que les Américains et les Anglais ravitaillent en armes et matériels apportés de Birmanie. La guerre se poursuit sans relâche pour ne former bientôt qu'un des multiples théâtres d'opérations du conflit qui va s'étendre à tout l'Extrême-Orient.

La guerre d'Espagne va constituer une sorte de répétition générale du conflit qui ensanglantera l'Europe. Malgré l'enthousiasme des jeunes républicains idéalistes et des milliers de volontaires luttant à leurs côtés, la puissance de feu allemande assurera la victoire des armées du général Franco. Les pilotes allemands de la légion Condor perfectionnent la technique du bombardement en piqué qu'ils pratiqueront à outrance lors des raids dramatiques de 1940. Ici, un paysan nationaliste célèbre la victoire de Franco.

Hitler est convaincu que les démocraties européennes ne s'opposeront pas à l'annexion de l'Autriche

L'Autriche est parcourue par un fort courant d'opinion réclamant son unification au sein d'une grande Allemagne. La pression s'accroît avec l'arrivée au pouvoir du puissant parti nazi en Autriche. En 1934, ses militants assassinent le chancelier Dollfuss. En février 1938, Hitler convoque en Allemagne son successeur, Schuschnigg, et exige qu'il inclue dans son cabinet plusieurs ministres nazis. Schuschnigg refuse et, pour prendre Hitler de vitesse, organise un référendum sur la question de l'*Anschluss* («annexion»). Mais un ultimatum le contraint à retirer son projet. Il est alors remplacé par un pro-nazi, Seyss-Inquart, qui invite l'armée allemande à occuper le pays et qui proclame le rattachement de l'Autriche le 13 mars 1938. Les puissances occidentales se bornent à protester timidement.

ACCORD COMPLET
des «Quatre» à Munich

La crise sudète et les accords de Munich

Le territoire des Sudètes, partie ouest de la Tchécoslovaquie, république créée en 1918 par le regroupement de provinces de l'Empire austro-hongrois, compte une forte minorité d'Allemands. Financés en sous-main par les nazis, ils entreprennent une vigoureuse campagne et, après l'annexion de l'Autriche, réclament à leur tour leur rattachement à l'Allemagne.

Chamberlain revient de Munich (à gauche), ramenant «la paix pour notre temps». En France, nombreux sont ceux qui, comme ces Parisiennes (en bas, à droite), se réjouissent, alors que les hommes d'Etat n'ont en fait obtenu qu'un bref répit.

Ce soldat allemand reçoit un accueil enthousiaste de la population autrichienne. Cette petite république germanophone, érigée après la Grande Guerre sur les ruines de l'Empire austro-hongrois, n'est pas un adversaire de taille aux yeux de sa puissante voisine. Son intégration dans la grande Allemagne, en violation flagrante des clauses du traité de Versailles, est bien perçue et les troupes d'occupation ne rencontrent aucune opposition. Hitler trouve ainsi une base de départ pour son offensive contre la Tchécoslovaquie.

VIVE LA PAIX

En septembre 1938, se tient à Munich une conférence, à laquelle prennent part les chefs de gouvernement de France (Daladier), d'Angleterre (Chamberlain), d'Allemagne et d'Italie, mais les Tchèques en sont écartés. Les Sudètes sont abandonnés à l'Allemagne, toutefois les quatre puissances s'engagent à garantir l'intégrité des autres territoires tchèques. Les peuples d'Europe respirent, croyant avoir sauvegardé la paix, mais ils se gardent bien de mettre en balance son prix. Seul Winston Churchill, lord de l'Amirauté britannique, déclare : «Nous avons essuyé une défaite sans même avoir fait la guerre.»

À gauche, un bombardier allemand Heinkel. Ci-dessous, chars d'assaut allemands en manœuvres.

Les forces en présence

L'accord de Munich donne à la France et à la Grande-Bretagne le répit dont elles ont besoin pour parachever leur réarmement. Selon les dispositions du traité de Versailles, l'Allemagne ne peut constituer qu'une armée de 100 000 hommes et il lui est interdit de se doter de navires cuirassés, d'une aviation d'assaut et d'engins blindés. Au cours des années 1920, ces prohibitions ont été secrètement violées et de nombreux Allemands se sont rendus en Union soviétique pour s'entraîner. Dès sa prise de pouvoir, Hitler abroge les clauses militaires du traité et lance un vaste programme de réarmement qui lui vaut l'indispensable appui des généraux. Il met en chantier une flotte de guerre pour défier la suprématie navale de l'Angleterre, jette les bases d'une nouvelle armée blindée et met à contribution les ingénieurs civils pour concevoir de nouveaux avions de chasse.

Théoriquement, la France, première puissance européenne, dispose d'une armée plus forte et mieux dotée que l'Allemagne et son aviation est sans rivale. Pourtant,

La ligne Maginot avec, au premier plan, des rangées de rails formant un obstacle antichars et, à l'arrière plan, une casemate de flanquement. La conception des ouvrages est excellente

sur le plan politique, le pays est déchiré entre la droite et le Front populaire. De plus, la stratégie de ses généraux n'a pas évolué depuis la guerre de 1914-1918. Conséquence des pertes essuyées pendant le conflit et de la chute de la natalité qui en est résultée, le grand état-major s'attend à une baisse sensible des recrues à partir de 1938. Il opte alors pour une stratégie purement défensive et, à partir de 1934, entreprend la construction d'une ligne de fortifications le long de la frontière allemande : la ligne Maginot.

L'Angleterre, quant à elle, ne connaît pas le service militaire obligatoire, sauf en temps de guerre, et sa force repose essentiellement sur quelques régiments composés de soldats professionnels ainsi que sur la Royal Navy pour défendre ses possessions d'outre-mer. Tenue par traité de venir en aide à la France si celle-ci est menacée, son assistance se réduit à un corps expéditionnaire de six divisions. Les généraux anglais, dont les conceptions

mais leur implantation déplorable. Edifiée pour verrouiller la frontière avec l'Allemagne, la ligne Maginot ne dépasse pas Malmédy, à l'ouest. Comme l'écrivait Clausewitz, le plus célèbre stratège allemand, «si vous vous retranchez derrière de puissantes fortifications, vous contraignez l'ennemi à chercher une autre solution pour passer»; ce qui sera le cas en mai 1940.

sont aussi obsolètes que celles des Français, ignorent résolument les tactiques modernes de l'emploi offensif de l'arme blindée.

La diplomatie de la dernière chance : sauver la paix à tout prix

Bien qu'il ait solennellement affirmé à Munich qu'il n'a plus d'ambitions territoriales, Hitler viole à nouveau le traité en mars 1939, et occupe les provinces tchèques de Bohême et de Moravie. Ni la France ni l'Angleterre ne sont en mesure d'intervenir militairement; elles ne peuvent qu'élever une véhémente protestation. L'un des principaux arguments des gouvernements conservateurs est de tenir Hitler pour le dernier rempart contre le communisme. Pourtant, le cabinet britannique, dans un effort désespéré pour se trouver des alliés à l'Est, décide d'ouvrir au printemps des négociations avec l'URSS, sans enthousiasme il est vrai. De leur côté, les Soviétiques, dépités de n'avoir pas été conviés à la conférence de Munich, se méfient des puissances occidentales. Les négociations traînent tout l'été, alors que Français et Anglais sont convaincus que la Pologne est la nouvelle cible de Hitler. Mais Joseph Staline engage des pourparlers avec l'Allemagne. Le 23 août 1939, un pacte de non-agression est signé par les ministres des Affaires étrangères Molotov et Ribbentrop. Deux jours plus tard, les gouvernements français et anglais concluent avec la Pologne un traité de défense mutuelle.

La Pologne au rendez-vous de l'histoire

De tous temps, la Pologne a été convoitée par ses deux puissants voisins, l'Allemagne et la Russie. Démembrée à plusieurs reprises, elle constitue une république indépendante depuis 1918. Les traités lui accordèrent alors un débouché maritime à Dantzig et une voie d'accès à ce port, baptisé le «corridor», séparant la Prusse orientale du reste de l'Allemagne. Hitler exige le droit de passage à travers le corridor et se heurte au refus des autorités polonaises. Il décide donc d'agir en force et envoie des troupes en Prusse orientale, sachant parfaitement que les Soviétiques ne broncheront pas.

La raison de cette immobilité est que le pacte germano-soviétique contient diverses clauses secrètes qui délimitent les sphères d'influence à l'Est. L'Allemagne pourra s'emparer de la plus grande partie de la Pologne, le reste ira à l'URSS, de même que les trois républiques baltes. De plus, les Soviétiques auront les mains libres en Finlande et en Roumanie.

Cependant, Hitler a besoin d'un prétexte pour justifier son invasion auprès de l'opinion publique et, ses «forces spéciales» massées le long de la frontière lui en fournissent l'occasion. Une douzaine de prisonniers revêtus d'uniformes polonais sont tués devant une station de radio allemande à Gleiwitz. La propagande nazie clame que la station a été assaillie par les Polonais et en représailles, à l'aube du 1er septembre, cinq

Dès son accession au pouvoir, le maréchal Joseph Staline (1879-1953) entreprend la campagne de collectivisation des terres. Entre 1935 et 1938, il expurge les rangs du parti des anciens chefs révolutionnaires et des centaines d'officiers sont victimes de parodies de procès qui lui assurent la mainmise de fait sur toute l'Union soviétique. Le culte de la personnalité qu'il instaure est si fort qu'il gardera la haute main sur son empire pendant toute la guerre malgré les pertes effroyables subies au cours de l'invasion allemande.

À gauche, une caricature de l'époque montre Hitler crucifiant la malheureuse Pologne sur la croix gammée (svastika) avec la complicité de Staline qui attend son heure pour partager les dépouilles de la Pologne.

armées allemandes déferlent sur la Pologne pendant que la *Luftwaffe* (armée de l'air) bombarde Varsovie.

La déclaration de guerre

A la Chambre des communes, le 2 septembre, le Premier ministre britannique, Neville Chamberlain, parle encore de paix et de négociations, mais les parlementaires s'y opposent, estimant que l'honneur de l'Angleterre est en jeu. Ils exigent du gouvernement qu'il adresse à Hitler un ultimatum le sommant de retirer ses troupes de Pologne avant le lendemain, 9 heures. La France notifie un ultimatum identique, expirant à 17 heures. Dès lors, la France et la Grande-Bretagne sont en guerre contre l'Allemagne et l'ordre de mobilisation générale est donné. On entend, pour la première fois, les sirènes d'alarme dans le

MOBILISATION GÉNÉRALE

Premier jour de la mobilisation : 2 Septembre

BATAILLE SUR TOUT LE FRONT
GERMANO-POLONAIS

ciel de Londres et, la nuit venue, le *black-out* est imposé. En France, l'armée prend position le long de la frontière allemande et les six divisions du corps expéditionnaire anglais sont déployées à l'ouest de la frontière belge.

Le viol de la Pologne

Sauf à lui manifester leur sympathie, les nations occidentales sont impuissantes à apporter un réel soutien à la Pologne qui défend héroïquement son territoire contre des envahisseurs très

supérieurs. Le 19 septembre, la campagne prend fin lorsque le général commandant la dernière armée polonaise combattante capitule.

Deux jours plus tôt, les Soviétiques ont envoyé deux groupes d'armées sur la frontière orientale afin de s'emparer des territoires que leur a concédés le pacte germano-soviétique. Le 25 septembre, les deux envahisseurs signent l'arrêt de mort de la Pologne en tant qu'Etat.

Peu après, les Russes annexent les trois républiques baltes de Lituanie, d'Estonie et de Lettonie.

La «drôle de guerre» s'installe pour l'hiver sur le front occidental

Pour envahir la Pologne, Hitler a pratiquement dégarni ses positions face à la France, pensant à juste titre que les

Les Polonais supportent tout le poids de la guerre éclair (*Blitzkrieg*) lorsque les bombardiers allemands pilonnent Varsovie en massacrant la population civile. L'image de cet enfant, assis en larmes devant les ruines de sa maison, deviendra bientôt un spectacle commun tout au long de la guerre.

Lorsque la France et la Grande-Bretagne mobilisent, en septembre 1939, on ne retrouve pas la liesse qui avait marqué l'appel aux armes de 1914. Les hommes, en grande majorité, considèrent que la guerre est inéluctable et que la défaite de Hitler est imminente.

Alliés ne réagiront pas. L'armée française lance quelques offensives ponctuelles en Sarre mais se retire aussitôt derrière la ligne Maginot. Les généraux sont décidés à défendre le territoire national mais ne se sentent aucun goût pour l'offensive qui coûte, à leurs yeux, trop cher en hommes et en matériel. A l'approche de l'hiver, chaque camp s'enterre dans les tranchées et seule se poursuit une activité de patrouilles. Le général en chef, Gamelin, est sûr que les Allemands vont attaquer non pas en Alsace ou en Lorraine, mais que l'on assistera à une répétition des campagnes de 1914, avec l'invasion de la Belgique malgré sa neutralité. Il met au point un nouveau plan selon lequel les forces françaises et anglaises réunies se porteront au devant de l'ennemi dans ce pays. Les hostilités ne connaissent une phase vraiment active que sur mer. Dès le début, les *U-Boote* (sous-marins allemands) attaquent de nombreux navires français et anglais qui réussissent néammoins à couler le *Graf Spee*.

Le maréchal finlandais Mannerheim (1867-1951), vétéran de la Première Guerre mondiale, est rappelé au commandement suprême au moment de l'agression russe. Sa détermination suscite une résistance acharnée à l'envahisseur. Par la suite, il s'alliera aux Allemands contre l'URSS et sera nommé président de la République en 1944.

Finlande : la guerre en blanc

Mis en appétit par l'absorption d'une partie de la Pologne et des trois Etats baltes, le 2 octobre, Staline exige de la Finlande la cession de certains territoires. Les Finlandais refusent, cherchent à gagner du temps mais, le 30 novembre, environ un million de Soviétiques envahissent le pays défendu par seulement 175 000 hommes. Le monde s'attend à une issue rapide de la campagne, mais les valeureux Finlandais se battent opiniâtrement sous le haut commandement du maréchal Mannerheim. Les unités russes, trop lourdes, s'empêtrent dans les forêts impénétrables, harcelées sans arrêt par les fantassins finlandais à skis. Cependant, irrésistiblement, le poids des envahisseurs finit par prendre le dessus. En mars 1940, alors que la glace est encore suffisamment épaisse, les blindés russes contournent et enfoncent les

Les troupes conduites par Mannerheim sont parfaitement entraînées aux combats d'hiver ; l'infanterie se déplace à skis (à gauche). La petite armée finlandaise fait payer aux Russes, malhabiles dans un terrain difficile, un très lourd tribut avant que leur supériorité en nombre n'arrache la victoire. Pour leur part, les fantassins français et anglais s'exerçaient dans les Alpes avant de partir au secours des Finlandais, lorsque les Allemands attaquèrent à l'ouest.

fortifications finlandaises. L'héroïque résistance de la Finlande suscite la profonde sympathie de l'Ouest.

Le Danemark et la Norvège proclament aussitôt leur neutralité. Mais, à l'approche du printemps 1940, tous les belligérants prennent conscience que, très bientôt, la «drôle de guerre» prendra fin. Les Etats-Unis, officiellement neutres, acceptent de vendre des armements aux Alliés selon le système du *cash and carry* («payez et emportez»), malgré une vive opposition du Congrès. La Grande-Bretagne bénéficie de l'appui inconditionnel des nations du Commonwealth, mais les Alliés souffrent d'un dramatique manque de préparation, face aux offensives qui se trament.

Les démocraties (en vert) isolées par les dictatures espagnole, allemande et russe (brun). En gris, les nations neutres en cette fin d'année 1940.

Namsos

NORVÈGE

FINLANDE

SUÈDE **Helsinki** • **Leningrad**

Oslo • **Stockholm** •

ESTONIE

Mer Baltique

• **Göteborg**

Riga • LETTONIE

DANEMARK

Copenhague • **Malmö**

LITHUANIE U.R.S.S

Dantzig • PRUSSE ORIENT.

• **Minsk**

ANGLETERRE • **Amsterdam** • **Berlin** • **Varsovie**

Londres • ALLEMAGNE

Dunkerque • **Cologne** SUDETES POLOGNE **Kiev** •

Bruxelles •

RHENANIE **Prague** •

• **Paris** **Nuremberg** • TCHECOSLOVAQUIE

RUTHENIE

Munich • **Vienne** •

Zurich • AUTRICHE • **Budapest**

FRANCE SUISSE HONGRIE

ITALIE

ROUMANIE

Bucarest •

Belgrade •

YOUGOSLAVIE

• **Sofia**

• **Madrid** BULGARIE

ESPAGNE • **Rome** **Tirana** •

ALBANIE

GRÈCE

Mer Méditerrané **Athènes** •

Mer du Nord

Atlantique

En une manœuvre éclair, les forces allemandes s'emparent du Danemark et de la Norvège avant de se lancer à l'assaut de la France, bientôt contrainte de demander l'armistice. La Grande-Bretagne se retrouve seule, face aux nazis, uniquement défendue par les chasseurs de la Royal Air Force. C'est seulement dans les sables du désert d'Afrique du Nord que les Anglais recueillent des succès aux dépens des troupes de Mussolini.

CHAPITRE II
LA GRANDE-BRETAGNE ISOLÉE

On peut dire que la détermination d'un seul homme a sauvé l'Europe : Winston Churchill (1874-1965). Premier ministre en novembre 1940, sa propagande est percutante ; en hommage à la RAF, il dit : « Jamais tant d'hommes n'auront contracté une dette aussi grande envers si peu d'entre eux. »

La campagne de Norvège

La Grande-Bretagne, la première, va violer la neutralité de la Norvège lorsque le commandant d'un destroyer intercepte dans ses eaux territoriales un ravitailleur allemand suspecté de retenir des marins britanniques prisonniers à son bord. Le 16 février, après un duel d'artillerie, les 300 marins sont libérés, mais cet incident décide Hitler à envahir le Danemark et la Norvège pour prévenir toute tentative d'occupation par les Alliés et protéger les transports de minerai de fer, vital pour son industrie, en provenance de Narvik.

L'offensive allemande démarre le 9 avril. En un jour, le Danemark tombe aux mains des Allemands dont les soldats déferlent sur la Norvège, appuyés, pour la première fois dans la guerre, par des unités parachutistes. Dans le fjord d'Oslo, l'artillerie côtière réussit à couler un croiseur lourd allemand, mais le gouvernement est contraint de se replier dans les montagnes. Un débarquement anglo-français à Namsos, le 14 avril, est rejeté à la mer quelques jours plus tard par les Allemands et une opération amphibie anglaise à Andalsnes subit le même sort. 2 000 chasseurs alpins allemands débarquent à Trondheim, mais une escadre anglaise au large coule huit des dix torpilleurs engagés dans l'opération ainsi qu'un sous-marin dans le fjord de Narvik. Les Alliés, auxquels se sont jointes des unités polonaises, débarquent et dispersent la garnison allemande. Malheureusement, avant que la position de Narvik ne soit consolidée, les armées allemandes passent à l'offensive sur le front de l'Ouest et envahissent la France. Les Alliés décident, début juin, de se retirer.

La place devenue libre, le Reich occupe la Norvège, installe au pouvoir

Un «Tommy» anglais, qui semble un peu perdu, monte la garde à un carrefour dans la région de Namsos en Norvège.

Pour envoyer des forces au secours des Finlandais, les Franco-Anglais doivent débarquer à Narvik (ci-contre) et traverser la Norvège, ce qui signifie violer la neutralité de ce pays. Les Alliés envisagent cette offensive pour couper la route aux Allemands, mais ces derniers vont les devancer.

Un amiral danois, les yeux bandés, est conduit auprès du général allemand commandant les troupes ayant pris Copenhague, pour discuter des termes de sa reddition.

le «traître» Quisling qui se heurte bientôt à une farouche résistance des habitants, soutenus par le roi Haakon exilé en Angleterre. Cependant, la défaite terrestre des Alliés en Scandinavie va peser très lourd sur le cours de la guerre.

Churchill : l'homme providentiel

A Londres, à la Chambre des communes, les parlementaires anglais éprouvent autant de honte que de colère devant les mécomptes de la campagne de Norvège. Ce ressentiment explose lors d'un débat, les 7 et 8 mai 1940, au cours duquel Chamberlain et son gouvernement conservateur subissent les attaques de l'opposition travailliste et même de certains membres de leur

parti. Après d'intenses discussions de couloirs, Winston Churchill est nommé Premier ministre à la tête d'une coalition rassemblant conservateurs et travaillistes. L'alliance occidentale compte enfin un chef clairvoyant, au courage éprouvé et reconnu. La haine qu'il voue à Hitler soutiendra le moral des peuples asservis d'Europe au cours des années sombres à venir.

A l'origine, l'intention des nazis était de suivre une nouvelle fois le plan Schlieffen de 1914 passant par la Belgique puis marchant vers le sud pour prendre à revers le gros de l'armée française, mais ils changent leur tactique.

La chute des Pays-Bas et de la France

L'assaut général est donné par les Allemands à l'aube du 10 mai 1940. Les unités spéciales de la Wehrmacht et les parachutistes s'emparent des ponts vitaux sur le Rhin et des aérodromes de Hollande. La IIe armée s'enfonce en Belgique le long du canal Albert et les unités aéroportées, dont les planeurs se posent près des casemates,

neutralisent la forteresse d'Eben Emael sur la Meuse. Pendant que les régiments français et anglais se hâtent vers le nord pour occuper des positions défensives le long de la Dyle, les chars Panzer du général Guderian se fraient un chemin dans l'épaisse forêt des Ardennes. A l'aube du 13 mai, protégés par le brouillard, ils franchissent la Meuse à Dinant et à Sedan, ne rencontrant qu'une opposition sporadique.

Progressant de près de 60 kilomètres par jour, sur

Von Manstein (en haut) et Guderian (à droite), ont remarqué très justement que le secteur des Ardennes constitue le point le plus faible du dispositif français : une zone de forêts peu fortifiées, que Pétain jugeait, en 1934, «impénétrable».

des routes encombrées de réfugiés, les Allemands atteignent les côtes de la Manche à Abbeville le 20 mai. En France, le général Gamelin installe son quartier général au château de Vincennes, qui ne dispose même pas de transmissions par radio convenables si bien qu'il perd rapidement toute notion de l'évolution dramatique de la situation. Les quelques divisions placées en réserve restent confinées derrière la ligne Maginot, que les

Allemands n'ont pas jugé efficient d'attaquer.

En quatre jours, la Hollande, submergée, capitule et la reine s'embarque avec son gouvernement à destination de l'Angleterre. Le gros de l'infanterie allemande fait aussitôt mouvement vers le sud, sur la Dyle, contraignant les Alliés à une retraite précipitée. Le seul moyen pour les troupes franco-britanniques de contenir l'ennemi serait de monter une contre-attaque en tenaille, venant à la fois du nord et du sud d'un couloir de 70 kilomètres laissé béant par l'ennemi. Gamelin, le 19 mai, donne ses ordres, mais l'absence de moyens de communication l'empêche de coordonner les combattants.

Au soir, le Premier ministre Paul Reynaud limoge Gamelin et le remplace par le général Weygand. Celui-ci rapporte les instructions de son prédécesseur pour se donner le temps d'évaluer la situation. Un sentiment d'impuissance et d'irréalité s'empare des états-majors et des troupes en campagne. Les Anglais, poussant au sud depuis l'Escaut sept de leurs neuf divisions, attaquent en direction d'Arras le 21 mai, appuyés par la cavalerie française, et infligent quelques pertes à l'ennemi. Mais c'est

Guderian estime qu'il pourra lancer ses chars à travers les Ardennes et, en fonçant ensuite vers la Manche, séparer les forces alliées. Dans le même temps, l'invasion de la Hollande et une puissante poussée en direction de Liège vont certainement attirer les Alliés au cœur de la Belgique. C'est exactement ce qui se passe.

Pour des dizaines de milliers de soldats français, la guerre commence par une interminable marche vers les camps de prisonniers (ci-dessus).

trop peu et trop tard. Le lendemain,
Weygand ordonne une contre-offensive
générale qui échoue. A court de munitions,
harcelées sans répit par la Luftwaffe, les
divisions alliées sont d'ores et déjà battues.
Coupé des Français, lord Gort, chef du corps
expéditionnaire britannique, est refoulé vers la
côte et, le 23 mai, décide le repliement de ses forces
autour de Dunkerque et leur évacuation.

L'armistice

Paul Reynaud est partisan de poursuivre le combat
à partir des colonies d'Afrique du Nord, mais son
cabinet succombe au défaitisme. Churchill se démène
pour renforcer la détermination des Français alors
que les Allemands entrent dans Paris et que le
gouvernement s'envole pour Bordeaux. Les
Britanniques offrent même de former avec la France
un Etat unique mais il est beaucoup trop tard.
Reynaud démissionne et il est remplacé, le 16 juin,
par le maréchal Pétain. Grâce à plusieurs opérations
navales, les derniers soldats anglais sont évacués du

La suprême
humiliation
infligée à la
délégation
française est de
devoir signer la
convention d'armistice
(ci-dessus) dans le
wagon où, en 1918, le
maréchal Foch reçut
la reddition des
Allemands. Mais, peu
après, les premiers
graffitis de la France
libre fleurissent sur
les murs.

Havre, de Cherbourg, de Bordeaux, et Pétain demande l'armistice. Le général de Gaulle décide de gagner Londres d'où il lance un appel à la résistance sur les ondes de la BBC au soir du 18 juin. Le 22, les plénipotentiaires français se présentent en forêt de Compiègne et n'ont d'autre alternative que de signer les conditions imposées par les nazis. Les provinces d'Alsace et de Lorraine sont annexées au Reich et les départements du Nord et de l'Ouest sont occupés. La France ne conserve qu'une souveraineté limitée sur le reste de son territoire : la «zone libre». Pétain s'installe avec ses services à Vichy.

Au retour de sa conférence avec le général Franco, Hitler rencontre le vainqueur de Verdun à Montoire le 24 octobre 1940. Pétain décide d'entreprendre une politique de collaboration avec l'Allemagne, convaincu que l'Angleterre ne tardera pas à déposer, elle aussi, les armes.

Pour éviter que la flotte française ne tombe aux mains de l'ennemi, les Anglais attaquent les bases de Mers el-Kébir et de Dakar, ce que Vichy ne leur pardonnera pas.

Le dilemme de Hitler

Au milieu de l'été 1940, Hitler s'interroge. Au grand étonnement de ses généraux, il a défait en quelques semaines les nations les plus puissantes d'Europe et, aujourd'hui, seule la Grande-Bretagne peut

Chargé de l'évacuation des Anglais pris dans la nasse de Dunkerque, le vice-amiral Ramsay, commandant la base navale de Douvres, organise en toute hâte l'opération Dynamo. Il réquisitionne tout ce qui flotte et constitue une armada hétéroclite composée de petits navires de guerre et de commerce, de bateaux de pêche et même de plaisance. Bien que de nombreux bateaux soient touchés par la Luftwaffe, l'opération se poursuit jour et nuit, alors que les Français se sacrifient pour défendre le périmètre. Le 4 juin, quand l'évacuation prend fin, Dunkerque est en flammes mais 339 000 soldats sont sortis du piège. Outre une forte majorité d'Anglais, de nombreux Français, Belges, Polonais et Tchèques réussissent à gagner l'Angleterre. La brève campagne de France aura eu le mérite de mettre en lumière les qualités militaires de trois généraux anglais, Alanbrooke, Alexander et Montgomery, dont l'expérience acquise contre les nazis sera précieuse plus tard.

s'opposer à ses desseins
expansionnistes en Europe.
Hitler n'a pas envisagé de
débarquer en Angleterre et ses
amiraux s'opposent à une telle
opération, conscients de la
puissance de la Royal Navy.
Convaincu que l'Angleterre
va demander la paix, il envoie

Ici à Douvres,
le radar permet
de détecter
l'approche de
l'ennemi et
de guider les
pilotes de la RAF
(ci-contre) vers leurs
objectifs. Le radar sera
l'artisan de la victoire
dans la bataille

des émissaires pour «tâter le terrain». Toutes ses
tentatives sont repoussées avec mépris. Pendant
six précieuses semaines, il tergiverse alors que,
de l'autre côté de la Manche, ses adversaires
renforcent leur défense. Hitler prend sa
décision le 16 juillet et fixe le démarrage
de l'opération *See-Löwe* («otarie»), le
débarquement en Grande-Bretagne, au
15 septembre. La Wehrmacht doit
faire débarquer treize divisions sur
un front couvrant toute la côte sud
de l'Angleterre. La *Kriegsmarine* (marine
allemande) proteste, faisant valoir qu'elle
est incapable de protéger une zone aussi
vaste et qu'il n'existe aucun engin de
débarquement. Dans ces conditions,
tout repose sur l'aviation et sa maîtrise
du ciel. Fin août, le maréchal Goering
affirme qu'il est capable de l'assurer.

Le Spitfire,
qui a
effectué son
premier vol en
1936, ainsi que le
Hurricane constituent
les fers de lance de
la chasse anglaise.
Constamment amélioré
pendant la guerre, le
Spitfire sera toujours
en première ligne
jusqu'en 1945.

La bataille d'Angleterre

Dès les premiers jours de l'été 1940,
les bombardiers allemands ont
pilonné les navires croisant en Manche mais
la chasse britannique a refusé de mordre à l'appât,

dissimulant ses forces. L'assaut total conçu par Goering doit être lancé par 3 242 avions face auxquels la RAF (Royal Air Force) ne peut aligner que 1 350 appareils dont bon nombre ne sont pas aptes à ce genre de combat. Avec deux jours de retard, l'opération est engagée contre les terrains d'aviation et surtout les stations radar dont dispose l'Angleterre. Une seule d'entre elles sera détruite.

Au 26 août, les pertes allemandes sont deux fois plus élevées que celles de la chasse anglaise : les Spitfire dispersent les lourdes escadrilles de bombardiers et neutralisent les Messerschmitt d'escorte. Cependant, début septembre, les réserves d'avions anglais s'amenuisent et la RAF souffre d'un cruel manque de pilotes. Le 7 septembre, Hitler ordonne à la Luftwaffe de

L'un des tournants de la guerre est la décision de Hitler de pilonner Londres au lieu de concentrer ses attaques sur les stations de radar ou les terrains d'aviation de la Royal Air Force. Ses bombes causent des ravages parmi la population civile mais ne réussissent pas à briser le moral des Londoniens qui se réfugient dans les stations de métro. Les bombardiers nazis sont finalement détruits par les chasseurs de nuit de la RAF équipés de radar.

bombarder Londres. Mais les pertes allemandes ont atteint un seuil critique, au point que Hitler finit par comprendre que jamais il ne pourra acquérir la maîtrise du ciel. Le 17 septembre, il abandonne ses plans de conquête, car il a déjà décidé d'envahir

l'URSS l'année suivante, malgré le pacte de non-agression, pour éliminer la menace bolchévique à l'Est.

L'engrenage de la terreur nazie en Europe occupée

Pendant que l'Angleterre se bat pour sa survie, les peuples des pays occupés subissent l'oppression brutale des nazis et les effets de leur politique raciale. Si la Wehrmacht a peu ou prou respecté les lois de la guerre, les dirigeants nazis, civils ou policiers SS, se comportent avec barbarie. Leur objectif est de mettre toute l'économie des nations conquises au service de la machine de guerre allemande, avec ce que cela implique : inflation galopante, réquisitions et rationnement. Même si l'extermination des Juifs n'est pas encore systématique en 1940, les premiers signes de génocide apparaissent en Pologne où se succèdent massacres et déportations dans des ghettos et les premiers camps de concentration. Au Danemark, les Juifs bénéficient de complicités pour s'enfuir en Suède, mais dans d'autres pays, les autorités locales participent activement aux rafles de leurs nationaux juifs. Partout on voit éclore, se dressant contre la sauvagerie des nazis, des groupes d'hommes et de femmes résolus à résister et à se battre.

Les Alliés préparent leur retour en force

Le lendemain même de l'armistice français, une petite flottille de vedettes rapides appareille de ports anglais. A bord, ont pris place les premiers volontaires appelés à combattre au sein de nouvelles unités

Les peuples occupés souffrent des pénuries alimentaires (ici en France). Mais le sort des Juifs est bien pire. Les sbires de Hitler regroupent les Juifs et les enferment de force dans des ghettos (ci-dessus à Varsovie), et les nazis commencent leur sinistre besogne en procédant à des exécutions de masse. Trouvant ces méthodes trop lentes, les SS décident en 1942 d'exterminer les détenus dans des camps spécialement organisés. Les Juifs ne sont pas les seules victimes de cette terreur. Les nazis éliminent les résistants, les Tsiganes, les homosexuels et tous autres éléments dits «antisociaux» dans leur campagne de «purification ethnique» de l'Europe.

spéciales : les «commandos». Ils
organisent des raids ponctuels sur
Boulogne et Le Touquet, abattant
quelques soldats allemands. Ils sont
ce que Churchill appelle sa «carte de
visite», pour que l'ennemi n'oublie
pas son serment : «Nous
reviendrons.» Outre la création des
commandos, Churchill prend deux
autres initiatives. La première est la
formation du *Special Operations
Executive*, le célèbre SOE (état-major
des opérations spéciales), avec mission
de «mettre l'Europe à feu et à sang» en
armant et en entraînant les résistants.
Il crée également le quartier général
des *Combined Operations*, dont la
tâche sera de préparer et coordonner
entre les trois armes (terre, air, mer)
des incursions en territoire tenu par
l'ennemi.

L'attitude des Etats-Unis

Il serait impensable que l'Amérique
puisse rester les bras croisés. Pourtant,
nombreux sont ceux qui prônent la

non-intervention. Joseph Kennedy, ambassadeur des États-Unis à Londres, est convaincu que l'Angleterre est à l'agonie, mais le président Roosevelt est d'un tout autre avis. Si l'essentiel des intérêts américains se situe dans le Pacifique, on note dans la population, lorsque l'Allemagne et l'Italie signent le pacte de l'Axe avec le Japon, une prise de conscience grandissante : tôt ou tard, l'Amérique devra s'impliquer dans le conflit.

En novembre 1940, Roosevelt est réélu pour un troisième mandat avec une large majorité, ce qui lui laisse toute latitude pour agir. Malgré la neutralité proclamée des États-Unis, il propose en décembre la mise en place d'un programme de «prêt-bail» et en fait adopter la loi par le Sénat en mai 1941. Jugeant que l'Amérique se doit d'être l'«arsenal des démocraties», il prête à l'Angleterre, qui en a désespérément besoin, 50 torpilleurs pour assurer la sécurité des convois américains dans l'Atlantique.

La guerre au désert

Le seul secteur où les forces anglaises se mesurent sur le terrain avec l'ennemi est la frontière séparant l'Égypte des colonies italiennes d'Afrique du Nord. La Grande-Bretagne y maintient en permanence une puissante garnison pour protéger le canal de Suez. En septembre

1940, la Xe armée italienne s'avance en territoire égyptien. En décembre, le général O'Connor est prêt à prendre l'offensive et, en une campagne éclair, ses 30 000 hommes rejettent les Italiens jusqu'à Bedafomm en Libye, capturant 130 000 prisonniers et mettant près de 400 chars hors de combat. Hitler, qui ne s'attend pas à la déroute de ses alliés, décide d'envoyer à Tripoli, en février 1941, le général Erwin Rommel à la tête de deux divisions d'élite. Au même moment, O'Connor reçoit l'ordre de se séparer d'une grande partie de son armée appelée sur d'autres théâtres d'opérations.

La campagne de Grèce

En octobre 1940, les Italiens se lancent à la conquête de la Grèce mais, une fois de plus, ils échouent. Hitler est de nouveau contraint de se porter au secours de son allié et il décide d'occuper la Grèce en même temps qu'il «aidera» la Yougoslavie, où le régime pro-nazi au pouvoir est menacé par les partisans. Les Grecs appellent l'Angleterre à la rescousse. Le cabinet britannique, assez réticent – bien que Churchill soit un ardent défenseur d'une offensive contre l'Allemagne par les Balkans, le «ventre mou de l'Europe» – finit par donner son accord. Hélas, l'opération se solde par un désastre. Le général Wavell rassemble 60 000 hommes qui débarquent en Grèce le 5 avril 1941. Le lendemain, les Allemands, passés par la Bulgarie et la Yougoslavie, passent à l'attaque; en trois semaines, ils sont à Athènes

Le général allemand Student constitue une armada de 500 avions et de 70 planeurs. Disposant de l'absolue maîtrise du ciel, il largue ses hommes sur l'aérodrome de Maleme, en Crète, le 4 mai 1940. Dix jours plus tard, les Anglais battent en retraite, perdant neuf navires de guerre et des milliers de prisonniers.

La garnison britannique cantonnée en Egypte reçoit, dès 1939, des renforts provenant des Indes, d'Australie et d'Afrique du Sud (ci-dessous). Les forces italiennes stationnées en Libye sont considérables (en haut, à gauche) mais, mal commandées, elles n'ont aucune envie de se battre vraiment. Si le général O'Connor n'avait pas été contraint de détacher certaines unités pour combattre en Grèce, il aurait pu chasser l'ennemi d'Afrique du Nord avant l'arrivée de Rommel.

et les Anglais doivent abandonner le terrain. Ils maintiennent néanmoins 14 000 hommes en Crète. L'île est aussitôt assaillie par les troupes aéroportées allemandes. Appuyés par de constants renforts et bénéficiant de la maîtrise du ciel, les parachutistes contraignent les Anglais à réembarquer.

Au premier abord, la campagne de Grèce est une catastrophe, mais il faut prendre en compte ses conséquences. Hitler, qui a programmé d'envahir l'URSS le 15 mai 1941, perd en Grèce cinq semaines vitales. De plus, il devra laisser sur place des forces importantes pour conserver la mainmise sur les Balkans.

La bataille de l'Atlantique

Pendant l'hiver 1940 et le printemps suivant, la Grande-Bretagne se bat sur un autre front non moins périlleux. Sa survie dépend de sa capacité à maintenir libres et sûres ses lignes de navigation. Au début de la

Faisant route en zigzag dans l'Atlantique, les convois américains naviguent escortés par des navires de guerre.

En 1939, la Royal Navy est la plus puissante marine du monde, mais la guerre sur mer devait démontrer que l'ère des cuirassés est terminée. L'arme navale du futur est le porte-avions avec ses avions-torpilleurs, utilisés la première fois par les Anglais qui neutralisent la flotte italienne mouillée dans le port de Tarente.

guerre, la flotte de surface allemande n'était pas de taille à se mesurer avec la Royal Navy, mais les nazis disposaient d'un certain nombre de sous-marins encore difficiles à détecter. En septembre 1941, le Reich peut aligner 150 *U-Boote*. Basés en Norvège

et en France, ces submersibles menacent les convois dans l'Atlantique. La *Royal Navy* ne peut mettre en service qu'un nombre très insuffisant d'escorteurs pour les lents cargos et cette situation se perpétuera jusqu'à l'entrée en guerre de l'Amérique. Des hordes de sous-marins ennemis, les «meutes de loups», parviennent, au printemps de 1941, à couler plus de navires que les chantiers navals britanniques ne peuvent en construire. Alors que ses sous-marins collectionnent les succès, les navires de surface de la *Kriegsmarine* ne brillent pas par leurs exploits. Certes, divers vaisseaux de ligne isolés écument sporadiquement l'Atlantique. Ainsi, en mai, le cuirassé *Bismarck* réussit à couler le *HMS Hood*, mais il est détruit par la RAF.

La stratégie navale de l'Allemagne repose sur l'emploi massif des sous-marins pour isoler l'Angleterre et la capture des bases établies sur le littoral français va permettre d'accroître considérablement leur champ d'action. Dès septembre 1939, vingt-six navires anglais sont envoyés par le fond, notamment le paquebot *Athenia* qui entraîne dans la mort une centaine de passagers dont de nombreux Américains.

Depuis toujours, l'idée fixe de Hitler est d'envahir l'URSS. Mais, mal préparées à affronter l'hiver russe, ses armées seront prises dans les glaces aux portes de Moscou. A la même époque, à l'autre bout du monde, le Japon attaque Pearl Harbour. Ce qui amène les Etats-Unis à s'engager aux côtés de la Grande-Bretagne. Si au début les agresseurs collectionnent les succès, lorsque l'énorme machine de guerre américaine se met en branle, il devient évident que l'inversion de la marée victorieuse en faveur des Alliés n'est plus qu'une question de temps.

CHAPITRE III
LA GUERRE TOTALE

Franklin D. Roosevelt (1882-1945) réussit l'exploit d'être élu quatre fois de suite à la présidence des Etats-Unis. A gauche, les Allemands préparent l'attaque à l'Est.

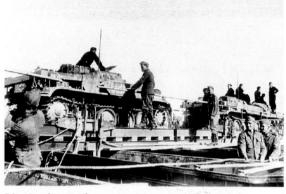

Au début, le matériel de guerre allemand se révèle de loin supérieur à celui des Soviétiques, mais la mise au point du tank T 34 donnera à l'Armée rouge un avantage décisif. Fabriqué en grandes séries dans des usines improvisées, il s'avère un blindé terriblement efficace. Ci-contre, chars d'assaut allemands au démarrage de l'opération Barberousse.

L'opération Barberousse, l'invasion de l'URSS

Au printemps de 1941, Hitler masse 3 000 000 d'hommes en Pologne et en Prusse orientale avant d'entreprendre la gigantesque opération d'anéantissement de l'Union soviétique. Ce sera une lutte sans merci. Bien que les Alliés aient prévenu Staline de l'imminence de l'invasion, les forces russes sont complètement prises au dépourvu. Les purges des années 1930 ont décapité le corps des officiers et la lourde bureaucratie est incapable de gérer les problèmes logistiques que pose la guerre moderne. Hitler divise ses forces en trois groupes. Le groupe d'armées Nord avance sur Léningrad et peut compter sur l'aide des Finlandais prêts à reconquérir leurs territoires annexés par l'URSS. L'objectif du groupe d'armées Centre est la prise de Moscou par Minsk et Smolensk. Le groupe d'armées Sud doit s'engager en Ukraine, conquérir la Crimée et finalement mettre la main sur les champs pétrolifères du Caucase.

A l'aube du 22 juin 1941, l'assaut général est donné.

Les bombardiers JU 87 constituent l'artillerie volante des divisions de *Panzer*.

Au début, les forces russes, incapables de coordonner sérieusement leur défense, sont écrasées. Progressant au rythme de quelque 75 kilomètres par jour, les Allemands capturent d'innombrables prisonniers et une énorme quantité de matériel. Pourtant les Soviétiques, retrouvant leur instinct de défense et leur confiance en la «sainte mère Russie», commencent à organiser leur résistance. Pendant les premiers jours, les soldats de la *Wehrmacht* sont souvent accueillis en libérateurs par une population heureuse de pouvoir secouer le joug communiste. Mais débarquent peu après tout l'appareil de la terreur nazie et les prédateurs du régime.

Rapidement, la fraternisation se change en haine et les Allemands sont bientôt aux prises avec les partisans qui harcèlent en permanence leurs lignes de ravitaillement, rendues d'autant plus vulnérables qu'elles s'allongent à mesure de la conquête.

Une colonne de cavalerie allemande franchit un pont flottant au début de la campagne de Russie. Hitler s'est bercé d'une sécurité illusoire en voyant la facilité de ses premières victoires et le nombre de soldats russes faits prisonniers. Mais il ne se rend pas compte de l'extraordinaire capacité de récupération des Soviétiques qui appellent la guerre à l'est la «grande guerre patriotique», et ce terme sera abondamment exploité par la propagande rouge pour stimuler la résistance des Russes. Staline se forge une image de «petit père des peuples».

A vant l'invasion de l'URSS, Hitler a diffusé l'ordre de liquider tous les commissaires politiques dans le cadre de sa lutte à outrance contre le bolchevisme. Après l'entrée en territoire soviétique, les ordres d'élimination s'étendent aux populations d'origine juive et nombreux sont ceux qui, parmi les soldats et surtout les officiers, sont choqués par la barbarie des *Einsatzkommandos*, les escadrons de la mort des SS. A Kiev, 34 000 hommes, femmes et enfants sont froidement abattus à la mitrailleuse dans le ravin de Babi-Yar, constituant ainsi le plus important massacre délibéré de civils de la guerre (ci-contre). Pour réconforter le moral de l'armée, le général von Reichenau publie un ordre du jour : «Le soldat doit bien comprendre qu'il faut exercer une vengeance sévère mais juste contre le Juif, ce sous-homme. L'armée doit aussi remplir un autre rôle, l'anéantissement des francs-tireurs harcelant nos arrières, car l'expérience prouve que ces actes de malveillance sont toujours le fait des Juifs».

A la mi-août, le groupe d'armées Centre investit Smolensk, ayant parcouru plus de la moitié du chemin de Moscou. Au nord, les Allemands ont presque complètement coupé les voies terrestres d'accès à Léningrad, alors que, au sud, 650 000 Soviétiques sont encerclés dans Kiev. A ce moment, Hitler paraît hésiter et la progression ralentit.

L'hiver russe

Au début d'octobre, la marche sur Moscou reprend mais, quinze jours plus tard, la pluie commence de tomber, transformant les pistes déjà mauvaises en torrents de boue dans lesquels s'enlisent véhicules et chars d'assaut. Les généraux espèrent que le gel viendra vite durcir les chaussées mais, mi-novembre, le grand froid paralyse les envahisseurs.

Napoléon disait qu'il avait été vaincu en Russie par le «général Hiver». Ci-dessus à gauche, des chars allemands ont été abandonnés dans la neige et, à gauche, un véhicule est embourbé jusqu'au plancher. Les Allemands sont contraints de stopper leur offensive, et leur ravitaillement est exposé aux coups de mains des partisans.

Le groupe d'armées Centre continue pourtant d'avancer et, en décembre, il est sur le point d'investir Moscou en un large mouvement de tenaille. Mais les divisions allemandes sont clouées sur place par le froid. C'est le moment que choisit le général Joukov pour contre-attaquer et forcer les nazis à faire retraite, au centre de leur dispositif, sur une ligne défensive à 90 kilomètres à l'ouest de Moscou. Pour effectuer la manœuvre, Staline a dégarni le front de Mandchourie, où il est aux prises avec les Japonais, de ses divisions sibériennes accoutumées aux grands froids. Bien que Hitler refuse de l'admettre, il vient d'essuyer, dans les faubourgs de Moscou, sa première défaite.

Utilisant la même tactique qu'en 1812, les Soviétiques pratiquent la politique de la terre brûlée, préférant livrer aux flammes leurs villages et leurs récoltes plutôt que de les voir tomber aux mains de l'ennemi. Ne trouvant ni abri ni ravitaillement, les nazis sont forcés de bivouaquer en rase campagne et de subir les rigueurs de l'hiver.

L'engagement américain s'accentue

Jugé victime d'une sauvage agression, Staline se change en allié du jour au lendemain dans l'opinion publique américaine. Bien que la presse s'apitoie sur le sort de la Russie et présente Staline comme un aimable «oncle Joe», celui-ci ne cesse de manifester envers les Alliés une profonde suspicion, même s'il est toujours prêt à amasser le matériel de guerre que ceux-ci lui envoient. Le 12 juillet, il signe avec la Grande-Bretagne un pacte d'assistance mutuelle dont l'exécution sera toujours «à sens unique», en sa faveur. A la mi-août, Churchill et Roosevelt – qui collaborent étroitement depuis le début – se rencontrent pour la première fois depuis la guerre à Terre-Neuve et signent la «charte de l'Atlantique». Ce document, plein de bonnes intentions, où est notamment consacré le droit des peuples à disposer d'eux-mêmes, ne sera jamais réellement mis en application mais ses principes formeront la base de la charte des Nations Unies. Outre les rapports difficiles qu'ils

Ci-dessous, Churchill et Roosevelt signent la charte de l'Atlantique à bord d'un navire de guerre à Terre-Neuve. A gauche de Roosevelt le général Marshall, chef d'état-major de l'armée américaine.

Après l'offensive de Hitler contre l'URSS, celle-ci devient un allié des Anglo-Américains. Un vaste programme d'aide est mis en place et de nombreux navires prennent la route maritime de Mourmansk. Sous la menace constante des sous-marins, des avions et des navires de surface allemands basés en Norvège, les convois subissent de très lourdes pertes.

entretiennent avec Staline, il existe cependant de nombreux sujets de discorde entre Américains et Anglais touchant au destin de l'Empire. Les Etats-Unis, qui n'oublient pas qu'ils furent autrefois colonie britannique, combattent pour faire triompher la démocratie et ils n'entendent pas appuyer les ambitions coloniales de leur alliée.

Rommel et l'Afrika Korps

En débarquant à Tripoli en février 1941, Rommel commence par regrouper l'armée italienne et, fin mars, il est prêt à prendre l'offensive contre la VIIIe armée anglaise. Les combats se déroulent essentiellement sur l'étroite bande côtière et chaque belligérant recule ou avance selon qu'il distend ou raccourcit ses lignes de ravitaillement. A la mi-avril, Rommel s'engage vers l'est, sur la route du canal

La seule autre voie de ravitaillement est le chemin de fer traversant l'Iran (ci-dessus et à l'extrême gauche). Les transports organisés par les Américains acheminent des milliers de tonnes de matériels, vivres et munitions. Des démarches sont entreprises, par la voie diplomatique, pour obtenir de la Turquie, neutre, le libre accès à la mer Noire par le Bosphore, mais en vain.

de Suez, et le commandant en chef britannique, le général Wavell, décide de s'accrocher à Tobrouk pour menacer le flanc de Rommel. Le «renard du désert», comme on le surnomme, prend conscience de ce qu'il s'est trop avancé et s'arrête pour assiéger Tobrouk. En juin, les Anglais tentent une percée mais échouent. Wavell est limogé et remplacé par le général Auchinleck qui, en novembre, repart à l'assaut et repousse Rommel sur 450 kilomètres, jusqu'à El Agheila, prenant Tobrouk au passage. Cependant, comme son prédécesseur, Auchinleck est contraint de se séparer de deux divisions australiennes envoyées en Asie pour affronter l'offensive japonaise. Fin janvier 1942, Rommel fait de nouveau mouvement mais, à court de ravitaillement, il doit s'arrêter à El Gazala où il reconstitue ses stocks. Fin mai, après seize jours de très violents combats et la résistance héroïque des Forces françaises libres du général Kœnig à Bir Hakeim, les Alliés font retraite en Egypte. La VIIIᵉ armée creuse des tranchées devant El Alamein et se prépare à défendre le canal de Suez.

Le général Erwin Rommel (1891-1944), fantassin de formation, assimile d'instinct les méthodes allemandes de la guerre moderne de mouvement et s'attirera le respect des Britanniques pendant la campagne du désert.

Le Japon se taille un empire en Asie du Sud-Est

L'invasion de la Chine n'ayant pas satisfait leur appétit de conquêtes, les Japonais rêvent d'étendre leur sphère d'influence. Ce qui inquiète les Etats-Unis qui possèdent de très importants intérêts dans le Pacifique. A partir de décembre 1940, les Américains prêtent assistance aux Chinois et décrètent un embargo sur les matières premières destinées au Japon. Cette sanction semble porter ses fruits : au printemps 1941, les Japonais viennent négocier à Washington, sans aboutir. Pendant ce temps, l'empire du Soleil levant poursuit ses préparatifs et son armée investit les colonies françaises d'Indochine. En représailles, les Anglo-Américains gèlent les avoirs nippons. En octobre, le bouillant général Tojo est nommé Premier ministre et son gouvernement adopte une ligne de conduite infiniment plus belliqueuse. Le 1ᵉʳ décembre, six

porte-avions
prennent
la mer et font
route sur les îles
Hawaï et la base
navale de Pearl Harbour
qu'ils attaquent à l'aube du 7 décembre.

La chute de Singapour

A l'extrémité de la péninsule malaise, les
Anglais ont puissamment fortifié leur
importante base navale de Singapour
en multipliant
les défenses

INDIE MOET VRIJ
WERKT EN VECHT ERVOOR!

contre une attaque par mer. On pense qu'aucune armée n'osera s'aventurer dans les collines couvertes d'une jungle épaisse et venir menacer la place forte.

Pourtant, le 7 décembre 1941, les Japonais débarquent au nord de la Malaisie et progressent rapidement à pied et à bicyclette. La garnison britannique, dépassée par les événements, s'avère incapable d'affronter l'ennemi dans la jungle. Elle se replie en hâte et se prépare à résister, mais Singapour est investie et se rend le 15 février 1942. Les Anglais, déjà pleinement engagés sur d'autres théâtres, n'ont pas pu renforcer suffisamment la Malaisie qui tombe aux mains de l'ennemi. Hong-Kong a connu le même sort au soir du 25 décembre 1941.

Le triomphe de l'empire du Soleil levant

Les Japonais se tournent alors vers les riches colonies hollandaises, investies sans coup férir, puis, en février 1942, leur aviation bombarde Darwin en Australie. Les Philippines sont, à l'époque, un véritable protectorat américain; leur armée est placée sous le commandement du général Mac Arthur. Les Japonais

Une bonne part des succès remportés par les Nippons est due à la résistance physique et à la frugalité des soldats, capables de subsister avec un simple bol de riz quotidien, n'emportant qu'un paquetage réduit au strict minimum. Sujets fanatiques de leur empereur, ils ignorent jusqu'au mot de reddition, préférant lutter et mourir sans jamais lâcher pied. Infanterie japonaise progressant ici dans la jungle.

Le 7 décembre 1941, les premiers des 350 appareils qui ont décollé des porte-avions japonais font leur apparition à l'aube dans le ciel de Pearl Harbour, principale base de la marine américaine dans le Pacifique. Quelques heures plus tard, trois cuirassés gisent par le fond et cinq autres sont gravement endommagés. Au même moment, les Japonais investissent les îles américaines de Guam, de Wake et de Midway. Ces coups de force, conçus dans leurs moindres détails par l'amiral Yamamoto, sont menés sans déclaration de guerre préalable et les pertes japonaises sont négligeables, alors que le moral des Américains en est très durement atteint. Par chance, les porte-avions de la Navy échappent à la destruction, car ils sont en manœuvres en haute mer. En solidarité avec son allié japonais, Hitler déclare officiellement la guerre aux Etats-Unis, alors qu'il n'en a nul besoin. Moyennant quoi, ce geste va faire basculer l'opinion publique américaine en faveur de l'ouverture des hostilités contre l'Allemagne et il donnera à Roosevelt le prétexte nécessaire pour préparer l'entrée en guerre de son pays.

Naufrage d'un navire japonais, vu par le périscope d'un sous-marin américain durant la bataille de Midway. Pour la *Navy*, la guerre dans le Pacifique consacre la revanche de Pearl Harbour. Bien que de nombreux navires de ligne soient coulés, l'intervention des porte-avions s'avère un facteur décisif en donnant à la marine les moyens de protéger les débarquements.

débarquent dans l'île de Luzon, au nord, le 22 février, et contraignent les Américains et leurs alliés philippins à se replier jusque dans la presqu'île de Bataan qui commande la baie de Manille. Mac Arthur quitte les Philippines début mars pour prendre la tête des forces américaines du Pacifique et son successeur, le général Wainwright, se maintient dans l'île de Corregidor jusqu'au 6 mai 1942. A bout de vivres et de munitions, il n'a d'autre choix que de capituler.

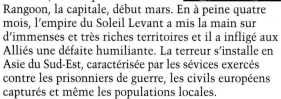

we here highly resolve that these dead shall not have died in vain…

REMEMBER DEC. 7th!

En une autre manœuvre, les Japonais envahissent la Birmanie, coupent la route des approvisionnements de Tchang-Kaï-chek, et s'emparent de Rangoon, la capitale, début mars. En à peine quatre mois, l'empire du Soleil Levant a mis la main sur d'immenses et très riches territoires et il a infligé aux Alliés une défaite humiliante. La terreur s'installe en Asie du Sud-Est, caractérisée par les sévices exercés contre les prisonniers de guerre, les civils européens capturés et même les populations locales.

La bataille de la mer de Corail

En avril 1942, les Japonais font mouvement vers le sud, avec pour objectif les archipels du Pacifique central et ils prennent pied en Nouvelle-Guinée, aux portes de l'Australie. Mais une escadre américaine

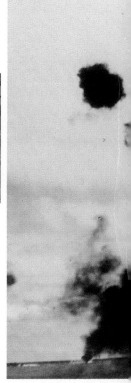

forte de deux porte-avions les empêche de débarquer à
Port-Moresby et contraint le convoi à faire demi-tour.
Commence la bataille de la mer de Corail où les
pilotes de l'aéronavale des deux camps se livrent
combat en plein ciel; les Américains remportent une
victoire décisive.

La provocation de Pearl Harbour va retourner l'opinion américaine, alors hostile à la guerre.

En juin 1942, les Japonais
essuient une nouvelle défaite,
encore plus lourde, à Midway. Les
Américains ont eu vent du projet
ennemi de débarquement dans l'île
et les attendent de pied ferme. Trois
porte-avions américains sont en
ligne, contre quatre nippons. Au soir

de la bataille, les Japonais ont perdu leurs quatre navires et un seul porte-avions américain est coulé. Les forces de l'amiral Yamamoto, désemparées, ont perdu l'initiative dans le Pacifique.

La conférence «Arcadie»

Le 22 décembre 1941, une conférence s'ouvre à Washington, sous la présidence de Roosevelt et Churchill, assistés de leurs conseillers militaires, où les Alliés s'accordent pour abattre prioritairement l'Allemagne tout en contenant les poussées japonaises dans le Pacifique, malgré l'opposition de la marine américaine qui brûle de venger Pearl Harbour. Pour atteindre ces objectifs, il est convenu de masser en Angleterre une colossale armée d'invasion et d'opérer, fin 1942, un débarquement en Afrique du Nord. Une autre disposition prévoit la constitution d'un état-major conjoint présidé par le général Marshall, chef d'état-major de l'armée américaine, pour coordonner au plus haut niveau les opérations. En apparence, la conférence est une belle démonstration de la parfaite unité de vues des Alliés mais, au fond, les tensions et les divergences entre Américains et Anglais subsistent.

Le général George Marshall (1880-1959), après avoir combattu en Europe en 1917-1918, est chargé de l'élaboration de la stratégie américaine et de l'organisation de l'armée qui ne compte, en 1939, que 200 000 hommes. En outre, lors de la conférence de Washington, en décembre 1941, il est nommé chef de l'état-major combiné. Choisi comme ministre des Affaires étrangères par le président Truman à la fin de la guerre, il met à exécution un plan pour la reconstruction de l'Europe (le «plan Marshall») qui lui vaudra le prix Nobel de la Paix en 1953. Ci-contre et à droite, les cuirassés d'escorte des convois de l'Atlantique.

La bataille de l'Atlantique

Pendant tout ce temps, la lutte pour la sécurité des transports dans l'Atlantique se poursuit. L'entrée en guerre des Etats-Unis amène la marine à prendre en chasse les *U-Boote* à l'ouest de l'Islande. Mais, entre ce secteur et celui des Anglais, s'étend un immense espace où la couverture aérienne est impossible. Ce vide est largement mis à profit par l'ennemi.

En surface, les sous-marins sont particulièrement vulnérables quand ils naviguent au diesel et rechargent leurs batteries, mais ils restent difficilement repérables car les radars sont encore trop volumineux pour être embarqués sur les avions de surveillance. Avec la découverte du radar miniaturisé,

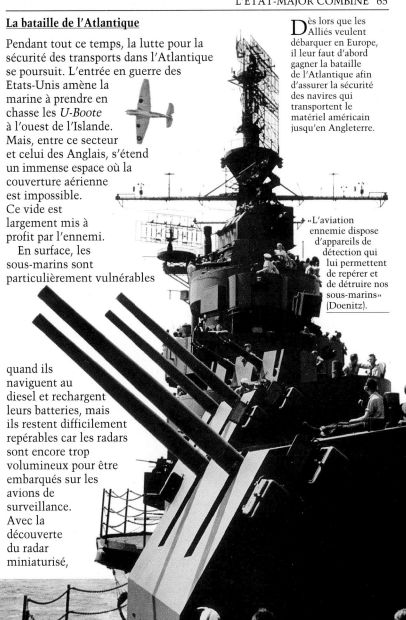

Dès lors que les Alliés veulent débarquer en Europe, il leur faut d'abord gagner la bataille de l'Atlantique afin d'assurer la sécurité des navires qui transportent le matériel américain jusqu'en Angleterre.

«L'aviation ennemie dispose d'appareils de détection qui lui permettent de repérer et de détruire nos sous-marins» (Doenitz).

le cours de la bataille tourne en faveur des Alliés. Mars 1943 marque le mois le plus noir pour ce qui est des pertes subies par les convois, mais désormais, le nombre de *U-Boote* mis hors de combat augmente de jour en jour, au point que l'amiral Doenitz décide d'abandonner la partie.

Les bombardements stratégiques sur l'Allemagne

De nombreux aviateurs, dont le maréchal de l'air Harris, commandant la flotte de bombardiers anglais, sont convaincus que des bombardements stratégiques peuvent contraindre un pays à demander la paix. La guerre a pourtant montré et montrera encore que ce n'est là qu'illusion. Le moral des Londoniens n'a jamais faibli pendant le *Blitz* de 1940-1941 pas plus que l'Allemagne ne capitulera quand elle sera la cible des raids alliés. Les bombardements sur l'Allemagne par la RAF commencent en mars 1942. La défense antiaérienne s'améliore, en particulier, grâce aux chasseurs de nuit. L'*US Air Force* commence d'arriver en Angleterre avec ses «forteresses volantes» B 17, évoluant à très haute altitude. Malgré leur armement défensif, ces appareils vont essuyer de lourdes pertes de janvier 1943 jusqu'à la mise en service du Mustang, chasseur d'escorte à long rayon d'action, début 1944.

Les premiers raids de la RAF sur l'Allemagne sont de peu d'effet mais quand les Lancaster quadri-moteurs entrent en service, un premier raid de mille bombardiers pilonne Cologne le 30 mai 1942 (ci-dessous). A partir de ce moment, en bombardant de nuit, la RAF va déverser un déluge de feu sur les villes allemandes. Malgré les radars perfectionnés et un système de navigation guidée plus précis, on se soucie assez peu de la précision des bombardements. Il s'avère impossible de ne frapper que les objectifs industriels ou militaires. Les pertes aériennes sont sévères mais les généraux pensent que le résultat en vaut la peine car les bombardiers détruisent les fabriques, les centres de communication, les usines d'aviation et les raffineries de pétrole, partout en Allemagne. Le 14 février 1945, la ville de Dresde, bien que dépourvue d'intérêt stratégique, est rayée de la carte et 60 000 personnes trouvent la mort dans l'ouragan de feu qui balaie les rues, anéantissant une ville qui constituait un monument unique d'architecture ancienne.

Les «opérations spéciales» et la Résistance en Europe

La première opération d'envergure des commandos britanniques est une incursion dans l'archipel norvégien des îles Lofoten en mars 1941, qui cause de graves dommages aux Allemands. Moins chanceuse est la tentative de débarquement à Dieppe, en août 1942, d'une division canadienne littéralement décimée par la défense allemande.

Plus les nazis oppriment les territoires occupés, plus ils se heurtent à la volonté de résistance des populations. Lorsqu'ils entreprennent de déporter des jeunes Français pour travailler dans leurs usines – le STO – en février 1943, nombreux sont ceux qui rejoignent le maquis. Pour les entraîner et les armer, des agents secrets anglais et français sont parachutés auprès d'eux. Beaucoup seront trahis et assassinés par la Gestapo, mais l'existence d'une résistance organisée oblige les Allemands à conserver sur place des divisions entières qui, sans cela, combattraient sur d'autres théâtres d'opération.

«Ouvrez maintenant un second front»

Sur le front de l'Est, les Allemands ont perdu la bataille de Moscou, mais ils n'ont pas pour autant perdu la guerre. Au printemps de 1942, Hitler limoge plusieurs généraux et décide de lancer au sud une offensive pour s'emparer du bassin du Don et des champs pétrolifères du Caucase. L'attaque n'est lancée que le 28 juin. Au début, les succès s'accumulent. Les nazis parviennent sur le Don, mettent le siège devant

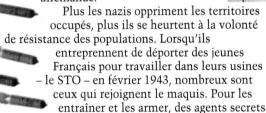

Lord Lovat en compagnie des commandos britanniques au retour de Dieppe. C'est la première opération d'envergure et, bien qu'elle se soit achevée par un désastre, les Alliés en tirent d'appréciables enseignements qui seront mis à profit le jour J. Parce qu'il est impossible de s'emparer d'un port bien défendu, ils mettent au point les ports artificiels Mulberry. Ils fabriquent aussi des engins blindés spéciaux pour neutraliser les obstacles plantés sur les plages. L'amiral Mountbatten, concepteur du raid, devait écrire par la suite : «Pour un homme tombé devant Dieppe, dix vies furent sauvées en Normandie le jour J.»

Sébastopol en Crimée et s'emparent de Rostov fin juillet. Les deux groupes d'armées Sud sont sur le point d'atteindre tous leurs buts lorsque Hitler décide d'y prélever des divisions qu'il envoie au nord, d'une part pour prêter main-forte aux assiégeants de Léningrad, d'autre part pour opérer une percée vers Stalingrad. Affaiblie, à court de munitions et de carburant, l'offensive sur le Caucase échoue.

Les Russes, qui sont dans une situation critique, demandent instamment aux Alliés d'ouvrir un second front à l'Ouest, pour obliger les Allemands à diviser leurs forces. Une grande partie de la presse britannique appuie cette politique, de même que les Américains qui mettent sur pied deux opérations majeures au printemps 1942. La première, baptisée *Sledgehammer* («marteau-pilon»), consiste en un débarquement massif en Normandie, cette même année, en raison du risque d'un effondrement de l'URSS. Pour 1943, sous le nom de code *Round-up* («rassemblement»), ils prévoient une offensive de grande envergure entre Dieppe et Calais.

Les Anglais préféreraient un débarquement en Afrique du

Hitler en compagnie des généraux Jodl et Keitel sur le front de l'Est. Convaincu d'être un stratège de génie, il décide de prendre la conduite de la guerre.

Nord. Cette opinion se renforce après l'échec sanglant du raid canadien sur Dieppe en août 1942. Les Américains, qui souhaitent «favoriser» le théâtre du Pacifique, désapprouvent l'envoi de forces importantes en Méditerranée. Finalement, Churchill et Roosevelt tombent d'accord, le 25 juillet, pour fixer à novembre la date d'une

Les soldats russes, opérant derrière les lignes, désorganisent les communications allemandes, ici en sabotant une voie ferrée.

opération amphibie au Maroc et en Algérie sous les ordres d'un officier général américain jusqu'ici inconnu, Dwight D. Eisenhower.

Le 10 août 1942, Churchill s'envole pour Moscou où il doit rencontrer Staline pour la première fois. L'ambiance n'est pas très cordiale; ce dernier accuse les Anglais d'être trop timorés face aux Allemands mais il se résigne, en fin de compte, à accepter la décision des Alliés, quoique de mauvaise grâce.

Cette carte donne une idée restreinte des opérations allemandes par rapport aux immensités de la steppe russe. Les trois groupes d'armées conquièrent d'immenses espaces complètement vides sans détruire pour autant les forces ennemies. Le général Halder écrit : «Nous pensions trouver en face de nous 200 divisions. Nous en avons déjà recensé 360. Sans doute ne sont-elles ni bien armées ni bien équipées, du moins à nos yeux, et elles manquent d'un commandement tactique, mais elles sont là. Et quand nous en avons détruit une douzaine, les Russes les remplacent aussitôt par une autre douzaine.»

Légende de la carte :

- Zone occupée par l'Allemagne en juin 1941
- Ligne de front août 1941
- Ligne de front novembre 1941
- Ligne de front décembre 1941
- Ligne Staline
- Poches russes encerclées
- Contre-attaques russes
- Frontière russe en 1939

mer de Barents

NORVÈGE · Mourmansk

ÈDE

· Belomorsk

FINLANDE · Petrozavodsk

Helsinki · · Leningrad
· Tallin · Novgorod

Riga · Velikije Luki · · MOSCOU
· Tula U.R.S.S.

Vitebsk · · Smolensk

Groupe d'armée Nord (Leeb) · Minsk

Bialystok · Guderian · Koursk
OLOGNE
· Varsovie · Kharkov
Groupe d'armée · Brest-Litovsk
Centre (Bock) · Kiev Stalingrad
Groupe d'armée Kleist
Sud (Rundstedt) · Ternopol · Rostov
· Uman
CHECOSLOVAQUIE mer d'Azov

· Budapest
HONGRIE · Odessa

· Sébastopol
ROUMANIE · Bucarest mer Noire

نصر الأمم المتحدة أقرب كل يوم

A la fin de 1942, le vent de la guerre commence de souffler en faveur des Alliés. Ils infligent à Rommel une défaite décisive devant El Alamein et débarquent en Afrique du Nord; à l'est, la VIe armée de von Paulus est assiégée dans Stalingrad. Dans le Pacifique, les Américains entament la longue et sanglante reconquête des îles annexées par les Japonais. A la conférence de Casablanca, les chefs alliés élaborent le débarquement en Normandie. Mais la route est encore longue qui conduira à la victoire.

CHAPITRE IV
LE TOURNANT DE LA GUERRE

Les Alliés débarquent en force sur la côte d'Afrique du Nord (à gauche), tandis que le maréchal Joukov (1896-1974) concentre douze armées qui vont frapper l'Allemagne nazie en plein cœur.

La bataille d'El Alamein

En juillet 1942, les Anglais réussissent à briser l'offensive de Rommel dans le désert égyptien sur la ligne de défense qui protège le canal de Suez. Cette ligne d'El Alamein s'étend sur 65 kilomètres entre la mer et la dépression de Quattara dont les pentes abruptes interdisent tout accès aux blindés. En août, Churchill se rend au Caire, limoge Auchinleck qu'il remplace par le général Alexander. Le général Bernard Law Montgomery est promu au commandement de la VIIIᵉ armée et il s'attache à relever le moral de ses troupes. Plus question désormais de parler de retraite!

Rommel est à l'extrême limite de ses lignes de ravitaillement alors que celles de Montgomery sont toutes proches du front. Fin août, Rommel tente de s'emparer de la crête de Alam el-Halfa mais les chars anglais l'attendent et il ne parvient pas à enfoncer le dispositif britannique.

Dans la nuit du 23 au 24 octobre, 1 000 canons déclenchent un feu nourri sur les positions allemandes en bordure de mer que Montgomery pulvérise. Le 3 novembre,

Le général Montgomery (à gauche), vétéran de la Première Guerre mondiale, a commandé une division en France en 1940. Son caractère impétueux et sa présomption lui valent de nombreuses inimitiés, aussi bien pendant qu'après les hostilités, mais il faut lui reconnaître qu'en quelques semaines il relève le moral de la VIIIᵉ armée, lui redonnant confiance.

L'opération Torch est la première manœuvre amphibie de grande envergure entreprise par les Alliés au cours de la guerre et elle fournit d'inestimables enseignements aux stratèges confrontés aux problèmes de transport sur de longues distances. Le gros du corps expéditionnaire appareille des ports de Grande-Bretagne, mais les troupes qui débarquent à Casablanca viennent des Etats-Unis. Eisenhower commande toute l'opération depuis son quartier général de Gibraltar. Pour la plupart des Américains, c'est un baptême du feu et la campagne ultérieure, en Tunisie, montrera que leur entraînement souffre de multiples lacunes. Eisenhower réussit à constituer un état-major homogène et fortement soudé qui demeurera auprès de lui, avec quelques rares changements, jusqu'à la victoire. Après la libération du littoral nord-africain, le succès de l'opération Torch rend possible l'engagement dans la mêlée de l'armée française aux côtés des Alliés, pour combattre en Italie puis en France.

l'ennemi décroche. Benghazi tombe le 20 novembre et la poursuite continue vers Tunis où les Allemands doivent être pris en étau entre Montgomery d'un côté et les armées de l'opération Torch, de l'autre.

Opération Torch : le débarquement en Afrique du Nord

Le but poursuivi par les Alliés est d'abord de chasser les troupes de l'Axe qui reculent sous la poussée anglaise venue d'Egypte, et de fournir un tremplin aux manœuvres futures en Italie et en Grèce. Des problèmes d'ordre politique se posent car le Maroc, l'Algérie et la Tunisie sont tenus par une administration inféodée au régime de Vichy et les Alliés veulent s'assurer de la loyauté des troupes françaises qui y restent cantonnées.

Sous le commandement du général Eisenhower, le débarquement a lieu le 8 novembre 1942 et ne rencontre pratiquement pas d'opposition. En représailles, les Allemands occupent la «zone libre» en France; ils envoient également de puissants renforts aéroportés en Tunisie à la demande des autorités françaises. L'ordre de mission du général Anderson, commandant la Ire armée britannique, est d'avancer vers l'est pour chasser les Allemands de Tunisie et opérer sa jonction avec la VIIIe armée, enfin, le 13 janvier, la 2e division blindée de Français libres du général Leclerc, venue du Tchad, rejoint à son tour Montgomery.

La conférence de Casablanca

Le 14 janvier 1943, Churchill et Roosevelt se retrouvent à Casablanca et, une fois de plus, leurs divergences politiques se manifestent. Les Américains veulent d'abord chasser l'ennemi d'Afrique du Nord, puis concentrer leurs armées en Grande-Bretagne pour investir l'Europe. Les Anglais privilégient une invasion par la Méditerranée. On convient finalement de faire porter l'effort principal sur un débarquement en France pour l'été 1944, mais, pour maintenir les troupes d'Afrique du Nord en haleine et assurer la sécurité des convois en Méditerranée, il est décidé d'envahir la Sicile dès l'été 1943.

Pour préparer l'invasion dans la Manche, les Alliés mettent en place un état-major interarmes, le COSSAC. Ils décident également que la guerre ne prendra fin que par la reddition inconditionnelle des forces de l'Axe. Cette proclamation fait l'objet de vives critiques en ce qu'elle exclut toute possibilité de paix négociée avec un gouvernement allemand modéré qui se formerait après un coup d'Etat contre Hitler. Les chefs alliés cherchent par-dessus tout à prévenir toute émergence d'un sentiment militariste dans l'un des pays ennemis, qui tirerait argument de n'avoir pas connu la défaite par les armes, comme ce fut le cas en Allemagne après la Grande Guerre.

Les chefs militaires français posent des problèmes aux Alliés

Outre les questions de haute stratégie, les chefs alliés à Casablanca ont à cœur de concilier entre elles les

Pendant que les troupes américaines défilent dans les rues de Casablanca, Eisenhower doit traiter avec Darlan (ci-dessous), ce qui lui vaudra de nombreuses critiques.

diverses factions dont chacune clame qu'elle seule personnifie la France. Le général de Gaulle n'a pas été prévenu de l'opération Torch et, par ailleurs, les Alliés ont organisé l'évasion hors de France occupée du général Giraud pour qu'il prenne le commandement des troupes françaises d'Afrique du Nord. Mais en novembre 1942, on apprend que l'amiral Darlan,

Les chefs alliés, à Casablanca, avec de Gaulle. Il sera très difficile de le persuader de serrer, devant les journalistes, la main de son rival, le général Giraud (ci-dessous).

commandant la marine de Vichy, est à Alger. Eisenhower, disposé à coopérer avec n'importe quel chef militaire français qui ne s'opposerait pas aux troupes d'invasion, passe un accord avec Darlan, ignorant complètement Giraud qui ne sera tiré des oubliettes qu'après l'assassinat de l'amiral la veille de Noël.

En Grande-Bretagne, de Gaulle s'estime bafoué et insulté, jugeant que lui-même et ses Forces

françaises libres sont seuls à pouvoir parler au nom de la France. Le gouvernement de Vichy, quant à lui, estime avoir pour lui le fait d'avoir été reconnu par les Etats-Unis en 1940. Churchill, à force de diplomatie, finit par obtenir de de Gaulle qu'il se rende à Casablanca pour rencontrer Giraud.

La campagne de Tunisie

Au début, les divisions de l'opération Torch progressent rapidement le long de la côte, s'emparent de Bône et de Philippeville, et Montgomery, à l'est, continue de poursuivre l'Afrika Korps dans les montagnes de Tunisie. Le «renard du désert», cependant, est encore loin de la défaite. Ayant reçu l'ordre de défendre Tunis jusqu'au dernier homme, bénéficiant de la proximité de ses sources d'approvisionnement, il mène une campagne de retardement en

Ces chars d'assaut britanniques sont bloqués devant Gabès. Il aurait fallu, selon certains, débarquer bien plus à l'ouest, près de Bizerte, pour soulager Malte et empêcher l'envoi de renforts allemands en Tunisie.

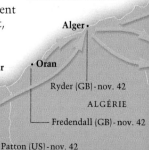

Alger •

• Gibraltar   • Oran

Ryder (GB) - nov. 42

ALGÉRIE

• Rabat   Fredendall (GB) - nov. 42

• Casablanca

Patton (US) - nov. 42

MAROC

Safi •

frappant alternativement ses adversaires à l'est et à l'ouest. La saison des pluies d'hiver marque un temps d'arrêt mais, dès la mi-février, Rommel attaque les Américains à Faïd. Ceux-ci, non aguerris, lâchent pied et les Allemands foncent sur le col de Kasserine. Des renforts constitués de troupes expérimentées montent en ligne en toute hâte et, le 3 mars, Rommel

En s'accrochant à la Tunisie, Hitler va y immobiliser (et y perdre) de nombreuses divisions d'élite qui auraient été bien plus précieuses sur d'autres théâtres d'opérations.

est renvoyé sur sa base de départ. Cependant, trois jours plus tard, il porte encore des coups très rudes à la VIIIe armée britannique devant Medenine.

C'est là le dernier assaut de Rommel en Afrique. Malade, il est rapatrié sur l'Allemagne. Les dernières divisions se battent avec acharnement mais, fin mars, Montgomery tourne la ligne Mareth et avance sur Sfax. Le 13 mai, le général von Arnim et ses 125 000 hommes capitulent.

En Europe de l'Est, les Allemands s'engluent dans l'enfer de Stalingrad

En retirant ses divisions blindées du Caucase, pour les jeter contre Stalingrad, Hitler va sceller son destin. Ses généraux l'ont prévenu que ses lignes s'allongent dangereusement et qu'il ne disposera pas de forces suffisantes pour réussir. Pour toute réponse, Hitler les relève de leur commandement.

Fin septembre, la VIe armée du général von Paulus repousse les Russes à l'intérieur de Stalingrad. Ceux-ci vont se défendre farouchement, maison par maison.

Von Paulus demande des renforts et Hitler usera littéralement 22 divisions dans une vaine tentative de déloger des décombres la LXIIe armée russe du

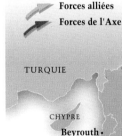

Forces alliées
Forces de l'Axe

TURQUIE

CHYPRE

Beyrouth •

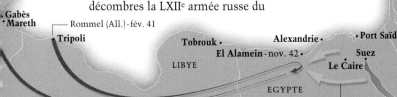

• Bizerte   • Palerme
• Tunis   SICILE

• Sousse

UNISIE   MALTE
43 • Sfax

• Gabès
• Mareth

—— Rommel (All.) - fév. 41

• Tripoli   Tobrouk •   Alexandrie •   • Port Saïd

El Alamein - nov. 42 •   Suez

LIBYE   Le Caire •

EGYPTE

Montgomery (GB)

général Tchouikov. Les Allemands subissent de telles pertes qu'ils doivent faire monter en ligne des unités hongroises et roumaines pour tenir leurs flancs. Pendant les mois d'octobre et de novembre, les Russes massent leurs troupes et, dès que le gel durcit le sol, ils attaquent de tous côtés. Le 22 novembre 1942, von Paulus et ses 250 000 hommes sont encerclés. Goering promet de ravitailler les assiégés par les airs, mais l'opération se révèle impossible. Von Paulus, nommé maréchal, n'a d'autre issue que de capituler le 2 février avec les 90 000 survivants de son armée. Hitler ne se remettra jamais de cette perte.

Koursk, la plus grande bataille de chars de tous les temps

Après le désastre de Stalingrad, les lignes allemandes sont désespérément minces et il s'avère impératif de les réduire. Le maréchal von Manstein, chargé de l'opération, ramène ses troupes sur la base de départ de l'été précédent. Il lance ses escadrons de chars contre les armées russes, sans répit, désorganisant leurs mouvements. Plus au nord, cependant, le général Joukov s'enfonce profondément dans les positions allemandes autour de Koursk, une brèche que Hitler veut à tout prix colmater. Son plan consiste à masser la quasi-totalité des unités blindées disponibles, soit 17 divisions, et à attaquer le saillant russe en tenaille. L'opération, baptisée Citadelle, est finalement lancée le 4 juillet 1943. Au début, l'attaque est un succès, mais Joukov attend son heure, laissant les Allemands brûler leurs stocks de carburant et de munitions. Au bout d'une semaine, il passe à la contre-attaque avec des troupes fraîches. Les Russes étrillent véritablement les divisions de Panzer épuisées. Une fois de plus, Hitler autorise un repli stratégique.

A l'automne, les Allemands sont rejetés sur le

En URSS, toute la population est mobilisée pour participer à l'effort de guerre, souvent dans des usines improvisées. Les femmes prennent la relève des hommes partis se battre sur le front, encouragées sans relâche par les slogans de la propagande communiste.

Bien que l'équipement militaire soviétique soit passablement rudimentaire, il convient tout à fait à une armée de paysans. L'une des armes les plus performantes est le lance-roquettes multitube : l'«orgue de Staline» (ci-dessus).

En 1943, Stalingrad est un gros centre industriel implanté sur la rive ouest de la Volga. Résolu à s'en emparer, Hitler écarte les objections de ses généraux, dégarnit d'autres secteurs du front et concentre pour l'assaut 22 divisions. La ville est défendue par la LXIIᵉ armée soviétique commandée par le général Tchouikov, soldat pur et dur, adoré de ses hommes. Le général von Paulus jette vainement toutes ses forces dans la bataille, transformant la ville en un champ de ruines, mais il n'obtient pas de résultats décisifs face à un adversaire déterminé. Tchouikov devait écrire plus tard : «Nous nous battons en tenant l'ennemi au contact rapproché, ce qui empêche son aviation de bombarder les positions de nos unités avancées. Chaque soldat allemand vit avec l'impression qu'il est en permanence au bout d'un fusil russe.»

Dniepr et les événements d'Italie contraignent Hitler à retirer des troupes du front de l'Est. Au centre, les Russes reprennent Smolensk et au sud le groupe d'armées B échappe de justesse à l'encerclement. Seule la Crimée est toujours aux mains des Allemands.

L'opération Husky : l'invasion de la Sicile

Les premières unités de deux armées anglo-américaines prennent pied en Sicile le 10 juillet 1943 sans rencontrer de forte opposition. Seules deux divisions allemandes sont stationnées dans l'île et le gros des forces italiennes capitule tout de suite. A mesure que les Alliés progressent dans l'intérieur des terres, la résistance allemande s'intensifie mais, le 22 juillet, les Américains s'emparent de Palerme. Trois jours plus tard, Mussolini est renversé et

Lors de l'opération Husky, un millier de bateaux mettent à terre 8 divisions qui découvrent que les Italiens les accueillent en libérateurs.

On utilise les gros «Landing ship tanks» pour débarquer les blindés directement sur les plages d'assaut.

remplacé par le maréchal Badoglio. Ce dernier souhaiterait demander un armistice mais la présence des forces allemandes sur son territoire l'en empêche. Eisenhower veut saisir l'occasion car il manque de moyens pour tenter une invasion. Il ordonne à la VIIIe armée de traverser le détroit de Messine le 3 septembre et le gouvernement Badoglio signe subrepticement un armistice. Quand ils l'apprennent, les nazis occupent aussitôt Rome.

Forcés, presque malgré eux, de porter la guerre sur le sol italien, les Alliés en tirent toutefois une consolation : les Allemands doivent y affecter des régiments qui, sinon, viendraient se battre en Normandie l'année suivante.

La guerre dans le Pacifique s'intensifie

Début août 1942, les Américains ont achevé la concentration de leurs forces et, en liaison avec les Australiens, ils préparent la campagne qui doit faire refluer la marée japonaise.

Ce seront principalement des opérations amphibies, des sauts d'île en île, chacune défendue jusqu'au dernier homme par un ennemi fanatisé.

La première étape sera la reconquête de la Papouasie et des îles Salomon. Partant de Port-Moresby, les Australiens livrent dans les montagnes de Papouasie des combats acharnés contre les Japonais qu'ils repoussent graduellement jusqu'à les assiéger dans Buna qui tombe en janvier 1943. De leur côté, les Marines débarquent à Guadalcanal et à Tulagi, dans les Salomon, le 7 août 1942. Ils résistent aux vagues successives des contre-attaques ennemies et achèvent enfin la conquête de Guadalcanal en février de l'année suivante. MacArthur lance alors ses troupes vers la Nouvelle-Guinée avant de s'emparer, à l'automne 1943, de l'importante base aérienne stratégique de Rabaul. En novembre, les GI's débarquent dans l'archipel des Gilbert où ils se heurtent à une très forte résistance. Les généraux réclament plus d'engins de débarquement, sans se préoccuper des besoins des Alliés pour leur invasion de l'Europe.

L'épopée de la reconquête du Pacifique est une longue succession de batailles acharnées, menées dans des conditions climatiques épouvantables, contre un ennemi bien entraîné au combat. Les Marines américains furent souvent obligés d'avancer sous le feu, au milieu des palétuviers ou dans une jungle épaisse. La campagne des îles Salomon demandera sept longs mois au cours desquels les Américains progressent d'île en île, sur 1 000 kilomètres, avant d'investir la principale base japonaise, Rabaul. Un des grands jours de cette campagne est celui où l'on apprend, en décodant un message, que l'amiral Yamamoto, l'homme du raid sur Pearl Harbour, doit effectuer un voyage d'inspection. Le 18 avril 1943, une escadrille abat le bombardier de l'amiral au-dessus de l'île de Bougainville. Fin 1943, la Navy a lavé l'affront de Pearl Harbour.

Guadalcanal

ÎLES SALOMON

mer de Corail

AUSTRALIE

N

• Port-Moresby

• Rabaul

PAPOUASIE

Darwin •

NLLE-GUINÉE

mer d'Arafoura

Le plan Cossac

A Casablanca, sir
Frederick Morgan a été
désigné pour préparer les
plans de l'invasion dans la
Manche baptisée opération
Overlord. Il constitue un état-
major mixte. Mais des divergences
d'opinion se font jour. Les Anglais,
épuisés par des années de combats
solitaires, penchent pour une stratégie
« à petits pas », alors que les Américains
privilégient une guerre à outrance
par les voies les plus courtes.

Le premier choix à opérer est
celui de la zone du débarquement.
Le plus logique aurait été de
prendre pied dans le Pas-de-
Calais où la Manche est la plus
étroite, mais c'est là que les
Allemands ont concentré leurs
fortifications. Après maintes
discussions, les stratèges
optent pour la côte nord du
Cotentin, en Normandie,
dans les limites du rayon
d'action des

▢	Etats-Unis
▢	Hollande
▢	Royaume-Uni
▢	Japon
⟨	Sphère d'influence Japonaise (juil. 42)

Océan Indien

mer de Banda

TIMOR

• Macassar

CÉLÈBES

• Surabaja

JAVA

Djakarta

BORNÉO

SARAWAK Palembang •

BORNÉO
NORD
BRITANNIQUE

BRUNEI

SUMATRA

Singapour •

PHILIPPINES

Kuala-Lumpur •

Corregidor

• Manille

MALAISIE

Bataan

mer de Chine Méridionale

LUZON

INDOCHINE
FRANÇAISE

OKINAWA

FORMOSE

• Bangkok

mer de Chine Orientale

• Hong-Kong

SIAM

• Canton

• Nagasaki

• Rangoon

• Shanghaï

mer Jaune

• Nankin

CHINE

• Mandalay

BIRMANIE

Golfe du Bengale

• Chung-King

• Calcutta

• Port Arthur

INDE

kden • Pékin

NEPAL

chasseurs basés en Grande-Bretagne. C'est l'opération
Overlord. Devant le manque d'engins de débarquement,
il est suggéré d'engager l'offensive avec trois
divisions transportées par mer et deux divisions
aéroportées, pour occuper un front de 50 kilomètres
entre Caen et Carentan. Comme il n'existe pas de
port utilisable avant que Cherbourg ne tombe, on
construira de toutes pièces deux ports artificiels,
baptisés «Mulberry». Le plan complet est soumis
aux gouvernants alliés à Québec, en août 1943,
Churchill donne son accord, mais de mauvaise grâce.

En reconnaissance du
succès de sa parfaite
coordination des
manœuvres en Afrique
du Nord et en Sicile,
Eisenhower reçoit
le commandement
suprême des forces de
l'opération Overlord.

Pendant les mois de l'automne 1943, les divergences entre les Alliés se font plus vives

Les Anglais, qui tenaient jusque-là une place
prépondérante, se rendent compte que, dorénavant,

la puissance militaire des Etats-Unis les ramène
à ne jouer que les «brillants seconds» au sein
de l'alliance. Churchill réclame instamment
une augmentation de 25% des effectifs de
l'opération Overlord mais les Américains
renâclent en proposant d'affecter de préférence
les engins utilisés par l'opération Torch à un
débarquement dans le midi de la France.

En novembre, les chefs alliés se réunissent
au Caire, avant de se rendre à Téhéran où ils
doivent rencontrer Staline. Churchill découvre
que les Américains ont jeté les bases d'une
offensive en Birmanie pour soulager la pression
exercée sur les troupes chinoises et ouvrir une
nouvelle route terrestre de ravitaillement. Roosevelt
se trouve pris entre les projets de ses généraux en

Birmanie et les arguments des Anglais qui jugent qu'Overlord n'est pas assez puissante. Toujours indécis, les Alliés se retrouvent à Téhéran où les Anglais continuent de plaider en faveur de nouvelles interventions en Méditerranée et dans les Balkans pour affaiblir l'Allemagne. Staline a des idées très personnelles sur le destin de cette région et il s'oppose vivement aux projets de campagnes en Yougoslavie et en Grèce. En contrepartie, il promet aux Américains de s'engager contre le Japon dès la défaite de l'Allemagne – ce qui plaît à Roosevelt –, et il est finalement convenu de reporter l'offensive en Birmanie et d'intégrer une division supplémentaire dans le dispositif d'Overlord.

Le 6 décembre 1943, le général Eisenhower est nommé commandant en chef des forces d'invasion avec instruction «de pénétrer en Europe et, en collaboration avec les autres nations alliées, de mener les opérations devant conduire au cœur de l'Allemagne et détruire ses forces armées».

En novembre 1943, Churchill et Roosevelt retrouvent au Caire le nationaliste chinois Tchang-Kaïchek (à l'extrême gauche). De là, ils se rendent à Téhéran pour rencontrer Staline. Les discussions sont d'ordre essentiellement politique. Le principe du découpage en quatre zones d'occupation de l'Allemagne, après la guerre, est adopté, de même qu'est scellé le destin de la Pologne sur laquelle Staline aura les mains libres, et ceci malgré les objections de Churchill.

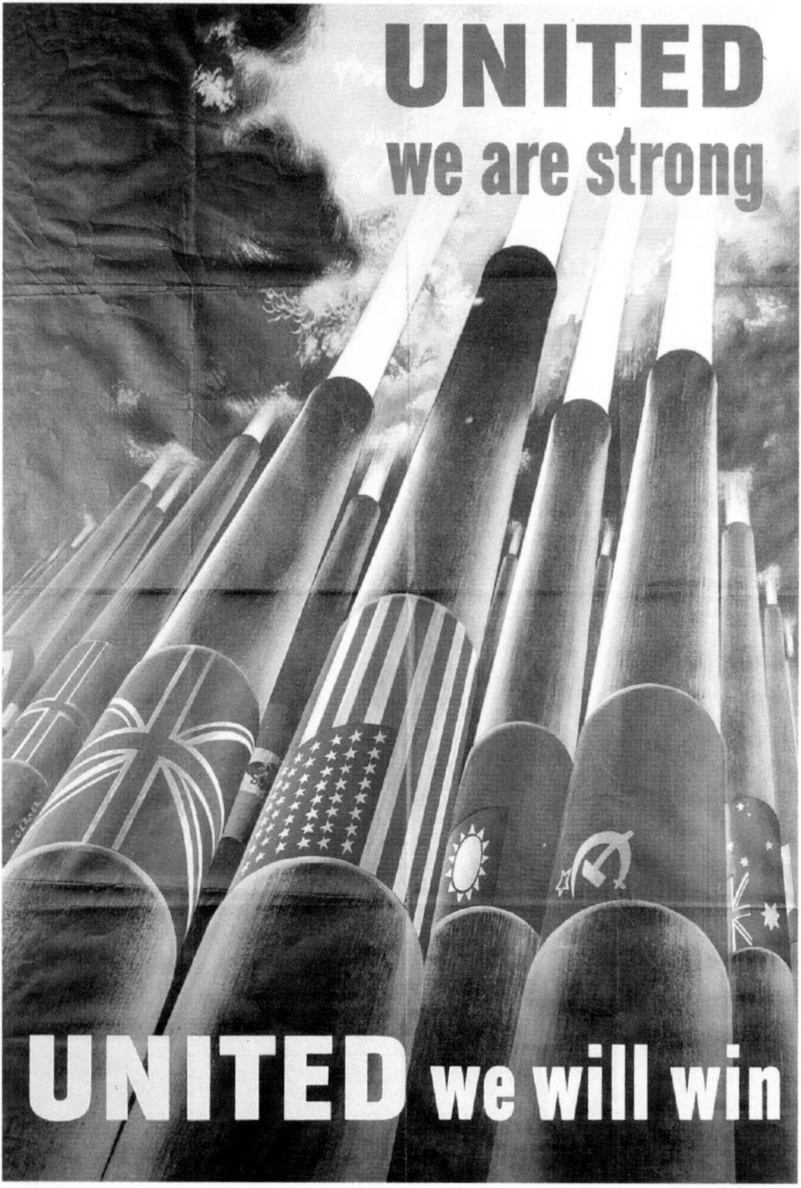
UNITED
we are strong
UNITED we will win

Au début de l'année 1944, les armées allemandes, qui ont subi de très lourdes pertes, ne sont nullement défaites. Les Alliés débarquent en Normandie. Malgré les divergences de vues entre les chefs militaires, Rome, Paris et Bruxelles sont libérées. Sur le front de l'Est, les nazis paient le prix de l'invasion de l'URSS et ils sont refoulés inexorablement vers leurs bases de départ. Dans le Pacifique, commence la reconquête de la Birmanie et les Américains progressent d'île en île vers le cœur de l'Empire japonais.

CHAPITRE V
LES GRAINES DE LA VICTOIRE

En récompense de ses succès, Montgomery est rappelé d'Italie pour prendre le commandement des forces terrestres d'invasion de la France

La tactique allemande

A la fin de 1943, et bien qu'il soit informé des concentrations de troupes sur le sol britannique en prévision d'Overlord, Hitler affiche une confiance inattendue, convaincu de l'invulnérabilité de son «mur de l'Atlantique». Il place aussi ses espoirs dans les nouvelles armes qui vont bientôt sortir de ses arsenaux : bombes volantes, missiles à longue portée, sous-marins pouvant ne pas faire surface pour recharger leurs batteries et avions à réaction.

A l'Est, ses généraux plaident sans relâche pour un raccourcissement de leurs lignes, afin de mieux répartir les efforts et de reconstituer des réserves,

mais Hitler refuse, pensant que les Russes seront bientôt à bout de souffle. Son aveuglement vient surtout du fait qu'il s'obstine à ne compter que le nombre des divisions dont il dispose, sans se préoccuper de leurs effectifs réels et de leurs qualités. Les unités d'élite des Panzer ont laissé dans les neiges russes les corps de milliers de soldats irremplaçables.

Les préparatifs d'Overlord

Pendant ce temps, le sud de l'Angleterre rapidement se transforme en un immense camp militaire en prévision du Débarquement. Des centaines de milliers de GI's (surnom des solats américains) arrivent avec leurs véhicules

A gauche, le Messerschmitt Me 262, le premier avion de chasse en service.

Rommel, le vieil adversaire de Montgomery, est désigné pour prendre la tête du groupe d'armées B qui tient tout le littoral européen entre l'Escaut et la Loire. Dès son arrivée, début janvier 1944, il entreprend de renforcer les défenses côtières. Il a la conviction que le seul moyen de battre les Alliés est de les écraser sur les plages et il donne ordre de disposer des millions de mines et d'édifier des obstacles antichars sur les plages.

et leur équipement. 20 000 ouvriers sont réquisitionnés pour construire les éléments préfabriqués des ports Mulberry et les usines tournent jour et nuit pour produire tout ce qui sera nécessaire aux troupes d'invasion, du char d'assaut aux boutons de guêtre. On pose en hâte des voies ferrées et des pipe-lines pour l'approvisionnement en carburant, on édifie des rampes d'embarquement et des baraques pour loger les hommes, le tout dans un temps record... et sans ordinateur.

L'inexorable recul des Allemands sur le front de l'Est

Le rude hiver 1943-1944 n'arrête pas la progression des Soviétiques dont le nombre est maintenant infiniment supérieur à celui des hommes de la Wehrmacht. L'Armée rouge maintient sans répit la pression sur tous les fronts et, au printemps, elle refoule l'ennemi

Les lourdes pertes enregistrées sur le front de l'Est, comme en témoignent ici ces chars abandonnés, incitent Hitler à rechercher d'autres méthodes de guerre et ses savants mettent au point les armes de représailles : le «programme V». Les premières – V1– sont des bombes volantes lancées sur Londres depuis les bases de la côte française. Celles de la génération suivante – V2 – sont des missiles balistiques, dont on voit ci-dessus un specimen prêt à être lancé de la base d'essais de Peenemünde.

Le monastère de Monte Cassino est la cible d'un terrible bombardement en février 1944.

entre le Dniepr et la Bug. En mars, une nouvelle poussée contraint les Allemands à reculer de plus de 220 kilomètres. La Crimée est reprise, Léningrad est libérée le 4 janvier 1944, après 900 jours de siège et au prix de plus de 1 600 000 morts et disparus. L'offensive s'enfonce en Ukraine. Une fois de plus, Hitler réagit en démettant ses meilleurs généraux et ordonne à ses armées de tenir. Lorsque, en juin à l'Ouest, les Alliés prennent pied sur le sol de France, Joukov lance une nouvelle offensive qui prend au piège 25 divisions nazies et ouvre la route de Varsovie. Les autres troupes russes atteignent la Baltique à Riga, coupant de ses bases le groupe d'armées Nord. Au début d'août, ils sont sur la Vistule, devant Varsovie, et se disposent à marcher sur les Balkans.

La bataille de Monte Cassino

Les renforts allemands envoyés en Italie seraient sans doute plus utiles sur d'autres théâtres d'opérations. Cependant, remarquablement menées par le maréchal Kesselring, les divisions contraignent les Alliés à disputer chaque pouce de terrain dans leur progression vers le nord. La VIIIe armée anglaise marche le long de la côte, séparée des Américains de la Ve armée et du corps d'armée française du général Juin, par la chaîne des Apennins, enfin les Polonais viennent du nord. La stratégie de Kesselring consiste à tenir les cours d'eau qui barrent la route des assaillants. Il prend appui sur la ligne Gustav, dominée par le monastère de Monte Cassino qui commande l'accès à Rome.

Pendant l'hiver 1943-1944, en des combats qui rappellent les tranchées de la Première Guerre mondiale, les Américains et les Anglais, mais aussi les Français, les Néo-Zélandais et les Polonais s'acharnent à déloger les défenseurs allemands du monastère de Monte Cassino.

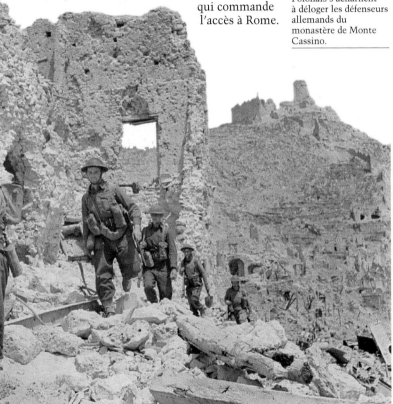

Se rendant compte que cette position est inexpugnable, les Alliés décident de tourner le verrou de Monte Cassino et de foncer sur la capitale. Mais l'opération se solde par un coûteux échec et les Alliés attaquent Monte Cassino, en plein hiver, provoquant

Ci-dessus, des soldats anglais patrouillent dans les ruines de Monte Cassino enlevé par les Polonais le 18 mai.

À gauche, un Liberty Ship en chantier. Les Américains ont construit en très grande série ces cargos assez rudimentaires en utilisant les méthodes de l'industrie automobile de travail à la chaîne, par assemblage d'éléments préfabriqués.

Ci-dessus, l'emblème du SHAEF. Des millions de tonnes de marchandises, d'équipements et de matériels sont acheminés en Angleterre en prévision de la plus grande opération amphibie jamais entreprise. Les responsables de la logistique sont les artisans indispensables, mais méconnus de la réussite du jour J. Tout le sud de la Grande-Bretagne est transformé en un gigantesque dépôt d'approvisionnement car les armées d'invasion doivent emporter avec elles tout ce dont elles auront besoin.

des pertes considérables. Réduit à un amas de décombres, le monastère est enlevé le 18 mai. Le 4 juin, les Alliés entrent dans Rome, mais déjà Kesselring s'est retranché sur une nouvelle ligne de défense.

Le jour J

Après un report de 24 heures dû au mauvais temps, aux premières heures du 6 juin 1944, trois divisions de parachutistes sautent sur le sol français. Dans le même temps, une immense armada de navires de guerre, de transports de troupes et d'engins de débarquement se présente devant le littoral normand. Un bombardement pilonne le mur de l'Atlantique et les unités d'assaut américaines, anglaises, canadiennes et françaises prennent pied sur cinq plages. Malgré les

Les hommes, entassés à bord des navires de débarquement, souffrent du mal de mer et ils seront heureux de prendre pied sur la terre ferme. Si de nombreux chars amphibies sont submergés par les vagues, les pertes seront plus faibles que prévu. Disposant de la maîtrise de l'air, les Alliés concentrent leur feu sur les ouvrages de défense côtière.

The New York Times.

"All the News That's Fit to Print"

6 A.M. EXTRA

ALLIED ARMIES LAND IN FRANCE IN THE HAVRE-CHERBOURG AREA;

GREAT INVASI

Un L.S.T. (navire de débarquement de blindés) américain.

N IS UNDER WAY

obstacles semés sur les grèves par les Allemands, les opérations sur quatre plages se déroulent relativement bien et les pertes sont nettement moins importantes que prévues. Mais, à Omaha Beach, secteur américain, les défenseurs retranchés dans leurs bunkers manquent de repousser les assaillants et ce n'est qu'en soirée qu'une étroite tête de pont est établie.

Les Allemands sont pris par surprise. La seule division blindée, près de Caen, reçoit des ordres contradictoires et ne peut intervenir. Dans la soirée, les Alliés ont atteint presque tous les objectifs fixés mais Caen, le plus important, est toujours aux mains de l'ennemi, ce qui aura des incidences dramatiques sur le déroulement de la bataille.

Le 6 juin, les Allemands sont paralysés par leur système de transmission qui exige que les ordres viennent uniquement du quartier général de Hitler en Poméranie. En outre, ils sont complètement mystifiés par la manœuvre de diversion, baptisée «Fortitude», montée par les Alliés qui les persuadent que les «vrais» débarquements auront lieu dans le Pas-de-Calais. Les officiers sur le terrain ne peuvent faire avancer les divisions blindées tenues en réserve sans la permission de Hitler et ceci permet aux Alliés d'établir leurs têtes de pont sur le littoral.

La bataille de Normandie

La priorité, pour le général Montgomery, commandant les forces terrestres d'Overlord, est d'abord de réunir en une seule les diverses têtes de pont et de pousser l'armée du général américain Bradley vers l'ouest pour s'emparer de Cherbourg. Mais les Allemands ne tardent pas à se manifester. Dans les combats qui s'engagent, les Alliés sont handicapés par les haies infranchissables du bocage normand, qui favorisent par contre la tactique défensive des Allemands. Montgomery fixe les Panzer autour de Caen pendant que les Américains prennent Cherbourg le 27 juin et se dirigent vers le sud sur Saint-Lô.

Montgomery continue de se battre dans Caen en ruines et, à la mi-juillet, Bradley se place sur la ligne de départ d'une offensive qui doit le conduire, au-delà de la Normandie, en Bretagne et sur la Seine. L'opération Cobra démarre le 25 juillet et, cinq jours plus tard, les chars du général américain Patton entrent dans

Avranches, ouvrant la route du Mans et de la Loire. Dans leur secteur, les Anglais progressent malgré une contre-attaque et les Allemands sont sur le point d'être encerclés.

Pendant que les Canadiens se fraient un chemin sur Falaise, les Américains pivotent vers le nord, s'efforçant de prendre au piège la VIIe armée allemande. La boucle est bouclée le 22 août.

La grande poursuite

Partout, on commence à parler d'une victoire finale pour Noël, alors que les armées foncent à travers la France. A l'extrême gauche du dispositif, les Canadiens remontent le long de la côte vers Calais, détruisant au passage les rampes de lancement des V1, et la IIe armée britannique, sur leur flanc droit, avance sur Bruxelles. Plus à droite encore se trouvent les Ire et IIIe armées américaines. Patton atteint la Seine le 19 août bien qu'une partie de ses hommes continue de se battre en Bretagne. Le 24 août, la 2e division blindée française débarquée le 1er août en Normandie, soutenue par les Parisiens et les Américains, libère la capitale. Le 3 septembre, Bruxelles en liesse accueille les Anglais qui, dès le lendemain, prennent Anvers. Les divisions américaines et françaises débarquées dans le midi de la France le 15 août – opération Anvil – remontent la vallée du Rhône en bousculant les unités ennemies. Dans le même temps, les chars de Patton traversent la Champagne mais, le premier septembre, devant Verdun, s'arrêtent brutalement, à court de carburant, accordant à l'ennemi un inestimable répit.

Le flanc droit de Patton, sur la Loire, n'est couvert que par des unités formées

Le port artificiel d'Arromanches (en haut, à gauche), bien que fortement endommagé par la tempête, joue un rôle capital en permettant le déchargement rapide du ravitaillement et du matériel.

Le maréchal von Rundstedt (à gauche, en bas) est le commandant en chef des troupes de l'Ouest.

L'ennemi mène une très habile guerre défensive dans le bocage qui contraint les Alliés à se battre mètre par mètre. A gauche, une affiche apposée par les Anglais en l'honneur de la Résistance française qui joua un rôle décisif lors de la bataille de Normandie.

FRENCH RESISTANCE
HELPS THROTTLE THE BOCHE

de résistants français et des brigades de cavalerie. Entre ces forces et celles d'Anvil s'étend un large couloir jusqu'aux Vosges par lequel les garnisons allemandes font retraite sans encombre.

Le général Eisenhower décide de prendre personnellement le commandement des opérations. Montgomery, promu maréchal, demeure à la tête du 21e groupe d'armées anglo-canadien, à statut égal avec le général Bradley; chef du 12e groupe d'armées américain. Bien qu'ils aient remporté une victoire décisive, les Alliés sont confrontés à des difficultés d'approvisionnement. Chaque kilomètre de l'avance allonge d'autant les lignes de communication et les bombardements du jour J, en détruisant ponts et voies ferrées, entravent lourdement les transports. Eisenhower est partisan de conserver le plus large front possible. Montgomery, bien meilleur stratège, privilégie une offensive menée par le gros des troupes en direction de la Ruhr, le cœur de l'industrie lourde allemande. Les Anglais se sont certes emparés d'Anvers, mais l'estuaire de l'Escaut n'est pas encore dégagé, et jusqu'à ce que le port soit utilisable en toute sécurité, n'importe quelle offensive risque de tomber en panne de ravitaillement.

La résistance des Balkans

En septembre 1944, pris en tenaille par les Russes et les Alliés, les Allemands commencent de se retirer de Grèce et Churchill saisit l'occasion pour accélérer ce processus qui soustrairait cette région

Les commandos britanniques débarquent en Grèce pour tenter de mettre un terme à la guerre civile entre les troupes royalistes et les communistes. A gauche, un soldat anglais pose devant l'acropole d'Athènes.

A droite, Tito avec un groupe de chefs de partisans dans une cachette de montagne en Yougoslavie.

à la convoitise de Staline. Les forces spéciales sont parachutées pour s'emparer d'un terrain d'aviation et, le 14 octobre, Athènes est libérée. Les Allemands se replient vers le nord, talonnés par les Britanniques. Lorsqu'ils pénètrent en Yougoslavie, une guerre civile, qui couvait depuis longtemps, éclate.

Les nationalistes croates – les Oustachis d'Ante Pavelitch – ont collaboré ouvertement avec les nazis alors que, en Serbie, le général Mihaïlovitch a rassemblé une armée de partisans, les Tchetniks. Dans le sud du pays, des unités communistes commandées par Tito se battent tant contre les Allemands que contre les Tchetniks.

Depuis l'invasion en 1941, les Anglais ont soutenu Mihaïlovitch mais, en septembre 1944,

Le 20 juillet 1944, une bombe, placée par un officier opposant au régime nazi, explose au quartier général de Hitler. Celui-ci en réchappe par miracle. Ici, il montre à Mussolini les vestiges de son abri.

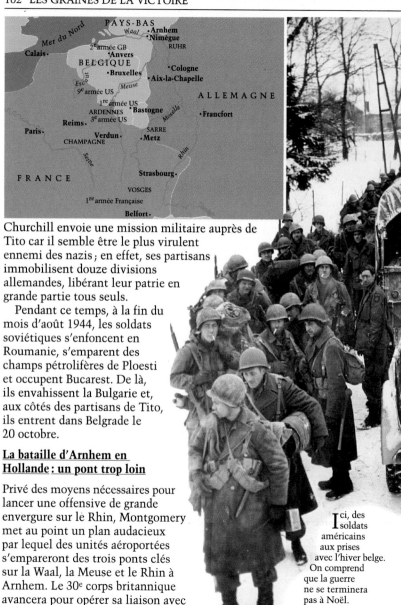

Churchill envoie une mission militaire auprès de Tito car il semble être le plus virulent ennemi des nazis ; en effet, ses partisans immobilisent douze divisions allemandes, libérant leur patrie en grande partie tous seuls.

Pendant ce temps, à la fin du mois d'août 1944, les soldats soviétiques s'enfoncent en Roumanie, s'emparent des champs pétrolifères de Ploesti et occupent Bucarest. De là, ils envahissent la Bulgarie et, aux côtés des partisans de Tito, ils entrent dans Belgrade le 20 octobre.

La bataille d'Arnhem en Hollande : un pont trop loin

Privé des moyens nécessaires pour lancer une offensive de grande envergure sur le Rhin, Montgomery met au point un plan audacieux par lequel des unités aéroportées s'empareront des trois ponts clés sur la Waal, la Meuse et le Rhin à Arnhem. Le 30ᵉ corps britannique avancera pour opérer sa liaison avec

Ici, des soldats américains aux prises avec l'hiver belge. On comprend que la guerre ne se terminera pas à Noël.

elles et établira une tête de pont sur le Rhin. Le 21 septembre, il s'empare effectivement de Nimègue et forme une tête de pont sur la Waal. Malheureusement, la 1re division aéroportée britannique larguée sur Arnhem ne s'en tire pas aussi bien. Malgré leur héroïsme, les Anglais sont encerclés et 2 400 hommes seulement réussissent à regagner leurs lignes. Plusieurs planeurs transportant l'armement lourd et des véhicules ne sont pas parvenus à destination et surtout, ce que les parachutistes ignoraient, deux divisions de Panzer, au repos dans les parages, mais informées de la manœuvre, les attendent de pied ferme. Malgré cela, Montgomery a enfoncé le flanc des défenses allemandes.

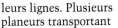

A gauche, la progression des armées alliées vers l'Allemagne, au nord les Britanniques, au centre et au sud, les Américains et les Français.

Sur l'Escaut, les Allemands ont installé deux puissantes garnisons dans l'île de Walcheren au nord et à Breskens, sur la terre ferme, au sud, qui commandent l'accès à Anvers. Il faut les déloger pour utiliser le port. Le secteur, inondé, est impraticable pour les blindés ; aussi la mission de nettoyer le terrain est-elle confiée à l'infanterie canadienne. Les deux places fortes résistent jusqu'en novembre et il faut trois semaines de plus pour déminer le chenal avant d'utiliser le port.

Montgomery, Eisenhower et Bradley examinant une carte. Ike doit tenir la balance égale entre ses chefs d'armées qui réclament, chacun, une priorité d'approvisionnements. En 1944, à l'arrivée de l'hiver, la Grande-Bretagne n'est plus le «numéro 1» de l'alliance, bien que Montgomery demeure convaincu que seule sa stratégie soit digne d'être suivie. Pourtant, l'échec de sa tentative de nettoyer l'estuaire de l'Escaut ne fait que rendre plus difficile le ravitaillement et prolonge la campagne jusqu'en 1945. La presse commence à remarquer les divergences entre les stratèges.

La pause hivernale

A la droite du dispositif allié, les chars de Patton sont à cours d'essence sur la Meuse et les Allemands, qui

Ci-dessus, la «route de Birmanie» qui serpente à travers la chaîne de l'Himalaya. C'est la seule voie terrestre d'approvisionnement des nationalistes chinois et elle est coupée quand les Japonais envahissent la Birmanie. Pour la rouvrir, il faut porter la guerre dans ce pays. Le général William Slim (1891-1970) – à droite – est envoyé en Birmanie en 1942 pour superviser la retraite de Rangoon et d'Imphal, puis il s'attelle à l'entraînement de la XIVᵉ armée aux Indes. Homme modeste et pondéré, il marque la campagne de sa personnalité et reprend l'initiative des opérations contre les Japonais. Le dégagement des centres d'Imphal et de Kohima, investis, lui fournit le tremplin nécessaire pour lancer une offensive générale dans le sud de la Birmanie, sans tenir compte de la mousson diluvienne, et il bat les Japonais sur leur terrain.

gagnent ainsi six jours de répit, en profitent pour constituer, sur la Moselle, une ligne défensive autour de Metz. Patton ne franchit la Moselle qu'en novembre et avance sur la Sarre à travers une région dévastée par la guerre. A sa droite, la Iʳᵉ armée française du général de Lattre de Tassigny doit livrer de très durs combats, dans la pluie et la neige, pour franchir les Vosges.

Au centre, la Iʳᵉ armée américaine du général Hodges poursuit sa marche sur Aix-la-Chapelle, mais il n'a qu'une faible couverture sur son flanc droit, le long des Ardennes. Montgomery, à gauche, se bat sur l'Escaut et avance dans d'épouvantables conditions météorologiques. Plus les Alliés s'approchent des frontières de l'Allemagne, plus la résistance de l'ennemi s'intensifie. Jusqu'à ce que le port d'Anvers soit opérationnel et que les stocks soient reconstitués début 1945, les Alliés ne peuvent guère entreprendre que des actions ponctuelles. Pendant que leurs troupes creusent des abris pour ne pas mourir de froid, Hitler leur prépare pour Noël un cadeau inoubliable.

Opérations en Birmanie

A l'autre bout du monde, depuis que les Japonais ont coupé la route terrestre de Birmanie, le seul moyen pour les Alliés d'approvisionner les Chinois est un pont aérien par l'Himalaya et les tonnages transportés sont calculés au plus juste. Une expédition conduite par le colonel Wingate démontre qu'il est possible à une troupe de se battre et de survivre dans la jungle et, aux Indes, les Anglais organisent leur XIVe armée – baptisée l'«armée oubliée» – placée sous les ordres du général Slim.

Fin 1943, les Japonais lancent une offensive contre les Indes, cherchant à couper la voie ferrée d'Assam au Bengale qui complète le pont aérien. Au début, ils remportent quelques succès, mais Slim résiste dans les villes clés d'Imphal et de Kohima, barrant la route des plaines aux Nippons. Ceux-ci mettent le siège devant les deux places stratégiques, qui vont tenir pendant six mois de très violents engagements, ravitaillées par avion. Les Japonais, affaiblis par de lourdes pertes, commencent à se replier, talonnés sans relâche par la XIVe armée qui les poursuit à travers la jungle jusqu'à la rivière Irrawaddy en décembre 1944.

Les Gurkhas, ces petits hommes des montagnes, infatigables, servent aujourd'hui encore dans certains régiments britanniques ; ils se sentent chez eux dans la jungle. Chacun porte un *koukri*, terrifiant coutelas que leurs ennemis redoutent.

Alors que l'«armée oubliée» du général Slim se fraie péniblement un chemin vers l'Irrawaddy, une offensive parallèle est lancée par les forces américaines et chinoises au nord, sous les ordres du général «Vinegar Joe » Stilwell. Son objectif est de s'emparer de la ville de Myitkyina, d'où les avions peuvent gagner la Chine sans être forcés de franchir de hautes montagnes. A gauche, des soldats lors de la bataille de Meiktila en Birmanie ; cet important nœud de communication commande la route et la voie ferrée le long de l'Irrawaddy, au sud de Mandalay. Les Japonais livrent de violents combats pour reprendre la ville, mais après que Mandalay est tombée aux mains des Anglais en avril, ils sont forcés de décrocher et font retraite vers le sud, le long du fleuve. La reconquête de la Birmanie est un des épisodes les plus horribles de la guerre car les hommes doivent lutter dans un environnement éprouvant pour les Européens : des conditions météorologiques épouvantables, une jungle à peu près impénétrable, les maladies tropicales, les animaux sauvages et toutes sortes d'insectes venimeux.

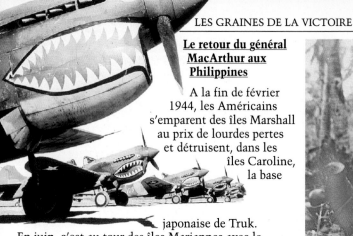

Le retour du général MacArthur aux Philippines

A la fin de février 1944, les Américains s'emparent des îles Marshall au prix de lourdes pertes et détruisent, dans les îles Caroline, la base japonaise de Truk.

En juin, c'est au tour des îles Mariannes avec le débarquement de deux divisions de Marines à Saïpan. Une escadre japonaise qui tente d'intervenir perd trois porte-avions ainsi qu'un grand nombre de pilotes expérimentés. La bataille des Mariannes fait rage jusqu'en août, avec sa sauvagerie habituelle, mais quand elle prend fin, les Américains disposent enfin d'un terrain d'aviation pour attaquer le Japon.

L'étape suivante permet au général MacArthur de tenir sa promesse de revenir aux Philippines : ses troupes débarquent à Leyte en octobre. Cette opération est marquée par la dernière sortie sérieuse de la flotte japonaise. Dans le golfe de Leyte, les Américains subissent la première attaque des *kamikazes* – ces avions pilotés par un homme et bourrés d'explosifs se précipitant sur un bateau –, mais ces actions suicidaires n'influent guère sur le cours de la bataille. C'est là le dernier engagement naval de la guerre classique, où des navires de surface s'affrontent à coups de canons. La flotte

En haut, un chasseur Curtiss P40 de l'escadrille des «Tigres Volants» en Chine. Ci-contre, le général MacArthur, qui, dès son retour aux Philippines, dresse les plans de l'offensive finale contre le Japon.

japonaise est détruite : à l'issue de la bataille, elle ne conserve qu'un navire en état de combattre.

La conquête des Philippines se poursuit et l'île de Luzon tombe aux mains des Américains au début de 1945. A partir de cette base, MacArthur propose de lancer l'invasion de l'archipel japonais, mais cette perspective n'enchante personne, sachant par expérience quelle résistance fanatique les Japonais opposeront pour défendre leur patrie.

Marines américains à Guam. Les Japonais ont disposé de deux années pour fortifier leurs positions dans l'île et ils n'ont aucune intention de capituler, fût-ce devant des forces incomparablement supérieures.

Dans les Ardennes, l'hiver 1944-1945, Hitler va tout miser sur un coup de force... et il perd tout. Ses armées sont refoulées vers le Rhin tandis que, sur le front de l'Est, l'Armée rouge marche sur Berlin. Dans le Pacifique, les Américains sont engagés dans de très violents combats et les canons ne se taisent que lorsqu'une bombe atomique est lancée sur Hiroshima. Alors que les nations libérées célèbrent la victoire et comptent leurs morts, les vainqueurs traduisent les vaincus devant le tribunal de l'histoire.

CHAPITRE VI
LA LONGUE ROUTE DES VAINQUEURS

Troupes américaines rangées, toutes bannières déployées, sur les gradins du stade de Nuremberg, geste hautement symbolique qui marque la fin du grand Reich. A droite, Staline, un des grands vainqueurs.

Les dernières cartes de Hitler

N'ayant plus confiance en ses généraux après l'attentat perpétré contre lui le 20 juillet 1944, Hitler perd complètement le contact avec la réalité. A l'automne 1944, il se convainc que les divergences entre les Etats-Unis et la Grande-Bretagne peuvent être mises à profit. Dès septembre, il jette les plans d'une contre-attaque massive à l'ouest qui doit franchir la Meuse et se porter sur Anvers. Il nomme Heinrich Himmler, chef de la SS, à la tête de l'«armée de substitution». Avec brutalité, Himmler écume les zones de l'arrière, enrôle d'autorité les personnels de l'intendance dans les divisions de *Volks Grenadiere* (les «grenadiers du peuple»), ainsi que de nombreux adolescents.

Les Alliés ont le regard fixé sur le Rhin, objectif prioritaire de l'hiver 1944-1945

A gauche du dispositif, Montgomery prépare une offensive partant de Nimègue, traversant la forêt de Reichswald pour s'emparer du carrefour de Wesel, soutenu par la IXᵉ armée américaine à sa droite. Au centre, la Iʳᵉ armée de Hodges est sur la frontière allemande, le Westwall, et au mois de novembre, de durs combats se déroulent dans la forêt de Hurtgen pour enlever les barrages de retenue d'eau sur la Roer.

Au sud, Patton réussit à faire sauter le verrou de Metz et il progresse dans des conditions très difficiles sur la Sarre et le Rhin, dans le secteur de Francfort.

Les soldats américains dans les forêts de Lorraine et autour de Bastogne souffrent de gelures, notamment des pieds, faute de disposer de chaussures imperméables et d'équipement approprié.

A sa droite,
la VIIᵉ armée
américaine se débat
dans les Vosges, mais
continue d'avancer.
Le 22 novembre, elle
débouche en Alsace et la
2ᵉ division blindée française fonce
pour libérer Strasbourg. Dans le
même temps, la Iʳᵉ armée de De
Lattre de Tassigny force le réduit
de Belfort et atteint le Rhin à
Mulhouse.

En enrôlant de force des enfants d'âge scolaire (ci-dessus) et des invalides, Hitler recomplète les rangs de ses divisions. Bradley pense que le secteur des Ardennes ne présente pas de risques et la longue ligne de front n'est tenue que par la Iʳᵉ armée. Les Allemands font d'abord de rapides progrès, mais les GI's résistent. Le général MacAuliffe, dont la division aéroportée est encerclée dans Bastogne (à l'extrême gauche), est sommé de se rendre et répond du même mot que celui qu'on prête au général Cambronne à Waterloo. Des soldats allemands, revêtus d'uniformes américains, s'infiltrent derrière les lignes alliées, jetant une certaine panique et, à Malmédy, massacrent de nombreux prisonniers.

La contre-offensive des Ardennes et l'irrésistible avancée soviétique

Les mauvaises conditions atmosphériques
ont empêché l'US Air Force d'effectuer des
reconnaissances et Hitler en profite pour réunir trois
armées, totalisant 22 divisions, sans que Bradley
détecte leurs mouvements. L'offensive est déclenchée
le 16 décembre et les Américains sont pris au
dépourvu. Au nord, la VIᵉ armée de Panzer avance en
direction de Liège mais elle se heurte à la résistance
des GI's. Au centre, la Vᵉ armée blindée creuse une
profonde brèche dans les lignes américaines, mais
le carrefour stratégique de Bastogne ne tombe pas.
Eisenhower ordonne à Patton de faire pivoter une
partie de son dispositif vers le nord pour faire lever
le siège de Bastogne et il confie temporairement
à Montgomery le commandement de toutes les forces
opérant sur le flanc nord.

Le 23 décembre, le beau temps s'installe et les
chasseurs-bombardiers découvrent les véhicules

ennemis sur les routes étroites des Ardennes. Confrontée à une dramatique pénurie de carburant, l'avance allemande est clouée sur place. Les Alliés passent à l'offensive. Bastogne est dégagée le 26 décembre et, à la fin de janvier 1945, tout le terrain perdu a été reconquis.

Bien que les Alliés aient connaissance de l'ampleur des atrocités nazies dès le début du conflit, aucune information ne filtre, soi-disant par crainte des représailles que les Allemands pourraient exercer sur les prisonniers de guerre. Le 27 janvier 1945, les Soviétiques libèrent le camp d'Auschwitz (à droite) mais ils ne révèlent rien avant début mai.

Pour leur part, en occupant les Balkans, les Soviétiques ont assuré la sécurité de leur flanc sud et se sont emparés d'objectifs politiquement inestimables. Au centre du front, après l'écrasement impitoyable du soulèvement du ghetto de Varsovie par les nazis, ils sont contraints de s'arrêter car leurs lignes de ravitaillement, tendues à l'extrême, ne permettent plus de reconstituer leurs stocks. A l'automne 1944, ils regroupent leurs forces, et envahissent la Prusse orientale, portant le combat pour la première fois sur le sol germanique. Varsovie en ruines est libérée le 17 janvier, dégageant ainsi toute la ligne de la Vistule. De cette base, deux groupes d'armées s'élancent vers l'Oder où ils établissent, début février, des têtes de pont. Au nord, les divisions russes atteignent la Baltique et la défense allemande est coupée en deux.

Cependant, les Occidentaux sont confrontés à l'horreur des camps de concentration et d'extermination; ils ne peuvent conserver le secret plus longtemps. Les Anglais libèrent Bergen-Belsen et les Américains Buchenwald, que Eisenhower visite avec Patton et Bradley (en haut).

La conférence de Yalta

La dernière réunion des chefs d'Etat alliés se tient à Yalta, en Crimée, en février 1945. Staline est euphorique car ses armées approchent à grands pas de Berlin alors que, à l'ouest, les Alliés se battent toujours pour sortir du bourbier des Ardennes. Il est clair pour tout le monde que le Reich est d'ores et

déjà battu mais le président Roosevelt veut obtenir la garantie que l'URSS viendra donner le coup de grâce au Japon. En échange, Staline a les mains libres dans les Balkans et la Pologne, une nouvelle fois, est démembrée. Les trois grandes puissances, auxquelles se joint la France, conviennent que l'Allemagne paiera les réparations exigées par Moscou et décident de la forme de gouvernement que les Alliés mettront en place après la guerre. Churchill réussit à obtenir carte blanche en Grèce.

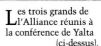

Les trois grands de l'Alliance réunis à la conférence de Yalta (ci-dessus).

HITLER DEAD IN C

Le Rhin est franchi

Sur le front Sud tenu par Bradley, les Allemands font sauter les barrages de la Ruhr et inondent toute la vallée. C'est seulement le 23 février que le retrait des eaux permet de reprendre les opérations. La IXᵉ armée du général Simpson peut alors avancer sur Düsseldorf et, le 5 mars, la Iʳᵉ armée américaine entre dans Cologne. Hitler donne ordre à ses troupes de tenir à tout prix la rive droite du Rhin.

Eisenhower veut se porter sur le centre du Reich, laissant aux Russes qui n'en sont d'ailleurs pas loin la prise de Berlin. Au nord, Montgomery regroupe ses forces et traverse le Rhin entre Rees et Wesel le 23 mars. Entre-temps, les chars de Patton ont franchi le massif de l'Eifel et se dirigent sur Coblence et Mannheim. Dans la nuit du 22 au 23 mars, ses hommes occupent une tête de pont sur le Rhin. Le 18 avril, les troupes allemandes de la Ruhr sont encerclées par Montgomery au nord et Bradley au sud. Le général Model qui les commande se donne la mort.

La capitulation des Allemands

Sur le front italien, en avril, les Alliés traversent les

Comme les mâchoires d'une tenaille, les Alliés resserrent leur emprise sur le Reich.

HANCELLERY

Apennins et déferlent sur la plaine du Pô. Le 29 avril, les Américains entrent dans Milan et, le même jour, les Allemands se rendent sans condition.

Sur le front de l'Est, ces derniers résistent encore en Hongrie ainsi que le long des fleuves Oder et Neisse, arrêtant pour un temps le «rouleau compresseur» russe.

Le problème est posé de l'avancée des Alliés jusqu'à Berlin, mais Truman, le successeur de Roosevelt à la présidence des Etats-Unis, confirme à Eisenhower l'ordre de ne pas franchir l'Elbe. Le 16 avril, Joukov traverse en force l'Oder et, le 21, ses éléments avancés se battent dans les faubourgs de Berlin, cependant qu'à sa gauche le général Koniev approche de Dresde.

Les Occidentaux décident néanmoins de continuer de progresser dans certains secteurs et c'est ainsi que Montgomery reçoit l'autorisation de marcher sur Hambourg et la Baltique en s'emparant de la péninsule du Schleswig pour interdire aux Russes l'accès au Danemark.

Dans l'univers irréel de son bunker de Berlin, Hitler épouse sa maîtresse, Eva Braun, le 29 avril.

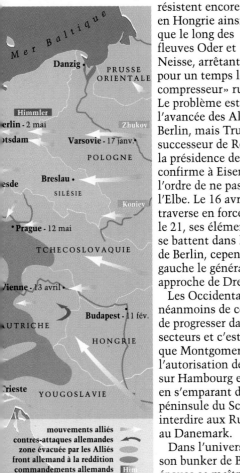

Aux yeux de Eisenhower, Berlin ne présente aucun intérêt stratégique et il n'est pas mécontent de laisser la capitale aux Soviétiques qui en ont fait le symbole de leur victoire. Dans son bunker, Hitler continue de diffuser ses ordres à des armées fantômes, cependant que l'Armée rouge fonce sur la ville défendue par un dernier carré de SS et d'adolescents des *Hitler Jugend* (pages suivantes). Son entourage l'incite à s'envoler pour la Bavière, mais dans sa folie, Hitler refuse. Abandonné même par Himmler qui s'échappe vers Flensburg, il décide de se suicider. Quand les Soviétiques atteignent la Chancellerie, ils ne trouvent que l'orgueilleux symbole du IIIᵉ Reich gisant dans les décombres (ci-dessus).

Carte :

Mer Baltique

Danzig
PRUSSE ORIENTALE
Himmler
erlin - 2 mai
Zhukov
tsdam
Varsovie - 17 janv.
POLOGNE
esde
Breslau
SILÉSIE
Koniev
Prague - 12 mai
TCHECOSLOVAQUIE
ienne - 13 avril
Budapest - 11 fév.
UTRICHE
HONGRIE
rieste
YOUGOSLAVIE

mouvements alliés
contre-attaques allemandes
zone évacuée par les Alliés
front allemand à la reddition
commandements allemands
commandements alliés

Le drapeau rouge flotte sur Berlin

Selon les accords d'occupation, Berlin, au milieu de la zone soviétique, est soumise à un régime spécial par lequel chacun des Alliés gouverne un secteur de la capitale. Le général Jodl signe l'acte de la reddition finale, après quoi il déclare : «Par cette signature, le peuple et les armées allemandes sont livrés, pour le meilleur et pour le pire, aux mains des vainqueurs. [...] A cette heure, je peux seulement exprimer l'espoir que ceux-ci les traiteront avec magnanimité.» Avec la fin de la guerre, les frontières de l'Union soviétique ne se trouvent plus qu'à 160 kilomètres du Rhin mais, dans l'euphorie de leur triomphe, les chefs d'Etats occidentaux, à l'exception de Churchill, ne comprennent pas qu'un nouveau conflit, la guerre froide, couve. Le vœu pieux de Roosevelt, afin que des élections libres soient organisées en Pologne, sera purement et simplement ignoré par les Russes qui font tomber dans leur sphère d'influence la quasi-totalité des Etats de l'Europe de l'Est.

Dans l'après-midi du lendemain, le couple se suicide alors que les obus russes pleuvent sur la capitale en ruines.

Le pouvoir, ou ce qu'il en reste, est dévolu, selon les dernières volontés de Hitler, au grand-amiral Doenitz retranché à Flensburg. Le 4 mai, au quartier général de Montgomery, une délégation allemande signe la reddition des forces nazies de Hollande, du Danemark et de la partie nord-ouest du Reich. La capitulation inconditionnelle de l'Allemagne est prononcée, trois jours plus tard, au grand quartier général de Eisenhower, dans une salle de classe d'une école de Reims.

A gauche, les Britanniques débarquent sur la côte birmane.

La reconquête de la Birmanie

Si l'Europe libérée est en liesse, les troupes combattantes d'Extrême-Orient ne connaissent aucun répit ; la chaleur et les moustiques sont toujours aussi insupportables. L'«armée oubliée» du général Slim se taille péniblement un chemin dans la jungle contre un environnement hostile et un ennemi toujours irréductible malgré les attaques des Américains et des Chinois au nord de la péninsule. En dépit de la mousson, les hommes avancent au cœur de la Birmanie méridionale en procédant à des débarquements sur les côtes pour tourner les positions ennemies. Basés sur l'Irrawaddy, ils descendent le long de la voie ferrée menant à Rangoon qui tombe le 3 mai.

L'une des images les plus émouvantes de la guerre, qui va devenir le symbole de la combativité américaine : des Marines plantant la bannière étoilée sur Iwo Jima.

Les derniers combats : Iwo Jima et Okinawa

La fin de la guerre en Europe permet aux Etats-Unis de transférer en Extrême-Orient toute la flotte des engins de débarquement. Une lourde escadre anglaise est également envoyée dans le Pacifique pour reprendre possession de Hong Kong et de la Malaisie.

L'US Air Force a besoin d'installer ses bases les plus près possible de l'archipel japonais pour que ses chasseurs puissent escorter les bombardiers. Bien que le feu ravage, l'une après l'autre, les grandes villes, le Japon ne donne

Selon leur code de l'honneur, les *bushido*, les prisonniers japonais ont failli à leur devoir en n'étant pas morts pour leur empereur. Ce fanatisme persuade Truman, qui a succédé à Roosevelt disparu le 12 avril, qu'un assaut contre l'archipel japonais très peuplé provoquerait d'énormes pertes. Malgré des bombardements pratiquement quotidiens, le moral des Japonais ne donne aucun signe de faiblesse et Truman sait que son opinion publique veut qu'il soit mis rapidement fin aux hostilités. Mais les Japonais ignorent que, depuis 1942, une équipe scientifique travaille dans le plus grand secret à Los Alamos, dans le désert du Nouveau-Mexique, sur le «projet Manhattan», la fabrication de la bombe atomique. Au début de l'été 1945, tout est prêt pour une première expérience.

aucun signe d'affaiblissement, d'où la décision
d'envahir la petite île d'Iwo Jima. On a compté
que quatre jours suffiraient, mais il faut
en réalité cinq semaines de rudes combats
et, lorsque l'île est conquise à la mi-juin,
6 000 Marines y ont trouvé la mort.

Le 1er avril, un autre débarquement est
effectué sur Okinawa, encore plus puissamment
défendue, qui tombe enfin le 12 juin. Les
Marines compteront 12 500 tués à la fin de
la campagne. Truman et ses conseillers sont
alors amenés à envisager d'autres moyens pour
remporter la victoire finale dans le Pacifique.

L'apocalypse au Japon

Le 26 juillet 1945, les
gouvernements chinois et
américain adressent au Japon
un ultimatum, le sommant de
capituler sous peine de s'exposer
aux plus terribles destructions.
Onze jours plus tard, une escadrille
de trois superforteresses B-29
décolle de Tinian aux îles Marshall
et l'une d'elles – baptisée Enola
Gay – emporte dans sa carlingue
une bombe atomique. Le colonel
Tibbets, chef de la mission, se
dirige sur Hiroshima. Survolant
son objectif à une altitude de
11 000 mètres, il largue l'engin de
mort. 78 000 personnes sont tuées
sur le coup et plus de 80 000
autres blessées. Cependant, ce
cataclysme n'est pas suivi de la
reddition attendue et une seconde
bombe est lâchée sur Nagasaki.
Le lendemain, 10 août, le
gouvernement japonais demande
l'armistice. Au cours d'une
cérémonie imposante à bord du
cuirassé *Missouri* ancré en baie de
Tokyo, le général MacArthur,

accompagné des généraux alliés, reçoit la capitulation du Japon, le 2 septembre 1945.

Le tribut payé par l'humanité

On estime de 40 à 50 000 000 les victimes, civils et militaires, de la guerre. 6 000 000 de Juifs ont péri dans l'Holocauste, les pertes russes se chiffrent à quelque 20 000 000. En fait, ce n'est qu'une évaluation car personne n'est capable de les dénombrer. L'Allemagne compte 5 000 000 de disparus dans la tourmente. Toutes proportions gardées, les nations occidentales ont beaucoup moins souffert puisque la guerre aurait fait 570 000 victimes en Angleterre et 450 000 en

A gauche, le colonel Paul Tibbets saluant depuis la cabine de son avion *Enola Gay* avant de larguer la bombe sur Hiroshima (ci-contre). Ci-dessus, le sceau de l'empereur Hirohito apposé sur l'acte de capitulation. Lorsque, le 26 juillet, les Alliés exigent une capitulation sans condition, ils expriment l'intention de convertir le Japon en une démocratie, laissant dans le vague le statut de l'empereur ; c'est seulement après le languace des deux bombes atomiques, suivi par une déclaration alliée précisant qu'il ne sera pas déposé, que Hirohito, passant outre aux objurgations de ses conseillers militaires, accepte de se rendre. Pour la première fois de son histoire, le peuple japonais entend la voix «divine» de l'empereur à la radio, le 14 août. La Seconde Guerre mondiale est terminée.

France. Il est impossible de déterminer les pertes subies par les pays d'Europe centrale, mais il est certain que la Pologne fut la plus touchée en raison des massacres collectifs perpétrés tant par les nazis que par les Soviétiques. Les Etats-Unis ont recensé 290 000 tués, presque exclusivement des combattants. Nul ne sait combien de Chinois ont trouvé la mort pendant les hostilités, mais on pense que le chiffre est proche de 10 000 000. Quant aux Japonais, on a compté environ 2 000 000 de morts. Mais il faut aussi compter des millions d'habitations détruites, des familles entières arrachées à leur terre et jetées sur les routes de l'exode ou de l'exil.

En 1945, pour juger les coupables, on institue de nouveaux chefs d'accusation tels l'instigation à une guerre d'agression ou les crimes contre l'humanité. L'opinion publique internationale exige que les auteurs de ces crimes passent en jugement et soient châtiés. Au procès de Tokyo (ci-dessus), le principal accusé est le général Tojo (ci-contre), limogé de son poste de Premier ministre en juillet 1944 après avoir perdu Saïpan. Il est accusé d'avoir fomenté «les attaques criminelles du Japon contre ses voisins» et d'avoir laissé infliger des traitements barbares aux prisonniers de guerre. Avec six autres généraux, il est condamné à la peine de mort par pendaison, ce qui constitue l'ultime déshonneur pour un membre de la caste militaire nippone.

Le tribunal de l'histoire

Fin 1945, au terme de longues discussions, les quatre grands – Angleterre, Etats-Unis, France et URSS – décident d'instituer une Cour internationale de justice militaire pour juger les principaux criminels de guerre. Les trois plus grands, Hitler, Himmler et Goebbels, sont morts. Goering fait alors figure de principal accusé ; il est entouré de vingt et un autres dignitaires nazis, politiciens, dirigeants du parti et de deux généraux de la Wehrmacht. La Cour se réunit en novembre 1945 au palais de justice de Nuremberg.

Les Alliés veillent scrupuleusement à la plus grande impartialité du procès pour éviter d'être accusés de pratiquer une justice sommaire. Trois accusés sont acquittés, douze sont condamnés à mort, les autres à diverses peines de prison. Quelques heures avant que la sentence soit exécutée, Goering échappe à son bourreau et se suicide. A Tokyo, une cour de justice similaire fait le procès des chefs japonais. En Europe, dans leur zone d'occupation respective, les tribunaux militaires alliés jugent un nombre considérable de nazis pour crimes de guerre mais beaucoup échappent à la justice. L'exemplarité de ces procès disparaît bientôt devant les réalités de la guerre froide et la nécessité de réintégrer l'Allemagne dans le concert des nations occidentales.

Les accusés du procès de Nuremberg. Page suivante, «Installons-nous à Berlin», proclame l'Armée rouge.

TÉMOIGNAGES
ET DOCUMENTS

DATES	EUROPE DE L'OUEST	EUROPE DE L'EST
1939		
2 mars		
15 mars	► Entrée des troupes allemandes à Prague, démembrement de la Tchécoslovaquie	
28 mars	Fin de la guerre d'Espagne	Invasion de l'Albanie par l'Italie
7 avril		
22 mai		
30 juillet		Crise de Dantzig entre Allemagne et Pologne
23 août		
25 août		
1er septembre	Mobilisation générale en France	Invasion allemande de la Pologne ►
2 septembre	Ultimatum britannique à l'Allemagne	
3 septembre	Déclaration de guerre de l'Angleterre et de la France à l'Allemagne	
5 septembre		
6 septembre		Chute de Cracovie
17 septembre		Invasion de la Pologne par l'URSS
29 septembre		Chute de Varsovie
6 octobre		Fin de la campagne en Pologne
14 octobre	Torpillage du *Royal Oak* à Scapa Flow	
16 novembre	Les Français évacuent l'Alsace	
4 novembre		
30 novembre		Invasion de la Finlande par l'URSS
17 décembre	► Sabordage du cuirassé allemand *Graf Spee* après une bataille contre la Royal Navy	
1940		
1er janvier	Mobilisation générale en Grande-Bretagne	
12 mars		Fin de la guerre russo-polonaise
18 mars		
27 mars		Ouverture du camp d'Auschwitz
9 avril		Invasion allemande du Danemark et de la Norvège
15 avril		► Bataille de Narvik
1er mai		Capitulation de la Norvège
10 mai	▲Offensive générale allemande en France, en Belgique et en Hollande	
13 mai	Les Allemands franchissent la Meuse	
15 mai	Capitulation de la Hollande Défaite de l'armée française à Sedan	

MÉDITERRANÉE	ASIE/PACIFIQUE	POLITIQUE

Débarquement japonais à Canton

Election du pape Pie XII

Pacte d'Acier entre Allemagne et Italie

Pacte germano-soviétique de non-agression
Traité d'assistance mutuelle entre Angleterre et Pologne

Les Etats-Unis proclament leur neutralité

Pacte germano-soviétique pour le partage de la Pologne; pacte entre URSS, Finlande et Estonie. Vote par le Sénat américain de la loi *cash and carry*

Rencontre entre Hitler et Mussolini

◄ Churchill, Premier ministre

DATES	EUROPE DE L'OUEST	EUROPE DE L'EST
17 mai	Chute d'Anvers et de Bruxelles	
20 mai	Les Allemands atteignent la Manche	
26 mai	Début de l'évacuation de Dunkerque	
27 mai	Capitulation de la Belgique	
10 juin	Le gouvernement français quitte Paris	
	L'Italie déclare la guerre à la France et à l'Angleterre	
14 juin	Les Allemands entrent dans Paris ◄	
16 juin	Les Allemands franchissent la Loire	
18 juin		
22 juin	Armistice franco-allemand	
1er juillet	Le gouvernement français s'installe à Vichy	
3 juillet		
10 juillet	Début de la bataille d'Angleterre	
16 juillet	Premières mesures françaises contre les Juifs	
	Début des plans de l'opération *See-Löwe*	
7 septembre	Les Allemands bombardent Londres ▼	
13 septembre		
25 septembre		
27 septembre		
7 octobre		
24 octobre		
5 novembre		
11 novembre		
14 novembre		
15 novembre		
6 décembre		
1941		
19 janvier		
22 janvier		
6 février		
10 février		
14 février		
25 février		
1er mars		

Invasion allemande de la Roumanie

Bombardement de Coventry

Mise en place du ghetto de Varsovie ◄

Invasion allemande de la Bulgarie

MÉDITERRANÉE	ASIE/PACIFIQUE	POLITIQUE

▼ Tragédie de Mers el-Kébir

Sous la pression du Japon,
les Anglais ferment la route
de Birmanie ravitaillant la Chine

Pétain, chef du
gouvernement français
◄ Appel à la Résistance
du général de Gaulle
sur la BBC

Offensive italienne contre
les Anglais en Egypte
Attaque anglaise de Dakar

L'Italie envahit la Grèce

La flotte italienne détruite
à Tarente par la Royal Navy

Victoire grecque sur l'Italie
en Albanie
Offensive britannique dans
le désert égyptien contre les Italiens

Pacte de l'Axe entre
Allemagne, Italie
et Japon
Entrevue Hitler/Pétain
à Montoire
◄ Roosevelt réélu
président des Etats-Unis

Offensive franco-britannique
en Abyssinie ►
Prise de Tobrouk par les Anglais
Les Britanniques entrent dans
Benghazi
Prise de Kouffra par les Français
libres du général Leclerc
L'Afrika Korps du général Rommel
arrive à Tripoli

Darlan Premier ministre
du gouvernement de
Vichy

DATES	EUROPE DE L'OUEST	EUROPE DE L'EST
11 mars		
28 mars		
5 avril		
6 avril		
13 avril		
17 avril		
27 avril		
5 mai		
20 mai		
27 mai		

Le cuirassé *Bismarck* est coulé par la Royal Navy et la RAF

22 juin		▲ Opération Barberousse, l'Allemagne envahit l'URSS
26 juin		La Finlande déclare la guerre à l'URSS
27 juin		La Hongrie déclare la guerre à l'URSS
4 juillet		Bataille de Minsk
12 juillet		
14 juillet		
28 juillet		
5 août		Chute de Smolensk

12 août		◄ Marche de l'armée allemande sur Léningrad
19 août		Prise de Kiev par les Allemands, 650 000 prisonniers soviétiques
29 août		L'armée russe évacue la Carélie
31 août		Contre-offensive russe sur le Dniepr
5 septembre		L'armée allemande occupe l'Estonie / Léningrad est isolée
24 septembre		
26 septembre		Fin de la bataille de Kiev
13 octobre		Premier convoi allié vers Mourmansk

17 octobre		Les Allemands prennent Odessa
30 octobre		Offensive allemande sur Moscou et la Crimée
18 novembre		
2 décembre		Les Allemands enlisés dans les faubourgs de Moscou
5 décembre		Hitler renonce à s'emparer de Moscou
7 décembre		◄ Contre-attaque des troupes soviétiques

MÉDITERRANÉE	ASIE/PACIFIQUE	POLITIQUE

▼ Rommel s'empare de Benghazi
Les Anglais débarquent en Grèce
Rommel encercle Tobrouk
Les Allemands attaquent la Grèce et
la Yougoslavie aux côtés des Italiens

Capitulation de la Yougoslavie
Les Allemands entrent à Athènes
Les forces franco-anglaises
s'emparent d'Addis-Abeba
Les Allemands débarquent en Crète

Soulèvement populaire
en Yougoslavie

Fin de la guerre en Syrie

Reprise de l'offensive par
la VIIIe armée anglaise en Libye

Le Japon envahit l'Indochine
Embargo sur les produits japonais
par les Alliés

Tojo Premier ministre du Japon

Vote de la loi «prêt-
bail» aux Etats-Unis

Pacte de neutralité entre
URSS et Japon

◀ Traité d'assistance
mutuelle entre URSS
et Grande-Bretagne

Charte de l'Atlantique
entre Churchill et
Roosevelt

De Gaulle crée le
Comité national
français de Résistance

▼ Les Etats-Unis abrogent
le pacte de neutralité

DATES	EUROPE DE L'OUEST	EUROPE DE L'EST
7 décembre		
8 décembre		
9 décembre		
10 décembre		
11 décembre		▼ Succès de la contre-offensive russe pour désengager Moscou
19 décembre		Arrêt de la guerre de mouvement en URSS
22 décembre		
23 décembre		
24 décembre		
25 décembre		
1942		
2 janvier		
11 janvier		
15-28 janvier		
28 janvier		
15 février		
19 février		
26-28 février		
2 mars		
4 mars		
27 mars		
28 mars		
12 avril		
18 avril		
24 avril		
30 avril		
6 mai		
8 mai		Offensive allemande dans le Caucase
12 mai		Tentative russe pour reprendre Kharkov

▲ Hitler prend personnellement le commandement des forces allemandes

Premier raid de la RAF sur Lübeck

MÉDITERRANÉE	ASIE/PACIFIQUE	POLITIQUE

Attaque surprise par les Japonais de Pearl Harbour, des Philippines, de Hong-Kong et de la Malaisie
Siège de Hong Kong par les Japonais
Les Etats-Unis déclarent la guerre au Japon
La Chine déclare la guerre au Japon et à l'Allemagne
◄ Débarquement japonais à Guam, dans les Marshall, et aux Philippines; attaque de la Birmanie
Prise de Bangkok

L'Allemagne et l'Italie déclarent la guerre aux Etats-Unis

Première conférence de Washington « Arcadie »

Les Japonais s'emparent de Wake
Les Américains quittent Manille

▼ Les Anglais reprennent Benghazi
Repli de Rommel jusqu'à El-Agheila

Chute de Hong Kong

Les Allemands reprennent Benghazi

Les Japonais s'emparent de Manille
Le Japon attaque l'Indonésie

Conférence panaméricaine de Rio

Les Japonais s'emparent de Rangoon
Chute de Singapour
Les Japonais bombardent Darwin en Australie
Bataille de la mer de Java
Les Japonais s'emparent de Batavia

Bombardement de Malte

Premières déportations de Juifs français

Capitulation américaine aux Philippines

Retour au pouvoir de Laval

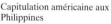

« 30 secondes sur Tokyo »
Premier bombardement
Débarquement américain en Nouvelle-Calédonie
Reddition américaine à Corregidor
Prise de Mandalay en Birmanie par les Japonais
Bataille de la mer de Corail

DATES	EUROPE DE L'OUEST	EUROPE DE L'EST

26 mai
27 mai

Les Allemands encerclent Kharkov et font 500 000 prisonniers

30 mai — Premier raid de la RAF sur Cologne ▼
3-6 juin

5 juin
19 juin
24 juin

Siège de Sébastopol

25 juin
3 juillet
4 juillet
16 juillet
23 juillet
7 août

Bombardement de Brême
Rafle du Vel-d'Hiv

Chute de Sébastopol
Les Allemands atteignent le Don

Les Allemands s'emparent de Rostov

12 août

18 août — Echec du raid allié sur Dieppe ▼
31 août
1er septembre
21 septembre
22 septembre
23 octobre
1er novembre

Début de la bataille de Stalingrad ▼

3-5 novembre
8 novembre

10 novembre
11 novembre

Les Allemands occupent la «zone libre» française

13 novembre
17 novembre

19 novembre

Attaque russe contre les troupes roumaines à Stalingrad

20 novembre
26 novembre

Sabordage de la flotte française à Toulon ▼

24 décembre
26 décembre

1943

2 janvier
2-3 janvier
14 janvier

Retraite des Allemands du Caucase

MÉDITERRANÉE	ASIE/PACIFIQUE	POLITIQUE

Début de la bataille de Bir-Hakeim

Bataille de Midway▼ ▶
Torpillage ▲
du porte-avions
Yorktown

Prise de Tobrouk par Rommel
Rommel atteint Sidi-Barrani
La VIIIᵉ armée se retire de Mesa-Matruk

Les Allemands atteignent El-Alamein

Bataille d'Alam el-Halfa

Débarquement américain
dans les îles Salomon

Conférence à Moscou
entre Churchill et Staline

Début de la bataille d'Arakan
Contre-offensive anglaise en Birmanie

Début de la bataille d'El-Alamein ▲

Débarquement américain
à Guadalcanal

Retraite allemande devant El-Alamein
Opération Torch
Débarquement allié en Afrique du
Nord
Reddition de Darlan aux Alliés
Les Allemands occupent la Tunisie
La VIIIᵉ armée s'empare de Bardia
Prise de Tobrouk par les Anglais
La Iʳᵉ armée anglaise se heurte aux
Allemands à Tabarka

Entrevue Hitler/Laval

Prise de Benghazi par les Anglais

Assassinat de Darlan à Alger
Giraud commandant en chef des
forces françaises d'Afrique du Nord

Capitulation japonaise à Guadalcanal

Jonction des Forces françaises libres
du Tchad avec la VIIIᵉ armée anglaise

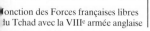

▲ Conférence de
Casablanca

DATES	EUROPE DE L'OUEST	EUROPE DE L'EST
16 janvier		
23 janvier		
27 janvier	Premiers bombardements de l'US Air Force sur l'Allemagne	
2 février		Les Allemands capitulent à Stalingrad
8 février		Les troupes russes reprennent Koursk
14 février		Les Soviétiques reprennent Rostov
6 mars		Les Allemands reprennent Kharkov
29 mars		
7-10 avril		
13 avril		Découverte du charnier de Katyn
18 avril		
19 avril		Soulèvement du ghetto de Varsovie
21 avril		
24 avril		
7 mai		
11 mai		
13 mai		
16 mai		Ecrasement du soulèvement du ghetto de Varsovie ▼
17 mai	Bombardements par la RAF des barrages de la Ruhr	
24 mai	Fin de la guerre sous-marine dans l'Atlantique ▼	
30 mai		
29 juin		
4 juillet		Opération Citadelle, bataille de Koursk
9-10 juillet		
17 juillet		▲ Offensive russe sur le Donetz
22 juillet		
24 juillet		
28 juillet	Bombardements de Hambourg	
13 août		
17 août		
23 août		Les Russes reprennent Kharkov
3 septembre		
12 septembre		

MÉDITERRANÉE	ASIE/PACIFIQUE	POLITIQUE

Offensive allemande en Yougoslavie
La VIIIᵉ armée prend Tripoli

Rommel contre-attaque à Faid

Rommel attaque Medenine
Bataille de la ligne Mareth

▲ L'amiral Yamamoto est abattu
par l'US Air Force

Conférence entre Hitler
et Mussolini

La VIIIᵉ armée attaque la ligne
d'Enfidaville en Tunisie

Nouvelle offensive japonaise
en Birmanie

Libération de Tunis et de Bizerte

Début de la libération des
îles Aléoutiennes

Capitulation des troupes allemandes
et italiennes en Afrique du Nord ▼

▲ 2ᵉ conférence de
Washington (préparation
de l'opération Overlord)

Débarquement allié en Nouvelle-
Guinée ▼

Arrivée de De Gaulle
à Alger

Opération Husky
Débarquement allié en Sicile

Prise de Palerme
Destitution de Mussolini
Badoglio Premier ministre

Rome déclarée ville ouverte
Les Alliés s'emparent de Messine
Libération de la Sicile

Débarquement allié en Italie
Armistice secret entre Alliés
et Badoglio
Les Allemands occupent Rome
Capitulation de l'Italie

▼ Conférence de Québec

DATES	EUROPE DE L'OUEST	EUROPE DE L'EST
12 septembre		
25 septembre		Les Russes reprennent Smolensk
1er octobre		
4 octobre		
13 octobre		
1er novembre		
6 novembre		Les Russes reprennent Kiev
18 novembre	Bombardements intensifs sur Berlin ▼	
22 novembre		
24 novembre		
28 novembre		
4 décembre		

1944

4 janvier		Offensive d'hiver, dégagement de Léningrad
19 janvier		Les Russes reprennent Novgorod
21 janvier		Les Russes libèrent Léningrad
22 janvier		
6 février		
15 février		

6 mars	Bombardement de Berlin	
18 mars	Bombardement de Hambourg	
20 mars	Combats des Glières entre Allemands et résistants français	Bombardement de Ploesti en Roumanie
29 mars		
2 avril		Les Soviétiques entrent en Roumanie
5 avril		
22 avril		
9 mai		Les Soviétiques reprennent Sébastopol
18 mai		
4 juin		
6 juin		

Opération Overlord; débarquement allié en Normandie ▲

9 juin		Les Soviétiques reprennent la Crimée
10 juin	Massacre d'Oradour-sur-Glane	
13 juin	Premiers V1 sur l'Angleterre	
14 juin	Libération de Bayeux	
15 juin		
17 juin		
18 juin		Les Soviétiques franchissent la ligne Mannerheim
22 juin		Offensive russe en Silésie

MÉDITERRANÉE	ASIE/PACIFIQUE	POLITIQUE

Les Alliés s'emparent de Salerne

Prise de Naples par les troupes françaises
Libération de la Corse
L'Italie déclare la guerre
à l'Allemagne

Débarquement allié à Bougainville

Conférence du Caire

Prise de Tarawa par les Américains ▼

Conférence de Téhéran
2e conférence du Caire

Les Alliés attaquent Monte Cassino ▲

Débarquement allié à Anzio
Contre-attaque de Kesselring à Anzio

Destruction de la base de Truk
dans les îles Caroline par les
Américains

Siège d'Imphal

Nouvelle offensive japonaise en
Chine

Débarquement américain dans
les Indes néerlandaises
Libération de l'île de Wake

Les Alliés entrent dans Rome ▲
Chute de Monte Cassino

Débarquement américain aux ▲
îles Mariannes à Tinian

Prise de l'île d'Elbe par les Français
La VIIIe armée s'empare d'Assise

DATES	EUROPE DE L'OUEST	EUROPE DE L'EST
27 juin	Libération de Cherbourg	
1er juillet		
3 juillet	Bataille du Vercors	Les Russes reprennent Minsk
9 juillet	La IIe armée anglaise prend Caen	
18 juillet	Les Américains atteignent Saint-Lô	
20 juillet	Attentat contre Hitler	
21 juillet		
25 juillet	Opération Cobra en Normandie	
1er août	Les Américains entrent dans Avranches	Soulèvement de Varsovie
	Débarquement de la 2e division blindée française en Normandie	
6 août	Libération de Brest	
10 août	Libération de Nantes	
15 août		
20 août	Pétain est emmené en Allemagne	Offensive russe en Moldavie
24-25 août	Libération de Paris	
29 août	Libération de Marseille	Soulèvement populaire slovaque
31 août		L'Armée rouge s'empare de Bucarest
3 septembre	Libération de Lyon	
	Libération de Bruxelles	
8 septembre	Premiers V2 sur l'Angleterre	L'URSS déclare la guerre à la Bulgarie
17 septembre	Parachutage sur Arnhem	Armistice en Finlande
21 septembre	Prise de Nimègue par les Alliés	
3 octobre		Capitulation des insurgés de Varsovie
9 octobre		
12 octobre	Libération de Bordeaux	
14 octobre		
20 octobre		L'Armée rouge et les partisans de Tito entrent dans Belgrade ▼
23 octobre		Les Russes entrent en Prusse orientale
28 octobre		Armistice soviéto-bulgare
12 novembre	Le cuirassé *Tirpitz* est coulé par la RAF ▲	
18 novembre	la IIIe armée américaine franchit la frontière allemande	
19 novembre	Les troupes françaises franchissent le Rhin	
23 novembre	La 2e DB libère Strasbourg	
24 novembre		
2 décembre	La IIIe armée américaine pénètre en Sarre	
8 décembre		
16 décembre	Offensive allemande dans les Ardennes	
26 décembre	La IIIe armée reprend Bastogne	Les Soviétiques encerclent Budapest

MÉDITERRANÉE	ASIE/PACIFIQUE	POLITIQUE

Conférence de Bretton-Woods

Les Français s'emparent de Sienne

Défaite japonaise à Imphal
Les Américains s'emparent de Saipan ▼
Démission du gouvernement Tojo

Débarquement à Guam
Prise de Tinian
Les Alliés s'emparent de Myitkyina

Opération Anvil ▲
Débarquement allié en Provence

Offensive générale en Italie ▼

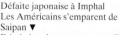

Libération d'Athènes

2ᵉ conférence
de Québec
Conférence de
Dumbarton Oaks
Conférence de Moscou

◄ Débarquement allié aux Philippines

Bataille navale de Leyte
aux Philippines
Premiers kamikazes ►

Bombardement de Tokyo

Débarquement américain à Iwo Jima

DATES	EUROPE DE L'OUEST	EUROPE DE L'EST
1945		
9 janvier		
12 janvier		Offensive russe en Allemagne
17 janvier		Entrée des troupes russes à Varsovie
22 janvier		
27 janvier		Libération du camp d'Auschwitz ▶
4 février		
9 février	Les Alliés atteignent le Rhin	
13-14 février	Bombardement de Dresde	Capitulation de Budapest
16 février		
23 février		
25 février		
5 mars	Les Américains entrent dans Cologne	
7 mars	Prise du pont de Remagen	
16 mars		
20 mars		
30 mars		Chute de Dantzig
1er avril	Les Alliés encerclent le bassin de la Ruhr	
4 avril		Capitulation de la Hongrie
9 avril	Bombardement de Kiel	
12 avril		
		Entrée des troupes russes à Vienne
13 avril	Libération des camps de concentration de Belsen et de Buchenwald	
16 avril		Offensive russe sur Berlin ▶
18 avril		Les Américains pénètrent en Tchécoslovaquie
25 avril	Liaison des Américains et des Russes à Torgau	
28 avril		
29 avril	Les Américains entrent dans Munich	Libération du camp de Dachau ▲
30 avril	Suicide de Hitler	
2 mai	Les Russes occupent Berlin	
3 mai		
4 mai	Capitulation allemande aux Pays-Bas, en Allemagne du Nord et au Danemark	
5 mai		Insurrection à Prague
8 mai	Capitulation de l'Allemagne; fin de la guerre en Europe	
13 mai		Les Russes écrasent la résistance en Tchécoslovaquie
14 juillet		

MÉDITERRANÉE	ASIE/PACIFIQUE	POLITIQUE

Débarquement américain à Luzon

Réouverture de la route de Birmanie

Conférence de Yalta

Les Américains reprennent
Corregidor
Prise de Manille par les Américains
Bombardement de Tokyo

Les Américains prennent Iwo Jima
Les Anglais reprennent Mandalay

Débarquement américain à Okinawa

Mort de Roosevelt
Truman président des
Etats-Unis

Conférence de
San Francisco
Création de la charte
des Nations Unies

Mort de Mussolini;
la Vᵉ armée prend Venise
Capitulation des Allemands en Italie;
la Vᵉ armée prend Milan
Les Anglais s'emparent de Trieste

Les Alliés libèrent Rangoon ▼

Les Américains encerclent le Japon

DATES	EUROPE DE L'OUEST	EUROPE DE L'EST
26 juillet		
27 juillet		
6 août		
8 août 9 août		
14 août		
29 août		
2 septembre		
6 novembre		
14 novembre		
1946		
29 avril		

MÉDITERRANÉE	ASIE/PACIFIQUE	POLITIQUE

◄ Première bombe atomique
sur Hiroshima
L'URSS déclare la guerre au Japon
Deuxième bombe atomique
sur Nagasaki
Le Japon offre une reddition
inconditionnelle
Capitulation japonaise en Birmanie
à Singapour
Capitulation du Japon à Tokyo
sur le cuirassé *Missouri*

Démission de Churchill
Conférence de Potsdam
Atlee, Premier ministre
britannique

Le général de Gaulle
devient chef du
gouvernement français
◄ Début du procès
des criminels de guerre
à Nuremberg

◄ Début du procès des
criminels de guerre à Tokyo

CHIFFRES

LES PERTES	Soldats mobilisés	Pertes militaires		Pertes civiles
Grande-Bretagne	4 600 000	271 311		60 595
France	5 600 000	210 000		400 000
Allemagne	10 800 000	2 850 000		2 300 000
Pays-Bas	500 000	13 700		236 300
Belgique	800 000	9 561		75 000
Autriche		380 000		145 000
Danemark		4 339		
Norvège	25 000	4 780		
Finlande	250 000	79 047		
Pologne	1 000 000	250 000		5 778 000
Yougoslavie	3 740 000		1 700 000	
Grèce	150 000	16 357		155 300
Italie	4 500 000	279 820		93 000
Tchécoslovaquie	180 000	6 683		31 000
Roumanie	600 000	519 822		465 000
Bulgarie	450 000	18 500		1 500
Hongrie	350 000		750 000	
Etats-Unis	11 490 000	292 000		
Canada	780 000	39 319		
URSS	20 000 000	14 500 000		7 000 000
Chine	50 000 000	1 324 000		10 000 000
Japon	7 400 000	1 506 000		300 000
Australie	680 000	29 395		
Nouvelle-Zélande	150 000	12 162		

in *Atlas de la Seconde Guerre mondiale* par John Keegan, *The Times*, 1994.

Une hécatombe humaine

Les soldats, mais surtout les populations civiles ont souffert de traumatismes irrémédiables dans leurs chairs et dans leurs âmes. Le bilan des pertes humaines reste effroyable, même si certains chiffres sont parfois contestables.

Durant la Seconde Guerre mondiale, les pertes humaines ont été presque quatre fois plus importantes que lors de la première (50 millions environ contre 13 millions). Cet écart s'explique par l'extention considérable des théâtres d'opérations, de l'Europe vers l'Afrique et surtout vers l'Asie (sur terre, sur mer et dans les airs), et par l'implication directe de toute la population dans la guerre. En effet, l'arme aérienne, dotée de longs rayons d'action, rend obsolète la notion de front, surtout quand la population de l'adversaire est un des objectifs prioritaires de l'aviation stratégique; il faut «casser» son moral par des bombardements terrorisants, afin de dissocier de ses gouvernants «jusqu'au-boutistes».

De même, les succès foudroyants des forces de l'Axe au début de la guerre ont conduit à l'occupation de vastes territoires, en Europe et en Asie, et ses corollaires : résistance, répression et conflits de type «guerre civile» résultant du caractère idéologique des hostilités.

D ieppe, août 1942, les victimes du raid anglo-canadien.

L'hécatombe sera aggravée par le non-respect de certains Etats (Japon et URSS principalement) de la convention de Genève sur les prisonniers de guerre (1929) et par les politiques racistes d'extermination systématique menées par le IIIe Reich, avec ses millions de victimes, Juifs, Tsiganes du grand Reich, «malades mentaux» et autres «vies indignes de vie» *(Lebensunwert)*, les persécutions qui ont touché les homosexuels, le traitement infligé aux Slaves, considérés comme «sous-hommes» *(Untermenschen)*… Elle le fut aussi par les crimes commis par l'URSS : massacres de prisonniers polonais ou déportations de peuples accusés collectivement d'avoir collaboré. Enfin, les innovations technologiques ont multiplié la puissance de feu et révolutionné les capacités de destruction. Si le bombardement de Hiroshima, le 6 août 1945, fit environ 100 000 morts (bilan en 1946), les pilonnages de Dresde, en février 1945, en firent 135 000. Cependant, au Japon, le «résultat» fut obtenu en une fois avec un seul avion.

Sur environ 50 millions de victimes, mortes ou disparues, moins de 20 millions sont des militaires. Toutes les générations ont donc été victimes de la guerre, sans distinction de sexe. Néanmoins, quand les pertes militaires sont très fortes (URSS et Allemagne) et les classes d'âge mobilisées nombreuses (de 17 à 50 ans), les structures démographiques du pays peuvent être bouleversées. En Union soviétique, le déséquilibre entre les sexes marque la population de l'après-guerre, ce dont témoignent la pyramide des âges issue du recensement de 1959 et ses profondes échancrures. […]

Dans certains pays, les civils ont subi des pertes bien plus élevées que les militaires. En Grèce (465 000 morts), elles ont principalement résulté d'une famine qui a ravagé la population (300 000 morts). En Yougoslavie (1,5 million de morts), trois facteurs sont intervenus : la répression aveugle de la guerre des partisans par les Allemands, les luttes internes entre les partisans de Mihaïlovitch (royalistes) et ceux de Tito (communistes), et les massacres interethniques (200 000 Serbes et Juifs furent éliminés par les Oustachis en Croatie). La Pologne enfin, dont 95 % de la population juive (soit 3 millions de personnes) a été exterminée, a connu, de 1939 à 1945, un impitoyable régime d'occupation mêlant massacres et déportations tant de la part de l'Allemagne que de l'URSS. Elle est la nation la plus meurtrie par la guerre (5 millions de morts).

L'abîme qui sépare les pertes subies par les deux grands vainqueurs de la guerre, les Etats-Unis (300 000 morts) et l'Union soviétique (20,6 millions de morts), mérite explication. Les premiers perdent 0,2% de leur population, les seconds 14%, véritable hémorragie. La partie européenne de l'URSS a subi par les deux fois le passage du «rouleau compresseur» des opérations militaires, la politique de terre brûlée à l'aller comme au retour, l'occupation, les massacres, la guerre des partisans, les famines (siège de Léningrad d'août 1941 à janvier 1944, 500 000 morts selon les sources soviétiques). Se sont ajoutées la mortalité et la répression, conséquences des déportations, ordonnées par Staline, de «peuples unis», comme les Allemands de la Volga ou les Tatars de Crimée. Quant aux pertes des Etats-Unis, elles sont restées relativement limitées (300 000) malgré la guerre du Pacifique, la bataille de l'Atlantique et les débarquements de l'Ouest. En effet, les

combats ne concernent pas le territoire américain. [...]

Les pertes françaises (580 000 morts) s'équilibrent entre civils et militaires. Ces dernières comprennent celles des forces régulières (192 000), des combattants de l'ombre (Forces françaises de l'intérieur, résistants fusillés ou morts en déportation) et les 31 000 Alsaciens morts incorporés de force dans la Wehrmacht. Parmi les pertes civiles, on compte 75 000 déportés raciaux.

Environ 400 000 Nord-Africains et tirailleurs de l'ex-empire français ont été tués dans les rangs de l'armée française et 50 000 originaires des Indes dans l'armée britannique. Les pertes civiles japonaises (680 000 morts), très inférieures aux pertes militaires (1,9 million de morts), connaissent une croissance exponentielle quand le Japon devient la cible de l'aviation stratégique après la conquête des îles Mariannes. Le 10 mars 1945, les bombes incendiaires font à Tokyo 84 000 morts, davantage

que la bombe atomique à Nagasaki.

A partir du 12 juin 1944, en Angleterre, tombent les V1 puis les V2. Ils provoquent 8 500 victimes civiles et ouvrent de nouvelles perspectives de destruction à distance et sans risques pour l'agresseur. Cependant, les effets des bombes atomiques des 6 et 9 août 1945 sont tels qu'ils arrêtent les hostilités et le massacre qui, contre toute règle du droit de la guerre, a ensanglanté l'Europe et l'Asie. Si des sinologues, «philosophes», constatent que les pertes chinoises dues à la guerre, mal connues, n'excéderont jamais les pertes des épidémies endémiques, l'hécatombe connue par certains pays européens est l'un des événements les plus tragiques du XXᵉ siècle.

Jean Delmas,
in *L'Etat du monde en 1945*,
sous la direction de Stéphane Courtois
et Annette Wieviorka,
La Découverte, Paris, 1994.

Des problèmes de méthode

Il est très difficile de dénombrer exactement les pertes subies par les belligérants. Les changements de frontières accompagnés de transfert de population (notamment en Pologne) rendent impossible la comparaison des recensements précédant les hostilités avec ceux qui les suivent. Les situations de guerre, mêlées de conflits internes, débordant, en amont comme en aval, les limites chronologiques de 1939-1945, en Chine par exemple, posent également problème. Le bilan des pertes pour ce pays, aggravé par l'absence de recensements précis, est particulièrement opaque. La répartition des pertes entre civils et militaires est parfois impossible, lorsque l'occupation de territoires se prolonge et que les résistances se développent. Le résistant peut être un militaire qui continue clandestinement le combat ; le plus souvent, il s'agit d'un civil qui lutte ou qui renseigne. Dans quelle catégorie est-il compté? Les bilans nationaux ne permettent pas toujours de le déterminer.

L'inclusion, ou non, dans les chiffres fournis, du déficit des naissances provoqué par l'état de guerre, c'est-à-dire l'accroissement du rapport décès/naissance dû à la guerre, est un autre motif d'incertitude. Or ce chiffre peut sensiblement modifier la somme de pertes : ainsi, si, pour prendre le cas français, aux pertes dues à la guerre (580 000), on ajoute le déficit des naissances pendant la même période, tel que l'évaluent les démographes (620 000), le bilan est deux fois plus élevé. (Encore ne faut-il pas oublier qu'en France les générations n'assurent plus leur renouvellement avant guerre : en 1938, le déficit des naissances est de 35 000.) On ne comptabilisera donc pas ce déficit, sans être sûr qu'il ne le soit pas dans certains bilans nationaux, en Union soviétique par exemple.

Jean Delmas, ibid.

Le sort des prisonniers de guerre

La fin des hostilités ne libère pas tous les prisonniers de guerre. Les 375 000 Allemands en captivité aux Etats-Unis sont rapatriés au printemps 1946. Leurs compatriotes internés en Union soviétique (plus d'un million) ne reviennent que de longues années plus tard ou disparaissent dans les camps sibériens (seulement 6 000 survivants sur l'ensemble des 100 000 prisonniers de Stalingrad).

Les 3,5 millions de Japonais qui se livrent aux Américains lors de la capitulation du Japon sont libérés presque immédiatement ; en revanche, les 600 000 Japonais capturés en Mandchourie en août 1945 par les Soviétiques sont internés en Sibérie. Seuls 100 000 en reviendront. Quant aux 2 270 000 prisonniers soviétiques libérés après la guerre et rapatriés en URSS, beaucoup d'entre eux furent dès leur retour envoyés dans des camps. La durée de détention fut de l'ordre de dix ans, pour ceux qui en supportèrent le régime.

Jean Delmas, ibid.

La Résistance en Europe

Chaque nation tombée sous le joug de l'occupant ou de l'oppresseur, a engendré ses combattants de l'ombre. Le tribut payé par la Résistance durant la guerre a teinté de sang les pages héroïques qu'elle a écrites.

La Résistance est un fait européen. Si elle n'a jamais été véritablement coordonnée, du moins a-t-elle connu à peu près dans tous les pays la même évolution et revêtu les mêmes formes.

Elle a consisté d'abord en diffusion de tracts et de journaux clandestins, guerre psychologique contre la propagande ennemie; la contre-propagande était assortie de collecte de renseignements pour les Alliés, d'aide aux aviateurs tombés en parachute, de sabotages de portée limitée. On a recensé en France plus de 1 100 journaux clandestins, quelques-uns tirant à plusieurs centaines de milliers d'exemplaires. Des réseaux d'évasion conduisent de Belgique en Espagne, à travers les Pyrénées, Juifs,

résistants menacés, prisonniers de guerre évadés, aviateurs alliés.

Les communistes, désireux de répondre à l'appel de Staline et d'aider l'URSS en difficulté, appliquent dans toute l'Europe occupée une autre tactique dite «d'action immédiate» et «d'action des masses», par attentats contre les collaborateurs et les soldats de la Wehrmarcht, grèves et manifestations de foules, destruction du potentiel économique pouvant être utilisé par l'occupant, création de «maquis» ruraux et urbains. Ce dynamisme, joint au langage patriotique qu'ils adoptent désormais, fait des communistes les incontestables animateurs de la Résistance, et souvent ses chefs.

En URSS, dans les zones occupées par la Wehrmarcht, existent des unités de guérilla ravitaillées et dirigées par l'Armée rouge; elles constituent l'avant-garde des unités régulières au cours de leur progression. En Yougoslavie, le communiste Tito, par son action inlassable, s'impose aux Alliés au détriment de Mihaïlovitch, jugé trop attentiste. [...]

En Pologne, la population est unanime dans l'hostilité à l'occupant. [...] Dans tous les pays, des milliers d'hommes jeunes, réfractaires à la réquisition, fuient les villes et se réfugient dans les campagnes, dans les montagnes surtout. [...] Les groupements de Résistance les aident et les [dotent d'une organisation]. [...]

En Allemagne, ce sont les opposants – catholiques, protestants, socialistes, objecteurs de conscience, communistes – qui remplissent les premiers camps de concentration (Buchenwald, Dachau, Ravensbrück). [...]

En France, la Résistance, d'abord spontanée, est peu à peu encadrée et dirigée par la France libre. Jean Moulin,

délégué du général de Gaulle, unifie les mouvements de zone sud, constitue une armée secrète unique, dote la Résistance de services communs de transmissions et de parachutage, crée enfin en mai 1943 le Conseil national de la Résistance, qui groupe toutes les tendances de l'opinion publique. [...]

La Résistance ne pouvait que harceler l'ennemi, sans le battre. Il est incontestable d'autre part que, livrée à elle-même, elle était condamnée progressivement à s'éteindre. Aussi bien les grands Alliés – les Anglais surtout – ont-ils armé et ravitaillé les groupes de résistants, mais ils ne l'ont fait qu'avec beaucoup de réticences et après de nombreuses hésitations. Ils se méfiaient d'une activité dont la direction leur échappait et dont ils redoutaient les engagements inconsidérés. Par suite, ils n'ont pas pleinement tiré parti de cette «cinquième colonne» que le comportement nazi leur avait en quelque sorte offerte.

La Résistance coûtait cher aux peuples qui s'y engageaient. Pour la réduire, irrités souvent par son caractère insaisissable, les autorités d'occupation multiplièrent les sanctions, les arrestations, les fusillades, les destructions d'immeubles, de villes entières parfois : un maquis français attaque une colonne, et le bourg d'Oradour est incendié, les femmes et les enfants enfermés dans l'église; la ville de Lidice est rasée parce qu'en est originaire un des auteurs tchèques de l'attentat contre le «protecteur» de la Bohême, Heydrich. Pour s'être toute entière soulevée, Varsovie sera rasée. On évalue en France le nombre de fusillés – résistants et otages – à 25 000.

Henri Michel,
in *La Seconde Guerre mondiale*,
Encyclopedia Universalis

Renseignement et guerre secrète

L'obtention de renseignements, leur interprétation ainsi que le faux renseignement eurent une énorme importance pour tous les belligérants. Du décodage des messages radio des résistants aux nombreux espions, parfois doubles, parfois triples, la guerre secrète a acquis ses lettres de noblesse durant la Seconde Guerre mondiale.

Les chefs de l'Intelligence britannique à Londres en salle de contrôle, 1943.

Avant toute chose, il s'agissait d'interroger les prisonniers de guerre et de faire des reconnaissances et des photos aériennes. Des méthodes plus raffinées, et plus secrètes, se virent classées en deux catégories par les Anglais : *Sigint* pour le décryptage des signaux radio et *Humint* pour les renseignements fournis par les espions et les organisations de la Résistance.

Un premier désarroi

Sigint commença mal. En effet, si les fonctionnaires des ambassades transmettaient régulièrement leurs renseignements, ces derniers étaient généralement sans intérêt. Ainsi, les informations transmises régulièrement à Tokyo par le consulat japonais d'Hawai sur les mouvements de la flotte américaine à Pearl Harbour étaient-elles immédiatement interceptées par les Américains. La guerre éclair menée par les Allemands à l'Ouest comme la percée foudroyante des Japonais en Extrême-Orient créèrent un désarroi total dans les services de renseignements alliés. Les réseaux d'agents qui n'étaient destinés qu'à opérer en temps de paix furent annihilés par les services de sécurité nazis qui se répandirent dans toute l'Europe. En Extrême-Orient, ce fut le même chose : les organismes de renseignement des puissances coloniales furent refoulés sur des bases situées aux Indes, à Ceylan, en Australie et à Hawai, à des milliers de kilomètres de leur zone d'opération. Un coup fatal pour MI 6 se produisit à Venlo, à la frontière séparant l'Allemagne de la Hollande, lorsqu'en novembre 1939, deux agents britanniques de haut rang furent enlevés et ne purent pas résister à l'interrogatoire des Allemands.

L'interception des messages radio était

devenue prépondérante. Armées, navires, diplomates ou agents secrets devaient rester en contact malgré l'éloignement.

Une machine « inviolable » violée

C'est alors qu'intervenait *Sigint*. Pour protéger leurs transmissions radio, les Allemands faisaient une confiance absolue à la machine à crypter *Enigma*, réputée inviolable. Elle servait à envoyer des messages à tous les niveaux ; mais une équipe de spécialistes anglo-franco-polonaise, basée à Bletchley Park, réussit à percer les codes si bien qu'une quantité d'information secrètes allemandes fut connue pendant toute la guerre. Ces informations furent désignées sous le nom d'*Ultra* et transmises aux états-majors. Elles jouèrent un grand rôle dans la victoire alliée, bien que la masse des signaux à décrypter ait souvent pris beaucoup de temps. Les spécialistes américains du chiffre réalisèrent un exploit identique en découvrant la clé du code japonais *Purple*. Les informations ainsi obtenues et baptisées *Magic* servirent à préparer les campagnes du Pacifique mais aussi à tendre une embuscade à l'amiral Yamamoto, commandant en chef de la marine japonaise, lors d'un vol vers les îles Salomon en avril 1943. L'amiral y laissa la vie.

Les agents opérant en territoire ennemi avaient besoin d'émetteurs radio. Les services de sécurité mirent donc au point des techniques élaborées d'interception, de décodage et de localisation. L'*Abwehr* et la *SD* allemandes étaient particulièrement douées pour les *Funkspiele* (jeux radio) tel que l'*Englandspiel*, lorsque les services de sécurité allemands en Hollande contrôlaient totalement les opérations de renseignement de ce pays,

de *SIS* et de *SOE*, à partir de 1941-1942. A la suite de la capture d'un agent en possession d'un émetteur, les Allemands purent arrêter 61 agents alliés envoyés en Hollande. MI 5 fit encore mieux pour empêcher les Allemands d'infiltrer des agents en Grande-Bretagne. Les agents pris étaient retournés, des réseaux « bidon » créés et de faux rapports envoyés tandis que les résultats de l'opération étaient contrôlés en permanence par l'écoute d'*Enigma*. Une bonne surveillance radio permit aux Allemands de se saisir d'un réseau d'espions soviétiques, l'*Orchestre rouge*, constitué à partir de cellules communistes d'avant-guerre et possédant des ramifications dans toute l'Europe occidentale.

Agents et résistants

Mais *Sigint* ne doit pas faire oublier le rôle de *Humint*. L'agent est irremplaçable pour certaines missions. Richard Sorge, espion soviétique opérant au Japon, fournit des informations capitales sur les plans japonais et allemands. Les Tchèques eurent un agent double, A-54, dans l'*Abwehr*, plusieurs années avant et pendant la guerre.

Outre ces professionnels, les Alliés disposaient d'une foule de réseaux de renseignements organisés par les résistants. Guidés par les services alliés, ils fournirent une masse de détails sur les activités ennemies : militaire, économique, technologique et politique. Dans toute l'Europe, des réseaux de toutes couleurs politiques envoyaient des renseignements dont les Allemands ne purent endiguer le flot.

John Keegan,
Atlas de la Seconde Guerre mondiale,
Larousse/The Times, 1994

L'holocauste

Plus de 5 000 000 de Juifs sont assassinés durant la guerre au nom de l'idéologie raciste d'Hitler. Marginalisation, exclusion, expulsion, transferts forcés, enfermement dans les ghettos... autant d'étapes vers la « solution finale », la « liquidation de la race juive » mise au point par les nazis. Par convois entiers, hommes, femmes et enfants sont déportés dans des camps d'extermination. Un holocauste qu'il ne faut pas oublier.

1933-1939, marginalisation et exclusion

L'antisémitisme est un principe essentiel de la « philosophie du monde » de Hitler, qui exprime une haine obsessionnelle à l'encontre des Juifs. Dès son accession au pouvoir, il met en place une politique antijuive.

A partir du 1er avril 1933, les nazis organisent le boycott des « commerces juifs ». Les « lois aryennes » (plus de 400 au total) chassent les Juifs de la fonction publique, des professions libérales, de l'armée et de la justice, de la presse. Les enfants sont exclus des écoles. Marginalisés par rapport à la communauté nationale allemande, les Juifs sont acculés à la ruine – car ils ne bénéficient pas des lois sociales.

Pour certains, il faut introduire une « séparation biologique » entre Juifs et « Aryens » : le 15 septembre 1935, les lois de Nuremberg « pour la protection du sang et de l'honneur allemands » interdisent les mariages mixtes. Pour définir qui est juif, l'arrêté officiel du 14 novembre 1935 prend en compte le critère « racial » et l'appartenance religieuse : « Est juif celui qui est issu d'au moins trois grands-parents juifs. Est juif celui qui appartient à la communauté religieuse juive. »

Aux yeux de certains radicaux, cette exclusion ne suffit pourtant pas à « assainir » véritablement l'Allemagne de la présence des Juifs.

Emigration et expulsion

On estime à 150 000 (sur 500 000) le nombre de Juifs qui quittent l'Allemagne entre 1933 et 1938. Or, l'*Anschluss* intègre dans le Reich 185 000 Juifs supplémentaires, dont les nazis veulent « se débarrasser ». Sous la responsabilité d'Eichmann, le Centre d'émigration juive de Vienne organise en six mois le départ forcé d'un quart des Juifs d'Autriche. Sur pression de l'Office central pour l'émigration juive, fondé à Berlin au mois de janvier 1939, plus de 80 000 Juifs d'Allemagne émigrent en 1939. Mais l'annexion de la Bohême-Moravie amène une nouvelle population juive au sein du Reich.

Ségrégation et expulsion sont menées de pair et les persécutions s'aggravent contre ceux qui refusent de partir. Dans la nuit du 9 au 10 novembre 1938, un véritable pogrom se déchaîne, commandité par Goebbels : 7 000 magasins pillés, des synagogues incendiées, des milliers de personnes agressées. Plusieurs centaines de Juifs sont envoyés dans les camps de concentration – ouverts dès 1933 pour y interner les opposants politiques. Des vitrines brisées jonchent le sol — d'où le nom de « Nuit de cristal ».

1939-1942, les transferts forcés

Après l'invasion de la Pologne, près de 2 000 000 de Juifs supplémentaires sont soumis au joug nazi. L'exclusion sociale et l'émigration ne suffisent plus ; ce sont des mesures policières et des actes de violence meurtrière qui vont bouleverser la vie des Juifs.

Dès l'automne 1939, les petites communautés sont dissoutes et regroupées dans les villes. On organise le recensement des Juifs de Pologne, dont les pièces d'identité sont frappées d'un tampon spécial. Ils doivent arborer un brassard blanc avec une étoile de David bleue ; dans le Warthegau, ils sont astreints au port de deux étoiles jaunes cousues l'une sur le côté gauche de la poitrine, l'autre dans le dos.

Cependant, dans les projets des dirigeants nazis, cette concentration ne constitue qu'une étape transitoire permettant de rassembler tous les Juifs de Pologne avant de les expédier vers une nouvelle destination. L'idée est alors de les installer dans une « réserve juive » près de Lublin, vers laquelle on commence à diriger des milliers de personnes, en de longues marches difficiles sur les routes enneigées.

Pour pouvoir organiser ces « évacuations » rationnellement, les Juifs devront être réunis, près des voies ferrées lorsqu'il s'agit d'un endroit éloigné de Lublin. Le processus de « ghettoïsation », commencé au cours de l'hiver 1939-1940, se développe. Les Juifs vont s'entasser dans les taudis surpeuplés du quartier le plus dégradé de la ville, d'où l'on fait partir tous les Polonais et les « Allemands ethniques ». Beaucoup sont enrôlés pour le travail obligatoire, dans des conditions extrêmement pénibles. L'approvisionnement en nourriture et en combustible ne cesse de se réduire. Par milliers, les habitants meurent de faim et de froid.

L'offensive allemande contre l'Union soviétique va offrir de nouvelles possibilités à l'Allemagne nazie, qui veut résoudre la conséquence paradoxale de ses victoires militaires : le nombre croissant de Juifs dans les territoires qu'elle domine.

A l'arrière des armées, des forces mobiles spéciales sont chargées de fusiller, sans jugement, les communistes soviétiques et les Juifs. Quatre *Einsatzgruppen* sont mis sur pied, soit 3 000 hommes. On estime le nombre de leurs victimes à 800 000 entre juin 1941 et janvier 1942. A partir de l'automne 1941, ils procèdent à des asphyxies par les gaz d'échappement de camions à moteurs diesel dirigés à l'intérieur des véhicules.

La « solution finale » de la question juive

Mais cela n'est encore qu'une étape dans l'escalade du massacre des Juifs d'Europe, avant qu'il soit décidé de procéder à une extermination systématique, organisée à grande échelle avec les procédés technologiques modernes.

Cette décision est arrêtée au plus haut niveau de l'Etat, entre le printemps et l'automne 1941. Elle n'est certes pas étrangère à la situation militaire sur le front de l'Est : l'échec de l'offensive éclair allemande commence à apparaître clairement et il n'est plus possible d'envisager une solution territoriale à la « question juive », par une extension de l'« espace vital » allemand.

Organisées par Heydrich et Eichmann, les déportations des Juifs du Reich commencent à la mi-octobre 1941. Plus de 20 000 Juifs sont transférés dans le ghetto de Lodz. Quelques semaines plus tard, 30 000 Juifs allemands, autrichiens et tchèques sont déportés vers Riga.

Le 20 janvier 1942, Heydrich préside une conférence interministérielle réunissant une quinzaine de « spécialistes » de la « question juive » à Wannsee, dans les faubourgs de Berlin. Il annonce qu'avec l'aval du Führer, les populations juives doivent être évacuées « vers l'Est », où elles seront astreintes au travail forcé, « avec des méthodes appropriées ». Il est certain qu'une grande partie de cette main-d'œuvre « s'éliminera naturellement par déficience physique ». Quant aux « éléments les plus résistants », il faudra « leur appliquer un traitement approprié » pour qu'ils ne puissent jamais constituer « les germes d'une nouvelle renaissance juive ». Les « inaptes au travail » seront parqués dans des « camps de transit » avant d'être expédiés « plus loin vers l'Est ».

Les modalités pratiques sont précisées pour « passer l'Europe au peigne fin », d'Ouest en Est : la conférence de Wannsee marque la mise en place des rouages de l'extermination des Juifs d'Europe.

Les déportations

On veille à maintenir le plus grand secret autour de la véritable finalité des transferts de Juifs « vers l'Est », qu'on désigne par un langage codé afin d'entretenir la fiction des camps de travail.

Les Juifs sont raflés à travers l'Europe entière, entassés dans des trains. Ceux qui arrivent vivants au bout du voyage découvrent un univers d'épouvante.

Les camps d'extermination

Des gazages ont été parfois pratiqués dans certains camps de concentration, mais il s'agit essentiellement de camps répressifs pour châtier les opposants et les « asociaux ». En revanche, les camps d'extermination ont pour seule finalité le massacre des êtres considérés comme « irrécupérables ».

Ces camps sont au nombre de quatre : Chelmno, qui fonctionne à partir de décembre 1941 où le nombre total de victimes excède 220 000 personnes ; Belzec, qui ouvre ses portes à la mi-mars 1942, où 580 000 Juifs furent assassinés ;

Sobibor, où le nombre total de Juifs gazés est de 250 000 environ ; Treblinka, où périrent 750 000 Juifs. La plus grande partie des déportés est immédiatement gazée. En dehors des quelques centaines de déportés nécessaires au fonctionnement des camps – et dont le sursis n'excède pas quelques mois –, il n'y a pas de survivants.

Auschwitz-Birkenau est à l'origine un camp de concentration, construit à partir du mois de mai 1940 pour des prisonniers politiques polonais.

Les bâtiments d'Auschwitz-Birkenau (II), à 3 kilomètres du camp d'Auschwitz I, sont édifiés à l'automne 1941. Les premières expérimentations de gazage au Zyklon B sont pratiquées au mois de décembre sur des prisonniers de guerre soviétiques. En juin 1942, Himmler choisit ce camp comme premier centre d'anéantissement des Juifs. L'aménagement des chambres à gaz s'intensifie

A l'arrivée des convois, les SS procèdent à une « sélection » entre ceux qui semblent susceptibles de travailler, et les autres – malades, personnes âgées, femmes enceintes, enfants… –, immédiatement gazés puis brûlés dans les crématorium. Au total, 1 000 000 de Juifs ont été assassinées dans ce camp.

A Auschwitz III, plusieurs dizaines de milliers de détenus travaillent pour des entreprises industrielles allemandes.

D'autres déportés meurent dans des souffrances atroces à la suite de pseudo-expériences médicales.

Construit à la fin de l'été 1941, à quelques kilomètres de Lublin, Maïdanek est également un « camp mixte » : 25 000 Juifs polonais considérés comme « aptes au travail » et des Polonais non juifs, des Biélorussiens et des Ukrainiens, y sont déportés. A partir de septembre 1942, on procède à des gazages massifs (plus de 50 000 en tout).

Devant l'avance de l'Armée rouge, les responsables de ces centres de mise à mort brûlent des documents compromettants, détruisent plusieurs installations comme les chambres à gaz de Birkenau et décident, à partir du printemps 1944, d'évacuer leurs prisonniers vers des camps situés plus à l'ouest. C'est le début des dramatiques « marches de la mort », au desquelles les prisonniers sont entassés à Gross-Rosen, Bergen-Belsen, Buchenwald, Dachau ou Ravensbrück, de plus en plus surpeuplés, en proie à la famine et parfois à des épidémies.

Le bilan

Entre janvier et mai 1945, les Alliés découvrent avec horreur la réalité du système concentrationnaire nazi.

On ne connaîtra sans doute jamais le nombre des victimes de la Shoah avec une absolue précision, par suite de la dispersion géographique des meurtres perpétrés pendant cinq ans, sous des formes diverses – cela d'autant plus que les nazis ont entouré du plus grand secret la « solution finale ». Toutefois, seuls ceux qui veulent nier ou minimiser l'ampleur du massacre des Juifs d'Europe arguent de calculs soi-disant fantaisistes. En réalité, des méthodes différentes, minutieusement élaborées, aboutissent à des chiffres très proches les uns des autres. Le tribunal de Nuremberg, parvenu au chiffre de 5 700 000 victimes juives, a donné le chiffre emblématique de 6 millions, souvent repris depuis lors. Par la suite, plusieurs chercheurs ont retravaillé sur ces évaluations numériques, pour conclure à des chiffres compris entre 5 100 000 et 5 800 000 – soit les deux tiers des Juifs vivant en Europe avant la Deuxième Guerre mondiale.

Anne Grynberg

La guerre pour mémoire

Des charges, sabre au clair, des hussards polonais contre les blindés nazis à la bombe atomique sur Hiroshima, l'imagination meurtrière de l'homme n'a pas connu de limites durant ces six années d'un conflit qui couvrit la presque totalité de la planète.

L es vainqueurs : Montgomery, Eisenhower, Joukov et De Lattre de Tassigny.

Enseignement de la Seconde Guerre mondiale

S'il y a des lieux de mémoire, il y a aussi des moments de mémoire et la Seconde Guerre mondiale est, de ce point de vue, un moment essentiel : celui où se nouent tous les enjeux du XXᵉ siècle et dont les échos façonnent les mentalités contemporaines. C'est un moment où l'histoire de l'Europe a atteint des sommets dans l'horreur; un moment où se sont affirmées des idéologies comme le racisme et l'antisémitisme qui, sous des formes parfois à peine renouvelées, resurgissent périodiquement dans le paysage politique européen. Ce qu'il y a de significatif dans le processus symbolisé par Auschwitz, c'est qu'on a voulu, en tournant le dos, au cœur même de l'Europe, aux acquis de la civilisation européenne, nier l'humain dans l'homme. C'est en cela que la Seconde Guerre mondiale a une portée universelle. [...]

Par rapport à toutes celles qui l'ont précédées, la guerre de 1939-1945 – qu'il faudrait peut-être appeler la guerre de 1937-1945, tant il est vrai qu'elle a commencé avant même que l'Europe ne s'embrase – apparaît comme une guerre essentiellement idéologique. Elle fut une sorte de guerre civile à l'échelle planétaire et il faudrait sans doute remonter aux guerres de Religion pour retrouver une guerre du même type en Europe.

in *Les Echos de la mémoire*,
textes réunis par Georges Kantin
et Gilles Manceron,
Le Monde Editions, Paris, 1991

Une nouvelle guerre

La Première Guerre mondiale avait convaincu les vainqueurs – mais pas les vaincus – que le tribut de la guerre est plus élevé que le gain de la victoire. La Deuxième Guerre mondiale apprit aux vainqueurs, comme aux vaincus, que «tout homme est un soldat». Ce principe, sue lequel les Etats évolués avaient organisé leurs armées et, dans une large mesure, leurs sociétés depuis la Révolution française, prit tout son sens en 1939-1945 et, de ce fait, engendra dans les pays fondés sur cette idée des souffrances assez terribles pour qu'ils bannissent le concept de la guerre de leur philosophie politique. Moins meurtris et plus avantagés par le conflit mondial, les Etats-Unis réunirent un consensus national suffisant pour entreprendre deux guerres coûteuses en Asie, en Corée et au Vietnam. L'Angleterre et la France, qui étaient sorties de la guerre sans trop de dommages, se laissèrent entraîner dans une série de guerres coloniales. L'Union soviétique, au contraire, malgré son attitude agressive, évita les affrontements qui risquaient de lancer

ses troupes dans des aventures dangereuses. Sa récente intervention en Afghanistan qui lui coûta un quart des pertes en vies humaines subies par les Etats-Unis au Vietnam semble renforcer ce jugement. Malgré la reprise de la conscription en Allemagne fédérale depuis 1956, pas un seul soldat allemand ne fut tué au cours d'un conflit depuis mai 1945. Quant au Japon, le plus pugnace des pays belligérants de la Deuxième Guerre mondiale, il est désormais lié par une constitution qui bannit le recours à la force en tant qu'instrument de politique nationale. Aucun des hommes d'Etat de la Deuxième Guerre mondiale n'a été assez fou pour prétendre, comme l'avaient fait ceux de la Première, qu'elle avait été entreprise pour mettre fin à toutes les guerres. Pourtant, depuis 1945, le monde n'a plus connu de conflit comparable.

John Keegan, *La Deuxième Guerre mondiale*, Perrin, Paris, 1990

BIBLIOGRAPHIE

● La sélection des ouvrages ci-dessous a été réalisée par l'auteur et l'éditeur en fonction de ceux utilisés pour la rédaction de ce livre.

– Archives du Mémorial pour la paix de Caen.
– Allen, Louis, *Singapore 1941-1942*, Davis Poynter, London, 1977.
– Arnold-Forster, Mark, *The World at War*, Collins, London, 1973.
– Badoglio, Marshal Pietro, *Italy in the Second World War*, Oxford University Press, 1948.
– Bradley, Omar N., *Histoire d'un soldat*, Gallimard, Paris, 1952.
– Bryant, Arthur, *The Turn of the Tide*, Collins, London, 1959.
– Carver, Michael, *Dilemmas of the Desert War*, Batsford, London, 1956.
– Churchill, sir Winston, *Mémoires de la Seconde Guerre mondiale*, (6 tomes) Plon, Paris, 1949-1953.
– Ciano, comte Galeazzo, *Journal politique 1939-1943*, Baconnière, 1946.
– Cole, H. M., *The Lorraine Campaign*, US Official History series, Washington, 1950.
– Courtois, Stéphane et Wieviorka, Annette (sous la direction de), *L'Etat du monde en 1945*, La Découverte, Paris, 1994.
– De Gaulle, général Charles, *Mémoires de guerre*, Plon, Paris, 1956.
– D'Este, Carlo, *Decision in Normandy*, Collins, Londres, 1983.
– Encyclopedia Universalis, *La Seconde Guerre mondiale*.
– Eisenhower, général Dwight D, *Croisade en Europe*, Robert Laffont, Paris, 1949.
– Ferro, Marc, *Questions sur la IIe Guerre mondiale*, XXe siècle, Casterman-Giunti, 1993.
– Grenville, JAS, *A World History of the Twentieth Century*, Fontana, London, 1980.
– Grynberg, Anne, *La Shoah, l'impossible oubli*, Découvertes Gallimard, 1995.
– Guderian, general Heinz, *Panzer Leader*, Michael Joseph, London, 1952.
– Halder, Franz, *Hitler as War Lord*, Putnam, London, 1950.
– Hamilton, Nigel, *Monty, Master of the Battlefield*, Hamish Hamilton, London, 1983.
– Horne, Alistair, *Perdre une bataille, France mai-juin 1940*, Plon, 1990.
– Kaspi, André, *La Deuxième Guerre mondiale, chronologie commentée*, Perrin, Paris, 1990.

– Keegan, John, *Atlas de la Seconde Guerre mondiale*, Larousse/The Times, 1994.
– Keegan, John, *La Seconde Guerre mondiale*, Perrin, Paris, 1989.
– Kemp, Anthony, *The unknown Battle, Metz 1944*, Warne, London.
– Kemp, Anthony, *6 juin 1944, le débarquement en Normandie*, Découvertes Gallimard, 1994.
– Leahy, Admiral William, *J'étais là*, Plon, Paris, 1950.
– Levisse-Touzé, Christine, *Paris libéré, Paris retrouvé*, Découvertes Gallimard, 1994.
– Liddell Hart, Captain Basil, *The Other Side of the Hill*, Cassel, London, 1951.
– Liddell Hart, Captain Basil, (ed.) *The Rommel Papers*, Collins, London, 1953.
– Luck, Hans von, *Panzer Commander*, Praeger, New York, 1984.
– MacDonald, Charles B, *A Time for Trumpets*, William Morrow, New York, 1984.
– Manstein, maréchal Erich von, *Victoires perdues*, Plon, Paris, 1958.
– Montgomery, Field Marshal Viscount, *Memoirs*, Fontana, London, 1960.
– Overy, RJ, *The Air War 1939-1945*, Stein and Day, New York, 1981.
– Patton, General George S, *War as I knew it*, Houghton Miflin, Boston, 1947.
– Rousso, Henri, *Les Années noires, Vivre sous l'occupation*, Découvertes Gallimard, 1992.
Rudelle, Odile, *De Gaulle, pour mémoire*, Découvertes Gallimard, 1991.
– Seymour, William, *British Special Forces*, Sidgwick and Jackson, 1985.
– Shirer, William L, *Le IIIe Reich*, Paris, Presses de la Cité, 1990.
– Shulman, Milton, *Defeat in the West*, Secker and Warburg, London, 1947.
– Stacey, colonel CP, *The Canadian Army, 1939-1945*, The King's Printer, Ottawa, 1948.
– Taylor, AJP, *The Origins of the Second World War*.
– Taylor, APJ, *The Second World War, an illustrated history*, Penguin Books, London, 1975.
– Tusa, John & Ann, *The Nuremberg Trial*, Macmillan, London, 1983.
– Whitaker, WD & S, *Rhineland, the Battle to End of the War*, Leo Cooper, London, 1989.
– Wilmot, Chester, *The Struggle for Europe*, Collins, London, 1952.

TABLE DES ILLUSTRATIONS

1939, par Kristof Chemineau.

33h Portrait du général Guderian, peinture de Wolf Willrich, août 1940. Bundesarchiv, Koblenz.

33m Prisonniers français emmenés dans un camp par les Allemands, octobre 1939.

34h Les généraux français signant l'armistice à Compiègne, mai 1940.

35h Entrevue entre Hitler et Pétain à Montoire, 24 octobre 1940.

34-35b Graffiti de la résistance française dans un village près de Bourges, 1941. Bundesarchiv, Koblenz.

35b Affiche de propagande anti-britannique en mémoire de Dakar et Mers el-Kébir, 1941. Mémorial de Caen.

36-37 L'évacuation de Dunkerque, peinture de Charles Cundall. Imperial War Museum, Londres.

38h Pilotes de la RAF après un raid, en arrière-plan un Spitfire, 1941. Imperial War Museum, Londres.

38m Radars le long de la côte d'Angleterre près de Douvres, 15 juin 1941.

38b Avion anglais Spitfire, dessin. Mémorial de Caen.

39 Avion allemand Heinkel 111 au-dessus de Londres lors de la bataille d'Angleterre. Imperial War Museum,

Londres.

40 Le rationnement des magasins français pendant l'occupation.

40-41h Les rafles de juifs polonais par les Allemands dans le ghetto de Varsovie, 1943.

41d Exécution de Juifs russes par les Allemands à Vinnitsa en Urkraine, 1942. YIVO, Institute for Jewish Research, USHMM Archives.

42h Epaves de chars italiens capturés par les Britanniques en Libye, 20 février 1941. Imperial War Museum, Londres.

42-43 Parachutages des unités allemandes sur la Crête, mai 1941. Bundesarchiv, Koblenz.

42b Parachutistes allemands en Crête, mai-juin 1941. Bundesarchiv, Koblenz.

43b Soldats indiens en Egypte, 1941.Imperial War Museum, Londres.

44b La Royal Navy montant la garde dans l'Atlantique, affiche de propagande, peinture de Frank H. Mason. Imperial War Museum, Londres.

44-45h Destroyer américain dans un convoi de l'Atlantique, juin 1943. National Archives, Washington.

44-45b Grande parade de sous-marins allemands.

45d Le commandant d'un sous-marin allemand regardant dans un périscope, mars 1942.

46 Obusier allemand, in Signal. Mémorial de Caen.

47 Le président Roosevelt lors de sa nouvelle investiture en 1941. National Archives, Washington.

48h Les Allemands traversant la rivière Bug en URSS, 22 juin 1941. Bundesarchiv Koblenz.

48-49 Avions allemands Junker 87 au-dessus de l'URSS, juin 1941. Bundesarchiv Koblenz.

49h Ponts artificiels construits par les Allemands lors de l'invasion de l'URSS, juin 1941. Bundesarchiv Koblenz.

49b L'avancée des allemands en URSS, juin 1941. Bundesarchiv Koblenz.

50-51 Les exactions des Allemands sur les Juifs russes, 1941, musée central des Armées de Moscou. Mémorial de Caen.

52h Chars allemands détruits dans la neige en URSS, hiver 1941, musée central des Armées de Moscou. Mémorial de Caen.

52b Camion allemand embourbé sur le front de Moscou, novembre 1941. Bundesarchiv Koblenz.

53 Attaque d'un village russe par les Allemands, hiver 1941, musée central des Armées de Moscou. Mémorial de Caen.

54h Transport de marchandises en Iran à

destination de l'URSS. National archives, Washington.

55h Convoi américain dans l'Atlantique vers Mourmansk. National Archives, Washington.

55m Train de marchandises en Iran. National Archives, Washington.

54-55b Le général Marshall en compagnie de Roosevelt et de Churchill à Terre-Neuve, lors de la signature du pacte de l'Atlantiqueaoût 1941.

56 Traces de chars allemands Panzer dans le désert libyen, 1942. Bundesarchiv Koblenz.

57 Le général Rommel en Afrique du Nord, 1942. Mémorial de Caen.

58-59 Soldats japonais dans la jungle de Malaisie, décembre 1941. National archives, Washington.

59h Affiche hollandaise sur la «pieuvre hollandaise», 1942. Imperial War Museum, Londres.

60-61 L'attaque des cuirassés à Pearl Harbour, 7 décembre 1941. National Archives, Washington.

62h Navire japonais entrain de couler vu dans le périscope d'un sous-marin américain, 1942. National Archives, Washington.

62b Affiche de propagande américaine en mémoire de Pearl Harbour. Imperial War Museum, Londres.

63h Soldat américain lisant l'annonce de l'entrée en guerre des

Museum, Londres.
93 Soldats anglais dans les ruines de l'hôtel des Roses à Monte Cassino. Imperial War Museum, Londres.
94 Chantier de construction des Liberty ships à Todo, Californie. National Archives, Washington.
95h Dépôt de bidons d'essence en Angleterre avant le débarquement en Normandie, avril 1944, photo de l'U.S. Army. National Archives, Washington.
95m Dépôt d'armes en Angleterre, avril 1944. Mémorial de Caen.
95b Dépôt de provisions diverses en Angleterre, 1944. Mémorial de Caen.
95d Insigne du SHAEF, photo Labardette. Musée mémorial de Bayeux.
96m La une du *New York Times* sur le débarquement en Normandie, 6 juin 1944.
96b Un LCT, engin de débarquement, américain attendant le signal du départ dans un port anglais, juin 1944. National Archives, Washington.
97 Le débarquement à Arromanches en Normandie, 26 juin 1944, peinture de Barnett Freedman. Imperial War Museum, Londres.
98h Débarquement du matériel sur un port artificiel Mulberry, juin 1944. Bibl. nat., Paris.
98b Le maréchal von Rundstedt en

Normandie, juin 1944. Bundesarchiv, Koblenz.
99m Soldat allemand en Normandie, juillet 1944. Bibl. nat., Paris.
99b Affiche alliée en l'honneur de la résistance française, photo Alain Gesgon. C.I.R.I.P.
100 Parachutistes anglais au Parthénon lors de la prise d'Athènes, octobre 1944. Imperial War Museum, Londres.
101h Tito en compagnie de ses partisans. Imperial War Museum, Londres.
101b Hitler faisant visiter son bunker de Rastenburg à Mussolini après l'attentat du 20 juillet 1944. Bundesarchiv, Koblenz.
102h Carte de la bataille des Alliés en Belgique et aux Pays-Bas, carte de Kristof Chemineau.
102-103 Les Américains sur la route du Rhin durant l'hiver 1944, photo U.S. Army Signal Corps. Mémorial de Caen.
103m Montgomery, Eisenhower et Bradley regardant la carte du Rhin avant l'offensive, fin 1944. National Archives, Washington.
104-105 Les Gurkhas dans la jungle de Malaisie. Imperial War Museum, Londres.
104h La nouvelle route entre Chunking et la Birmanie pour les convois de ravitaillement américain. National

Archives, Washington.
105 Le général Slim en Birmanie en 1945. Imperial War Museum, Londres.
106 Le 4e corps indien lors de la prise de Meitlika en mars 1945, Birmanie.
107 Soldats africains du Commonwealth dans un temple bouddhiste à Kalewa en Birmanie. Imperial War Museum, Londres.
108h Chasseurs américains P 40, «Flying Tigers», stationnés en Chine. National Archives, Washington.
108b Portrait du général Mac Arthur de retour aux Philippines, 1944. National Archives, Washington.
109 Les Marines en action à Guam, 31 juillet 1944. National Archives, Washington.

CHAPITRE VI

110h Les bras des Alliés brisant la croix gammée, affiche de 1945. Musée d'histoire contemporaine, Paris.
110b Les Américains dans le stade de Nuremberg en 1945. Bundesarchiv, Koblenz.
111 Portrait officiel de Staline durant la guerre.
112h Les parachutistes de la 101e division américaine dans les rues de Bastogne, photo New York Times. National Archives, Washington.
112-113 Les Américains aux prises de l'hiver dans les

Ardennes, début 1945. National Archives, Washington.
113h Jeune soldat allemand prisonnier en Belgique, 16 décembre 1944. Imperial War Museum, Londres.
114h Eisenhower visitant le camp de Buchenwald en compagnie de Patton et Bradley, avril 1945.
114-115m Churchill, Roosevelt et Staline à la conférence de Yalta, février 1945.
115h La libération du camp d'Auschwitz par les Soviétiques, janvier 1945.
115b Des soldats soviétiques aidant des femmes yougoslaves du camp d'Auschwitz. Ghetto Fighter's House.
116-117h La une du *New York Times* du 2 mai 1945 sur la mort de Hitler.
116-117b Carte de l'étau allié se resserrant sur l'Allemagne par Kristof Chemineau.
117h Soldat russe dans le bunker de Hitler à Berlin. Bundesarchiv, Koblenz.
118 Jeunes prisonniers allemands de l'Armée rouge, Berlin mai 1945, musée central des Armées de Moscou. Mémorial de Caen.
119 Soldat allemand dans les ruines de Berlin, mai 1945.
120-121 Le drapeau soviétique flotte sur Berlin, mai 1945, musée central des Armées de Moscou. Mémorial de Caen.

139b Roosevelt et Churchill à la conférence de Casablanca, janvier 1943. Imperial War Museum, Londres.

140h Offensive des soldats soviétiques, musée central des Armées de Moscou. Mémorial de Caen.

140mg Convoi dans l'Atlantique.

140md Reddition de combattants juifs pendant l'insurrection du ghetto de Varsovie, 1943. National Archives, Washington.

141mg Reddition du général von Arnhim en Afrique du Nord, mai 1943. Imperial War Museum, Londres.

141h Portrait du général Yamamoto. National Archives, Washington.

141md Portrait du général Eisenhower.

141mc Chars américains en Birmanie.

141mc Soldats américains en Birmanie.

141b Roosevelt et Churchill à la conférence de Québec, août 1943. Imperial War Museum, Londres.

142h Bombardier américain B17, coll. part. Mémorial de Caen.

142m Sabotage par la Résistance des lignes de chemins de fer en Normandie, 1944. Bibl. nat., Paris.

142b Embarquement de parachutistes américains le 6 juin 1944. Imperial War Museum, Londres.

143gh Les ruines du monastère de Monte Cassino. Imperial War Museum, Londres.

143gm Les soldats français entrant dans Rome, juin 1944. Bibl. nat., Paris.

143ch Les Marines dans l'atoll de Kawajalein, îles Marshall, février 1944. National Archives, Washington.

143dm Les Marines tués sur la plage de Tarawa, novembre 1943. National Archives, Washington.

143b Le débarquement des Marines dans les îles Marianne. National Archives, Washington.

144m Vue aérienne du *Tirpitz* dans les eaux norvégiennes. Imperial War Museum, Londres.

144b Les partisans yougoslaves marchent sur Belgrade, 20 octobre 1944.

145hg Débarquement des Alliés en Provence, 15 août 1944. National Archives, Washington.

145mg La VIIIe armée anglaise en Italie, 1944.

145md Les Marines à Saipan dans les îles Marshall, 1944. National Archives, Washington.

145bg Le débarquement du général Mac Arthur aux Philippines, janvier 1945. National Archives, Washington.

145bd Pilotes japonais *kamikaze*, 1945.

146b Les victimes du typhus dans le camp de Belsen au moment de sa libération, 1945. Imperial War Museum, Londres.

147hg La libération du camp d'Auschwitz par l'Armée rouge, janvier 1945. National Archives, Washington.

147d Patrouille américaine dans le Pacifique. National Archives, Washington.

147m Une escadrille de chasseurs soviétiques au-dessus de Berlin, 1945.

147gb Les chars soviétiques dans les ruines de Königsberg, 1945.

147db Un régiment de

la RAF débarque à Rangoon, juin 1945.

148h Les accusés allemands au procès de Nuremberg, 1945.

148b Les accusés japonais au procès de Tokyo, 1946. National Archives, Washington.

149h L'explosion de la bombe atomique sur Hiroshima, 11 août 1945.

150 Corps de soldats canadiens sur la plage de Dieppe après l'échec du raid en août 1942. Imperial War Museum, Londres.

152 La neige recouvrant les ruines de Léningrad, novembre 1941.

153 Soldats allemands prisonniers de l'Armée rouge, Berlin, 1945. musée central des Armées de Moscou. Mémorial de Caen.

154 Résistants français en Normandie nettoyant leurs armes, 1944, photo U.S. Army. Mémorial de Caen.

156 Contrôle Ss dans le ghetto de Varsovie, 1940-1943.

159 Déportation de Juifs de Solvaquie vers 1942. Yad Vashem, Jérusalem.

160 Les généraux alliés à Berlin en juin 1945, de gauche à droite Montgomery, Eisenhower, Joukov et De Lattre de Tassigny. Bundesarchiv, Koblenz.

161 Soldats anglo-canadiens récupérant les derniers vestiges du parti nazi à Kranenberg, février 1945. National Archives, Washington.

INDEX

CRÉDITS PHOTOGRAPHIQUES

Bibliothèque nationale de France, Paris 98h, 99m, 142m, 143gm. BDIC, Paris 70, 132db, 137db. Bundesarchiv, Koblenz 4ᵉ plat, 4, 7, 15h, 20h, 20b, 31b, 32h, 33d, 34-35b, 42-43, 42b, 48h, 48-49b, 49h, 49b, 52b, 56, 90, 91h, 91m, 98b, 101b, 110b, 117h, 129, 160. Jean-Loup Charmet, Paris 1ᵉʳ plat, 110h. C.I.R.I.P. 99b. ECPA 90-91. Imperial War Museum, Londres Dos, 6, 18g, 28, 30d, 30-31h, 36-37, 38h, 39, 42h, 43h, 44b, 59h, 62b, 66-67h, 67h, 72-73h, 72m, 72-73b, 75m, 75b, 76h, 77m, 82h, 84, 86h, 92b, 93, 97, 100, 101h, 104-105, 105, 107, 113h, 127, 130bd, 131h, 131bd, 132hd, 132dm, 132b, 133cb, 135h, 135h, 138h, 138gm, 139g, 139b, 141mg, 141b, 142b, 143gh, 144m, 146b, 150. Keystone 1h, 2, 3, 8, 9, 12h, 15b, 17h, 18-19h, 19b, 20-21, 23h, 24-25, 26g, 29, 33g, 34h, 35h, 38m, 40, 40-41h, 44-45b, 45d, 54-55b, 74b, 106, 111, 114-115m, 115h, 119, 124-125b, 126g, 130h, 130bg, 131bg, 132g, 132gm, 132ch, 135b, 136h, 136cg, 138dm, 138b, 139mh, 139dh, 139md, 140mg, 141md, 141mc, 144b, 145mg, 145bd, 147m, 147gd, 147db, 148h, 149h. L'Illustration/Sygma 12b, 25h, 134h, 134gm, 151. Mémorial de Caen 11, 14, 22-23, 24, 26d, 35b, 38b, 46, 57, 68h, 95m, 95b, 102-103, 142h, 154. Musée central des Armées de Moscou/Mémorial de Caen 5, 50-51, 52h, 53, 68b, 69d, 71, 78m, 79h, 79b, 80-81, 118, 120-121, 128, 134gd, 136cd, 140h, 153. Musée Mémorial de Bayeux 89, 95d. National Archives, Washington, DC 16h, 16-17, 44-45h, 47, 54h, 55h, 55m, 58-59, 60-61, 62h, 63h, 63b, 74-75h, 82, 83b, 86m, 86-87b, 89, 92h, 94, 95h, 96b, 103m, 104h, 108h, 108b, 109, 112h, 112-113, 120h, 121h, 122-123b, 125h, 126h, 132cm, 137h, 137gd, 140md, 141h, 143ch, 143dm, 143b, 145hg, 145md, 145bd, 147hg, 147d, 148b, 161. Roger Viollet 1b, 13, 18m. United State Holocaust Memorial Museum 41d, 114h, 115b, 133h, 137cd, 156, 159.

REMERCIEMENTS

L'auteur et l'éditeur tiennent à remercier particulièrement Françoise Passera et Franck Marie au Mémorial de Caen, Madame Kuhl aux Bundesarchiv de Koblenz.

COLLABORATEURS EXTÉRIEURS

DÉCOUVERTES GALLIMARD
DIRECTION : Pierre Marchand et Elisabeth de Farcy.
GRAPHISME : Alain Gouessant. FABRICATION : Violaine Grare. PRESSE ET PROMOTION : Valérie Tolstoï.
LA SECONDE GUERRE MONDIALE
EDITION : Nathalie Reyss. MAQUETTE : Vincent Lever (Corpus) et Dominique Guillaumin (Témoignages et Documents). ICONOGRAPHIE : Nathalie Reyss, Suzanne Bosman et Savina Lambert. CARTOGRAPHIE : Kristof Chemineau. LECTURE-CORRECTION : François Boisivon et Catherine Levine. PHOTOGRAVURE : Arc en ciel. MONTAGE PAO : Paragramme et Dominique Guillaumin.

De 1939 à 1945,
la Seconde Guerre mondiale
est bien un conflit total, planétaire.
De Varsovie à Paris,
de Pearl Harbour à Stalingrad,
de Singapour à El Alamein,
de Berlin à Hiroshima,
le monde s'est embrasé,
faisant des millions de victimes.
Des chefs ont émergé, pour le meilleur
et pour le pire, Churchill, De Gaulle, Staline,
Roosevelt, Hitler, Mussolini...
Un ouvrage de référence, conçu par Anthony Kemp,
pour appréhender les bouleversements
profonds et douloureux,
qui ont fait le monde d'aujourd'hui.

A 53320
ISBN : 2-07-053320-4

9 782070 533206

53, 55, 68, *76*, 82, 89, 90, 91, 100, 102, 111, 114, *114*, 115, 116, 117, *117*, *121*, 126, 127, *127*. US Air Force 66, 113, 123.

V

V1 *91*, 99.
V2 *91*.
Varsovie 24, *25*, *40*, 92, 114.
Verdun *35*, 99.
Versailles, traité de 13,

14, *19*, 20.
Vichy 35, 73, 74.
Vincennes, château de 33.
Vistule 92, 114.
Volga *81*.
Von Arnim, général Jürgen 75.
Von Manstein, général Erich *32*, 76.
Von Paulus, général Friedrich 71, 75, 76, *81*.
Von Rundstedt,

général Gerd 99.
Von Reichenau, général Walther *51*.
Vosges 100, 104, 113.

W

Waal 102, 103.
Wainwright, général 62.
Wake *61*.
Walcheren, île de 103.
Washington 57, 64, *64*.
Wavell, général Archibald 43, 57.

Wesel 112, 116.
Westwall 112.
Weygand, général Maxime 33, 34.
Wingate, colonel Orde 105.

Y

Yalta, conférence de 114, *115*.
Yamamoto, amiral Isoroku 61, 64, *84*.
Yougoslavie 43, 87, *100*, 101.

CRÉDITS PHOTOGRAPHIQUES

Bibliothèque nationale de France, Paris 98h, 99m, 142m, 143gm. BDIC, Paris 70, 132db, 137db. Bundesarchiv, Koblenz 4ᵉ plat, 4, 7, 15h, 20h, 20b, 31b, 32h, 33d, 34-35b, 42-43, 42b, 48h, 48-49b, 49h, 49b, 52b, 56, 90, 91h, 91m, 98b, 101b, 110b, 117h, 129, 160. Jean-Loup Charmet, Paris 1ᵉʳ plat, 110h. C.I.R.I.P. 99b. ECPA 90-91. Imperial War Museum, Londres Dos, 6, 18g, 28, 30d, 30-31h, 36-37, 38h, 39, 42h, 43b, 44b, 59h, 62b, 66-67h, 67h, 72-73h, 72m, 72-73b, 75m, 75b, 76h, 77m, 82h, 84, 86h, 92b, 93, 97, 100, 101h, 104-105, 105, 107, 113h, 127, 130bd, 131h, 131bd, 132hd, 132dm, 132b, 133cb, 135b, 135h, 138h, 138gm, 139g, 139b, 141mg, 141b, 142h, 143gh, 144m, 146b, 150. Keystone 1h, 2, 3, 8, 9, 12h, 15b, 17h, 18-19h, 19b, 20-21, 23h, 24-25, 26g, 29, 33g, 34h, 35h, 38m, 40, 40-41h, 44-45b, 45d, 54-55b, 74b, 106, 111, 114-115m, 115h, 119, 124h, 124-125b, 126g, 130h, 130bg, 131bg, 132g, 132gm, 132ch, 135h, 136h, 136cg, 138dm, 138b, 139mh, 139dh, 139md, 140mg, 141md, 141mc, 144b, 145mg, 145bd, 147m, 147gd, 147db, 148h, 149h. L'Illustration/Sygma 12b, 25h, 134h, 134gm, 151. Mémorial de Caen 11, 14, 22-23, 24, 26d, 35b, 38b, 46, 57, 68h, 95m, 95b, 102-103, 142h, 154. Musée central des Armées de Moscou/Mémorial de Caen 5, 50-51, 52h, 53, 68b, 69d, 71, 78m, 79h, 79b, 80-81, 118, 120-121, 128, 134gd, 136cd, 140h, 153. Musée Mémorial de Bayeux 89, 95d. National Archives, Washington, DC 16h, 16-17, 44-45h, 47, 54h, 55h, 55m, 58-59, 60-61, 62h, 63h, 63b, 74-75h, 82, 83b, 86m, 86-87b, 89, 92h, 94, 95h, 96b, 103m, 104h, 108h, 108b, 109, 112h, 112-113, 120h, 121h, 122-123b, 125h, 126h, 132cm, 137h, 137gd, 140md, 141h, 143ch, 143dm, 143b, 145hg, 145md, 145bd, 147hg, 147d, 148b, 161. Roger Viollet 1b, 13, 18m. United State Holocaust Memorial Museum 41d, 114h, 115b, 133h, 137cd, 156, 159**.**

REMERCIEMENTS

L'auteur et l'éditeur tiennent à remercier particulièrement Françoise Passera et Franck Marie au Mémorial de Caen, Madame Kuhl aux Bundesarchiv de Koblenz.

COLLABORATEURS EXTÉRIEURS

DÉCOUVERTES GALLIMARD
DIRECTION : Pierre Marchand et Elisabeth de Farcy.
GRAPHISME : Alain Gouessant. FABRICATION : Violaine Grare. PRESSE ET PROMOTION : Valérie Tolstoï.
LA SECONDE GUERRE MONDIALE
ÉDITION : Nathalie Reyss. MAQUETTE : Vincent Lever (Corpus) et Dominique Guillaumin (Témoignages et Documents). ICONOGRAPHIE : Nathalie Reyss, Suzanne Bosman et Savina Lambert. CARTOGRAPHIE : Kristof Chemineau. LECTURE-CORRECTION : François Boisivon et Catherine Levine. PHOTOGRAVURE : Arc en ciel. MONTAGE PAO : Paragramme et Dominique Guillaumin.

Table des matières

Luna Press
PUBLISHING

Text Copyright © 2023 LK Kitney
Cover © 2023 Jay Johnstone

First published by Luna Press Publishing, Edinburgh, 2023

LK Kitney to be identified as the Author of the Work has been asserted by
once with the Copyright, Designs and Patents Act 1988.

Tell Ourselves ©2023. All rights reserved. No part of this publication
duced, stored in a retrieval system, or transmitted in any form or by
ectronic, mechanical, photocopy, recording or otherwise, without prior
ission of the copyright owners. Nor can it be circulated in any form
cover other than that in which it is published and without similar
luding this condition being imposed on a subsequent purchaser.

www.lunapresspublishing.com
ISBN-13: 978-1-915556-02-8

THE LIES WE TELL OURSELVES

LK KITNEY

LUNA NOVELLA #17

THE
WE T
OURSE

LK KIT

LUNA NOVELL

Luna
Press
PUBLISHING

The right of
her in acco

The Lies W
may be rep
any means,
written per
of binding
condition i

For everyone who has ever given me
safe harbour from the storms.

Contents

Chapter One

There is an old shark in the waters around Keset. It is not the season for her; ice in the waters around this dirty city of narrow, overcrowded streets where snow lingers until high summer means her prey are schooling together for protection, unable to be picked off one by one. She should starve here.

She does not. Fed a fat appeasement, she is content to leave her usual targets for now. They, in exchange, do not dare to take the opportunity to turn their great strengths against her in a united front, more afraid of the repercussions of her wrath than the inconvenience of her interest.

I, too, would rather face her interest than her ire. That is why I have come to meet her, walking past behemoth ships of trade and conquest and ego tied to shore by rope and anchor. Crossed with planks and walkways they almost create a floating city of their own, their sailors taking advantage of the ice to take their fun in any way they please, forging contracts and contacts with their neighbours, each one of them with stories to tell and legends to claim.

One old woman with a gnarled walking stick and the stiff movements of the bitter northern winter in my bones is nothing remarkable but a sailor is a gossip. By the time I have done nothing more than walk past them, there are already six independent bets amongst the Keseti dockworkers, and eight across the crews of four different ships that I am about to face my doom. Even the Keseti guards patrolling the harbour have swapped coin against whether they will pull my corpse from the water before I feed what lives in the deep below.

All for approaching a single ship moored by herself; alone in a wide circle of dark water. The Black Shark of Nion.

She is *Golden Harvest*, a name as infamous as that of her captain; the shade of a man supposedly so evil, so vengeful, that even the Nightmare did not want him. She moors here now because no port authority has ever succeeded in preventing her and perhaps, if they tolerate this small evil of her presence, no further will fall on them.

I have never been one to fear stories of monsters. I have met my fair share in this long life and come through unscathed and often unimpressed. But I would be lying to say I did not share the concerns around me, for other reasons.

To the untrained eye, with her single mast, tidy ropes and neat sails that, even reefed, seem to make her dance in the cold winter wind, she looks like a toy compared to the giant trade vessels of Brindur, Aroda or Yana. To the trained eye, or the old one, it is clear to see that her narrow hull and sharp prow let her cut through waves like a fin: fast and nimble.

Once, ships like her were the sign of honest trade, news and exploration across the known world, enough so that Nion made the silhouette of this shark their national emblem.

They are all but vanished now, along with the people who built them — scuttled or burned. She may even be the last; a lingering shade twenty years out of time. As well as the solid purple of Esia, she still flies the Black Shark, though the colours have faded and the fabric is tattered from the wind. Many times patched and darned from different materials, I doubt anything is left of the original save the memory of it.

I could turn away and leave her sitting in Keset's harbour. I owe this city nothing. Its fate when the crew grow bored of waiting is no concern of mine. The abomination who runs this ship need never know I ever gave his request consideration. It is an outlandish truth he wishes to share with me: that I am the one he waits for.

My moment of hesitation robs me of the choice. The woman who delivered his message to me appears above the railings of the ship as two others lower a gangplank. Strong lines and hard muscle define her, and the smile she offers as she beckons me forward is a half-twisted thing. She does not approve of the methods her captain is employing, but believes in their necessity. To kill or cure, this will remove the last of the poisonous tumour within him for good. Her thoughts, not mine. Though she knows what to expect from me, and I her, I do not give away the thoughts that do not belong to me.

She keeps my feet steady as I step aboard to be shepherded across the deck towards the doors that signify the captain's private spaces.

A small ship needs only a small crew, yet this one is tiny. Despite the low numbers, there are faces from almost everywhere. No surprise; the captain is a man almost as well travelled as I am. I wonder what their stories are, to stay, but they are too full of curiosity of *me* to provide any clues. Even *they* cannot fully guess what he wants with me.

The messenger ushers me through the doors before closing me in, the sound of her body resting against them ensuring privacy for what comes next. Even amongst abominations, this could be poorly received.

I am in a small, sparse room with a small table set into the centre covered in maps and charts of places I do not recognise weighed down with rocks and weights. It is a theatre. I do not buy it for an instant. There is a door on the opposite side of the room, almost closed.

"Are you going to invite me in, Fiaer Dradorn — scourge of the seas, Shark from the East — or were manners the first thing you lost?"

He flies the Esian flag, and so I stay with a familiar language.

"Mother Kiera," he replies in kind, as the sounds of frantic shuffling come from the other side of the door, almost as if I had startled him. "Excuse my unreadiness. I was unsure if you would come."

The door swings open and I prepare for my first glimpse of a monster.

He has not dressed for company: wearing faded trousers, an open-necked shirt and a worn leather jerkin despite the cold. He goes barefoot on the wooden boards.

I met his father many years ago, before he took the title Dradorn. That he died near a decade ago is untrue. He lives on in the height and sharp features of his son, and in the dark, curly hair. The eyes are a little lighter, as is his skin tone.

The similarities are enough that I almost expected the son to be the same age his father had been when I had met him. He is not. Barely more than five and twenty.

The clearest differences are the scars, and not just physical ones. Those lighter eyes hold a depth his father had lacked the last I saw him and the son is guarded against me — wary — the worries he holds leaking through the edges of his resolve.

He does not want me to believe him. He needs me to. That does not stop the touch of mockery in his sweeping bow as he invites me into his chambers. He is not cowed by me, and does not see the appeal of formality, but is willing to pretend otherwise. That endears him to me, somewhat.

There is little evident in his sparse chambers to back up the rumours of his immense wealth, earned through blood. A single set of shelves keeps logs and ledgers safe. A simple desk fastened to the floorboards, bearing a closed logbook — bookmarked with blotting paper — ink and a pen, takes the centre of the room. An equally simple chair is tethered to the desk. In an alcove to one side is a fine hammock strung over a cot where, instead of a bed, he has stashed a simple sea-chest. The ends of a shirt stick out from the seam. The wooden walls are marred with deep gouges and light comes from tiny windows — small, to better weather heavy storms — and lanterns burning oil.

The only displays of wealth I have seen are the sword at his hip and a single ring on a finger. Inheritances, not prizes, and both worth more than he probably realises.

He offers me the single chair. It is exactly as it appears, without comfort. I suspect a sore backside will be the least uncomfortable thing either of us will endure today.

"Is–?" he starts as he continues to pace, unsure where to put himself or where to start.

"Not until I am sure of your intentions."

The look that flashes across his face makes me laugh. "Oh, I know you don't have those kinds of plans, and I doubt many old women have safeguarded their loved ones from your attentions with any measure of success — though perhaps they ought to. Don't look at me like that. I was young once too. I know what a handsome face and a quick smile can do, and son, you have both."

There is a blush there, under the attempt at blasé indifference. A crack between man and monster. A crack between the infamous man of war and a boy who does not know what to do with my compliment, his surprise breaking down his guard, just for a moment.

It is enough to reassure me that trusting myself to a man with such a reputation for recklessness may be worth it. For all the lies that surround him, I must know who *he* believes himself to be before I trust him with my own treasure.

I also understand his apprehension. It is a vanishingly rare person comfortable with what I am and a rarer one still willing to knowingly subject themselves to the things I can do. At my urging he stops pacing and leans against the desk, facing me, his fingers grip the wood tightly.

I share his trepidation. Snatching passing thoughts is one thing. To read a mind another. To enter it entirely... The risks are so high.

I am old. Cold bones are the least of my concerns, and my symptoms. There is a tugging at my heart I long to follow and, if I am not careful, I may yet follow that yearning. But some things must be risked, especially for those we love.

He scowls as accepts my safeguards: agreeing no attempts at deception, or manipulation of what he wishes me to see, and a forgiveness of my personal inexperience of the details of the life he leads. He will not endanger this plan, but there are parts where I may meet resistance. Fortunately I have always been a stubborn, wilful woman.

I take his hands: rough, calloused, scarred. So many broken bones that have healed more than once.

I breathe in and direct the threads of magery to the shape I need and, for a moment, I see myself as he does: an old woman, dark skin sagging with age, a headscarf over silver hair, a stoop in her back and a worn staff over her knees. I shine with a light that has no source and his wonder widens the door into his mind. Another moment, and he sees himself as I do. The oppositional views collide until we are outside of ourselves and each other, a third view of two still, quiet figures hand in hand, man and woman. Youth and age. Vigour and frailty. Neither knowing who we are, or who is invading.

For that moment, what we want is carried on a name whispered in the heart of us with longing, familiar and strange. That difference is enough. We find edges, definitions as we surrender, as we take control. We become You and I, interwoven, threaded through each other. You widen the weaving, leaving room for I to peer in, offering I — me — Your truth.

The taste of salt fills my mouth, the wind blows through my hair. A tropical summer sun, two years past, warms my skin as I slip into Your memories.

Chapter Two

The priest prays.

She has done this every day at noon for the twenty-one days since you left the Isian port of Ide, heading into the uncharted, unknowable East.

Despite the repetition of her actions you continue to watch her strange routines with more curiosity than you hope your crew realises.

The "great" Captain Fiaer Dradorn is meant to be a seasoned man. Enhancing the legend your father started, there is no port you would dare not sail into at least once. You know customs and languages most would never consider, yet the priest has you perplexed.

It is not an unfamiliar feeling, but it is unwelcome, one you have not felt this strongly since your father made you dance to his paranoid tunes.

You do not let your crew see your confusion. It would lend power to their own and you cannot afford to throw fuel on the latent dissatisfaction thrumming through *Golden Harvest*. You have too much to lose.

The priest raises her arms and shrills into the air, chanting in Isian, her bizarre pantomime not once deviating. You understand some of the words she uses; they are similar to Esian but make no sense in the context you would presume — another difference between the twin countries, though Esia and Isia have shared little more than a border for hundreds of years.

Esia is a home for when the sea grows too lonely. Isia is a secretive place even sailors do not cast many rumours about. You used that to explain your decision to sail there. A chance to put paid to what scant rumours did exist, and to add to your own. Fiaer Dradorn — the man who would sail east and return, chasing the next great adventure.

Your crew do not know the true reason you have brought them to forsaken waters. The secrecy sits poorly with you, a heavy knot in your gut that will not shift.

They are more than just hands to make *Golden Harvest* work. These people are your family. They have a right to know, but to speak of your true intentions here would be to make something as substantial as mist real, and if it fails to become solid it will destroy you, as it destroyed your father.

The priest takes a tiny dagger and lets a drop of blood fall from her sun-browned fingers into the water. The bird on her shoulder flaps its black wings and screams at the sky.

You are not sure what type of bird it is, too like a raven — but white — only its wings stained black. It is bad news having a bird like that on board. Ravens eat carrion, and a raven never goes hungry. You have been considering getting a ship's cat when next you make port, as an act of defiance.

Finished with her ritual for today, the priest turns and smiles at you. Her robes are as white as the sun on the water. It hurts to look at her. You do it anyway. If you look away she laughs, and there is no mirth there.

"Nisha blesses us this day," she says in Trade — the common language between all known countries. Her accent is heavy; it makes her words thick and slurred, but this script is something you understand. It is the only thing about the priest you do.

After all, neither you or your crew are entirely sure what a goddess is, or supposed to be. Deism is an ancient idea you have only come across a handful of times from the words and minds of oddball scholars on the run from something. Their own sense of reality, more often than not.

The priest has tried to explain it to you: this notion that there are beings no man or animal can see, touch, taste or hear possessed of incredible power and, of anything conceivable in the cosmos, they choose to watch the minutiae of people's lives on this one broken world.

She also does not seem to understand your confusion over why such beings require people like her to speak *for* them. If this Nisha has the power the priest claims, to shape whole worlds, it should not require human mouthpieces. That it does suggests it not worth veneration.

She is also unable to convincingly explain her insistence on something called conversion either, though you let her attempt it on your crew to see it in action. To her chagrin, it had gone nowhere.

She does not see how contradictory it is to suggest such powerful beings need people to fawn over them. Unless, instead, this Nisha's power is syphoned from the people who believe in it, in which case, a goddess is not truly possessed of power, great or otherwise.

There *are* certain creatures with the power the priest claims. They are not gods, but monsters — the Nightmare's own children. The very thought makes your skin crawl and, taking offence, the priest brings such discussions to an abrupt end.

You explain her as a strange custom from a land full of secrets and hope the whale in the hold of wondering if you are leading your family to doom can continue to be ignored.

The winds pick up once the priest finishes her prayers, pushing *Golden Harvest* further east than any ship has ever been and returned to sing stories about.

Only the foolhardy and the desperate come this far.

You are both.

Twenty one days since port, and seventeen since you last saw land — the promontory of the Horn of Truth dwindling into the sunset, and there are no charts for these waters. Your navigator, Cylin, a portly man with a fondness for frowning does his best to create them — and history — as you go, but there is precious little to go on. He swears at the priest and her goddess as his skills languish.

He has asked, more than once, why you are bringing them all so far from land, from sanity. There is nothing out here. Not even nothing of worth, just... nothing.

You have been left alone by all that should have befallen a ship in these waters at this time of year. Even squalls and gyres have moved out of your way to leave your passage smooth and easy. You have seen no rocky outcroppings, no corals. No pods of whales or dolphins have come near. There has not even been the silver glint of scale under the water from fish. No birds save for the priest's own hunt in the waters around you — though what it finds are a mystery.

The water is dead and you are a corpse floating on its surface, pushed and pulled on whims you cannot understand but must accept.

You remind Cylin that he will have what has been promised

to him in return for his trust in you. Not only would you rather have his goodwill, you will need him and his abilities should something go wrong.

He backs down, but he is not the only one nurturing discomfort. The whole ship is brittle, waiting to crack. If you do not do something soon, all you will be left with are splinters.

Your crew work as diligently as ever but their songs and the chatter and the insults you find comforting — the sounds of a ship's life — have faded. When they do break out, they are dark and full of menace. Your crew have little to do to distract themselves from their poor moods. Normally that would be the tinder needed to sink a ship, but even those in your ranks with argumentative natures have knuckled down and kept the peace — on the surface. They want what you have promised them. The real danger will come once they have it.

The priest wraps an arm around your waist as she heads towards your quarters. Teasing to irritate you. You have no interest in her. She is a fine-looking woman, and you have rarely been known to turn down a fine-looking anyone who showed enthusiastic consent, but rarely is not the same as never. Even if her very presence did not leave you uneasy, you need to show you are not sailing into obscurity for the sake of a pretty face. She is here only to oversee that you hold up your end of the bargain you struck in Isia. As envoy, she has your chambers as a sign of respect while you have been sleeping with the crew in the cramped hold. You prefer it there anyway.

As the priest leaves the deck you breathe in the saline air and smile — though it is false — to diffuse the tension. Someone must.

One hand flexes, itching for the hilt of the sword at your

hip. The thumb of the other runs over a patch of lighter skin on your ring finger. You wet salt-crusted lips with a lick of your tongue and your heart drops at the necessity of these little motions to keep your calm, hoping you show anticipation and not anxiety.

You have always tried to be if not a good man, then a decent one. One who knew the value of an oath. One your father would have recognised as ally — at least before the paranoia had destroyed him. One that your mother might have been proud of, if you had ever known who she was. Sure, there have been times you have strayed from that ideal: made a few enemies, been chased from one port or another, your name cursed by those you left behind, but you have never been a bad man. Driven, sometimes even ruthless, but always with reason.

As the days pass, it is getting harder for you to argue that you have stayed true to that. You once swore you would stay out of the politics of nations, no matter how desperate things become.

Yet, for what the Isians are offering you, you will break your vow a thousand times over if you must, despite knowing what will come from your actions here.

Once, you ran from the same thing, clinging to your father's shirt as he pushed through streets packed with frightened people to reach the ship you now, still, call home. Flames licked houses and tore through the districts you had known in the secret maps of a child's mind, ash swirling in a dark blizzard. You had seen your father kill men that night, fighting invaders while the palace on the hill burned. You had buried your head into your father's neck, feeling his sweat slick against your own skin — the piss where you had been so scared the first time he pulled you out of harm's way as he fought someone off running down both your legs. His hair tickled your cheeks as his tears soaked you on that hot, dry night.

He had stayed on the streets of Nion, screaming for his wives and your sister until the smoke had made you choke and invaders had gathered in groups too large for one man burdened with a small boy to beat back, forcing him to choose between his loves. Between his children. When the news filtered through that your family was dead — their heads on spikes on the road leading up to the palace on the hill along with every other Nionese who had fallen protecting their home — he had never let you forget he had chosen you.

At least the gold will be good for your crew. For you it is just an excuse — an easy reason to pretend you had a choice in becoming the man who will change the world.

You had not.

Just two months ago, you had harboured from a storm in a small Esian town close to the border with its secretive neighbour. Your crew had settled in quickly, making a nuisance of themselves in the taverns; a welcome trade on a night such as this. You had a drink — just enough to stop you going to check again that *Golden Harvest*'s ropes were tight and correct. They were. They always are, but without her you have nothing.

The drink served you was a stronger cut than usual; captain's share, perhaps. A generosity, or more likely a clever ploy as once a man is already drunk it is hard for him to say no to more. Bolstered by a liquid confidence you had not needed, you had approached a handsome young man who kept catching your eye, unsure in his stance and bearing if he wanted to take the chance on you.

You did not share his hesitation and offered yourself to him, your mind occupied only by how much you desired him. Your only hope that he would want you too. He did, and he led you to a private chamber upstairs from the tavern floor where you delighted in delighting him, aware of each other's wants before words, until you woke late in the morning, your head pounding — something very wrong.

Your lover held you down without trouble, too weak — too confused — to fight him, and gave you orders to meet him in Ide for a job, well compensated. He then took material things from you to ensure your compliance as if taking your pride was not enough.

Klaudai, your surgeon, stumped by the lingering effects of the drug you had been spiked with, declares you lucky to only have been robbed. She had noticed, of course, though she has kept her silence to avoid further embarrassment.

It is not even pride that keeps you from explaining to your crew how easily you had been manipulated. It is not even to recover the belongings you yourself once stole. Nor is it for the wealth promised to all these who stand beside you. The Isian man had known how to get into your head and abuse what he had found there, and that is something you cannot forgive. You cannot forgive how he still haunts your dreams, filling them with longing.

Your crow, Khleo, in her basket at the top of the mast calls down that there are strange sails on the horizon, right where the priest said they would be.

Golden Harvest picks up speed, pushed along by gathering winds, rocking against cresting white-caps in what had been glass-smooth waters moments ago.

This is the first real motion you have felt in near three

long weeks, your beautiful ship bursting into life, the way she pitches and yaws as familiar to you as your own face. Pushed and pulled on listless waters by unknowable forces, she has been dead this whole time, making ghostly progress and leaving the barest of wakes behind her.

Now, she breathes. Lives. Your crew come to life with her: their voices break out in rhythmic singing to keep each other in time. Some even jest. Samethi — chief under you — swears at those who slack, almost as if this was a normal hunt. They fix the sails to take advantage of the sudden winds, angling towards your quarry on the horizon. The beat of your heart speeds as you race towards the end.

How you will truly be remembered depends on if you live through the oncoming attempts to kill you: whether you live to claim your gold, or sink to the bottom of these crystal waters, abandoned and forgotten as if you never were.

Your prey is a Yannish ship, far from the northern islands she calls home. She is a boxy looking thing, sitting low, either full of goods or she has taken on water. Either will slow her down. Either works in your favour.

You have only seen ships like her a handful of times and have never dared take one on. The effort has never been worth the reward.

Now? You would take on a whole fleet.

The Yannish ship tries and fails to turn from your path. Paper sails swivel on all five of her tall masts, trying to catch the wind, sagging and sinking as the air shifts around them. The winds that fill your sails fail to catch hers, and she is too low in the water. She lacks the skill of your crew easing into the wind rising behind you. She lacks your intent and your determination. She lacks your need.

You grip the wooden railing of your ship and taste the sea as it sprays over the bow, showering you in a fine mist. This time, your grin is true, if short lived.

You give the orders for the flags to be changed, pulling down the unfavourable emblem of Nion and the deep purple of Esia and replacing them the pointed golden lotus of Isia.

The change goes against the priest's plans but the colours you fly are more than symbolic. Isia wants this, Isia can claim it. You have anchors that will not shift and you learned from your father a long time ago that not every rebellion needs to be loud to be effective.

The priest reappears, the bird on her shoulder. The glint in her eye matches your own. You look away in discomfort at the similarity, instead checking on your crew and your ship.

Being caught up in practicalities as you close the distance banks some of the lust for the fight. To allow the distraction and ignore your ship would mean failure. It also grants you the opportunity to spend quiet moments with your crew.

There are faces here you will not see again, voices you will not hear once the sun sets. You would spend your time no other way. You hold the title of captain now, but you know where you came from.

The red lacquer painted over the boards of the Yannish ship glistens in the afternoon sun, and as soon you can see the shapes of people on her broad deck, and they can see you, they request aid.

Storms half-beached them on rocks before lifting them off again. They are damaged, taking on water and trapped in doldrums, the winds refusing to carry them home. They need more pumps and materials for repairs and will pay handsomely to be out of these alien waters.

What they offer would make you all rich many times over. It is a pittance to what the Isians have promised. You would not waste your crews — your family's — lives on something this reckless for anything less.

Isia did not give you a reason you believed for this direct attack on a remote island nation, far from the borders of either. All you can do to soften the blow is accept that while Isia picked the target, they made no mention of how this hunt was to be completed. The guise of friendship will allow you to subdue the Yannish crew before they realise they *can* fight. Success here will best be served by sabotage.

The northern ships may be slow and tempting, but that is a deception. The crews are armed with bows made of some supple metal only the Yannish produce and do not sell. Their arrows fly further than you can return and even their smallest crews outnumber your largest.

The priest shakes her head and your crew ready bows, spears and javelins from the armoury, taking positions behind the thick cedar protection of *Golden Harvest* despite your orders to the contrary. You snatch weapons away from those closest to you. They turn and simply fetch more.

You do not understand what is happening, nor can you argue against it. The words gather in the back of your throat, burning your tongue but never moving past your teeth. You can only watch as your family continue to arm for battle.

They are willing to fight for you; for this ship. Yet you stand by like a coward. That is not the man your father made you into. You draw your sword, ready to fight alongside your family. Deception would not work. It is not even worth the attempt.

On the Yannish ship, your silence has prompted them to

reply in kind and the dread silence of the tension before a battle descends, unbroken even by seabirds, as you reef your sails to minimise damage and to keep your place on this too-still water, the wind that powered you now vanished, lest it offer aid to the Yannish vessel.

The notion of a glorious fight battles the sorrow of knowing the cost as you signal a volley from your archers. Yannish crew begin to fall, their screams echoing out across the unnatural waters. Then, the sky darkens as they return the favour.

The heads of Yannish arrows glint in the sun as they begin to fall on you like rain. You wait for the thuds of metal in wood and the screams of the wounded and dying, but silence, save for the lapping of waves against the two hulls comes instead.

The priest stands on your deck with her arms outstretched, glowing a painful, bright white. Her head is thrown back and she chants faster than you have ever witnessed. The arrows hold, frozen in the air, and you gape as they turn, as one, to face the Yannish and return as if loosed from your own side.

This is the work of no goddess, whatever one is, but something far more inherently unnatural.

A world-breaker. Mage. Blighted people who destroy everything they touch. Rumours say one was there the night Nion fell: that night your home burned and your father rescued the wrong child. Rumours gathered before the paranoia had claimed your father fully. That makes them all the more likely to be true.

Now one is on your ship.

What are you going to do about it, boy? Your father's voice echoes in the chambers of your mind. There are no good solutions, but one of them is at least the *right* thing to do.

It is just as well your father has been dead for many years.

He would never forgive you for what you are about to lose as you make for the mage, sword ready, your grip sure.

The ship creaks underfoot, reassuring. Alerting. Betraying. A fierce pressure builds around you and you are frozen mid-stride in nothing as if the very air has grown solid, a natural position made uncomfortable by how long you are made to hold it. Your heart pounds and sweat drips from your face in fear.

The priest turns, sparing no more mind for the Yannish attack; your own people are quick to press the advantage given to them, lost to a battle craze that is not theirs.

The priest brushes off arrows she cannot see, warping their paths around to embed near your feet, leaving scars on your ship. Your heart.

"You cannot kill me," she whispers in your ear, her breath breaking through the strange magery she has you caught in; the sensation of it sends shivers down your spine.

"I know your mind, *Captain* Dradorn." She spits the honorific, the way you do in your mind when times are dark. "I see your dreams and desires, Fiaer. I have helped myself to your secrets and pulled apart your many, many guilts. You cannot afford to lose what we are offering you."

The resistance around you fades.

"Prove me wrong, *boy*." She has not quite got your father's accent down right, but the intent is clear. The words that you live by, drilled into your mind as you fought through your clumsy young teens to break through his dissatisfaction with everything you were: too gangly, too broad. Too tall, too short. Too lean, too fat. Too lazy, too helpful. Too stupid, too smart. Walking rigging blindfold in a cyclone was easier than earning a compliment. *Prove me wrong, boy.*

You intend to. You spit at the mage's feet all the same. It is all you can do.

She grins and turns you back towards the fight, pushing you into the mess of clashing weapons and screaming people as both parties begin to board each other, hoping for dominance, swinging from ropes and laying down planks to cross the gap between sky and fathomless deeps.

The Yannish will *not* have your home. They will not capture her secrets, nor sink her. Not while you still draw breath.

You dance through your own people, pulling them away from strikes they had not noticed, helping them when they slip, teaming up to keep them safe. These are your family and they are all you have. You will mourn for those you lose in the privacy of your own space, in your own way, immortalised on the only place they have all belonged. For now, you save who you can.

It is tiring work, knocking people back and hacking them down when they will not stay put. It is hot, unforgiving torment. The smell of blood and salt is in your nostrils and the back of your throat. You have taken wounds — more scars, if you live that long — and you have been using your off-hand since a bad blow early on broke bones in your main.

Despite their numbers, the Yannish are defensive fighters by nature and their pre-emptive attempt to board *Golden Harvest* is quickly routed. They fall back onto the familiar surroundings of their own ship while you and yours press the advantage, the Yannish bows too big and awkward in these small battlegrounds. Before another hour has passed, the captain of the Yannish ship kneels before you, her weapons at your feet stained red and brown, like yours.

You are a match in other ways too. The laboured breathing,

the way she holds her wounds together with broken hands. The way she meets your eyes, knowing how this will end. She has given up only to spare the last of her crew.

You accept, to spare the last of yours. The decks of both ships are stained red with death and the desire to live and too many eyes lie open, glassy, unseeing. The whole world now is the stink of blood and salt. The water crests with pink foam and floating bodies are the only signs that life was ever here. You swallow bile.

Slaughter outside of a need to survive has never sat well with you. The torments of those times you have engaged in it will never leave you, and this one will join the rest. But that does not mean you will show this softer side — the one your father despised — before the battle is truly won.

Your sword hangs heavy in your hand. The hours of fighting in the heat of the sun have left you parched and trembling as the adrenaline fades. You should see the surgeon before you pass out. Let her see to the others first. You can hold out a little longer yet.

Most of the Yannish crew kneel with their captain, laying down their weapons. Those of your crew who remain able subdue the last rebellions, restraining them all with irons and chains and ropes — whatever comes to hand.

If it was up to you, you would face the ramifications of being known as a slaver. You prefer to take the cargo and run, to let your victims return home and try again. But when times are desperate, or you have no other choice, slavery is the best outcome for a bad situation. Distasteful, it is at least never personal. These Yannish sailors are now the political prisoners of Isia. Even if they are ransomed home, they will never earn out the debt their government puts on them for their "freedom", all with the temerity to call such a transaction patriotic.

It is not an outcome you wish on anyone, let alone someone you respect, and you do respect this nameless captain and her crew. They fought honourably in a dishonourable fight they could never have won. Not with the world-breaker on your side.

With a world-breaker not actively working against you at least.

Kill them all, your father whispers in your mind. You can almost feel the spittle as his paranoia barely holds him back. You can taste the hatred in his words as he urges you to be more like him. *It would be a mercy.*

The words and the tone are his, but that accent is still slightly off. As if summoned, the priest clambers towards you, stepping over friends and strangers to do so.

You know weariness. It claws through you now the battle is over, but you still stand tall. The priest leans on railings for support, pulling herself along ropes, slumping with the effort of motion. Her bird flies in circles above her head. You look for wounds that would explain her condition, but the only blood on her white robes is where the fabric has soaked up that of those she passes. You fail to find any sympathy for her exhaustion.

The Yannish captain, who has defiance and respect in her pale blue eyes for you and your crew, shifts entirely to fear as the priest approaches. She scrabbles for her weapons again, and you for yours, but neither of you are the ones to act.

It is the Yannish cook who grabs the priest from behind, a filleting knife to the world-breaker's throat. He looks about in wild panic as he struggles to do what is necessary to save you all.

Even as you wish with all your heart for him to drag the knife, you throw yourself across the deck. Before your thoughts can catch up to your feet, the cook is dead, cut down by your own hand, fresh blood dripping from your sword.

The priest, unharmed, leans against you. Her smile of thanks contains not one speck of gratitude.

Kill them all.

A boy: a young man, not much younger than you — and you are struck by how old you feel — falls to his knees to cradle the body of the cook in his arms. He spits at you and the priest. The urge to protect the mage brings the edge of your weapon to the boy's throat and lifts him to his feet.

Though the mage makes the memories of your father's words dance in your head, something stronger than her holds you back.

Where the cook was fair, like most Yannish — blonde, blue eyed and slight of frame — the boy either takes after his mother, or he is not the cook's own birth son. Not with that dark coppery skin, like yours. Or the black hair that curls at his nape. Or the broad shoulders, like yours.

You apologise, the words coming out in Nionese. Your father liked to hear you grovel in the language of the sea. The language of the ocean that lays its emotions out for all to witness. It was how he knew you were sincere. This is an old habit brought forth in love. In loss. In memory. Brought forth by your father's words echoing on the end of the mage's puppet-strings.

His age means the cook's boy would never have known Nion as it was. Even *your* memories are a child's faded dreams, but there is no denying that here is a piece of home stranded upon the sea. Your father was a violent man, but he would have embraced this boy.

The cook's boy does not grant you forgiveness. His Nionese is flaky, unpractised and the accent is warped by his more familiar Yannish, but the meaning is clear. What you are doing: fighting, stealing, killing, especially for something like that mage, is not the way of the Nion he was taught about. You agree.

You *try* to agree.

Once again your words stop before they form in your lungs, dead before they are given breath. You struggle against the magery, its touch now hammer blows against you. You bare your teeth to push through, showing the effort. Pleading with eyes alone that this boy understands this would not be your way, if you had a choice. You are as much a victim of the world-breaker as the Yannish are.

By the time the priest's grip on you falters, the cook's boy is gasping. Where you were struggling to push air out, he struggles to pull it in. He grabs at his throat, eyes wide as his skin flushes purple and the whites of his eyes turn scarlet. You can only watch in numb shock as his body goes slack, collapsing against the deck, lifeless.

Another piece of your fractured heritage lost in a matter of moments while you let it happen. As if you did not even care.

Your father screams in your mind.

"Why?" you yell, your own voice finally breaking through.

"We have no use for prisoners, Captain. We have no desire to bargain with governments or desperate families."

"Then let them go."

"You are not that naive."

It is in her eyes, in the set of her jaw: Isia has no intention of honouring their payment to you. They sent you out here to die with your quarry. Forgotten. Without story.

She laughs. "If you die here, it is not my doing. However, payment is only given for services rendered. A pauper's job earns a pauper's wage. Will your conscience be reason enough for your crew?"

You hesitate. You are here because you have no choice. Your crew are here for their promised wealth. To deny them that would be an unforgivable treason.

You could find the money another way. Trade to and from Keset will be peaking soon, and you have gone this long without the tantalising promises of Isia, if they are even true. What you do not know cannot haunt you.

You rub at the patch of empty skin on your finger. A loss that hurts, but it was only a ring. Only a signet of where you had come from. It was not even really yours.

You meet the mage's eye. You do not flinch.

"I am in your head, *boy*," she says, finding another angle. "I am in *everyone's* head. Perhaps going for a swim is the only thing they have ever wanted to do? It will be no harder than it was driving them to battle. No harder than driving you."

The urge to clamber onto the railings of the Yannish ship overcomes you, and you look down — so far down — into the depths of the sea. Despite the carnage of battle floating on the surface, it would be good to dive in and take the heat of the day off. You lean forward and stop, catching on a rope before you slip and fall.

The mage will not let you die this way. You are her way home. That does not stop your crew, leaping too quickly for you to even know where to look.

The sounds of bodies hitting the water are hammer blows to your heart. Not all of them can swim, and even those who can will tire quickly. You cannot save them all.

Samethi, the chief, climbs the railings, ready to dive and the panic you feel nearly brings you to your knees. He is more than your second. For all his cruelty, you loved your father, but Samethi is the one who loves you as a father should love a son. You cannot lose him. You try to pull him back, begging.

You fail.

The last time you screamed, your father was still alive. He had wormed it out of you, then beaten you for your weakness. Since then, you have yelled, you have shouted. You have learned to harness the cold danger of a lowered voice. But, as Samethi hits the water, swallowing the sea as he begins to sink, a scream escapes you again. High pitched and desperate as you throw ropes, preparing to dive in and haul him back to the surface knowing you cannot stop the rain of people following Samethi into the deep.

There is only one thing you can do. The Yannish captain backs away. She does not want to die. You do not want to kill her, but you have been stripped of your choice. It is her crew or yours. You beg her forgiveness, not noticing the slip into Nionese, into old habits, as your blade meets her flesh and stops her heart.

The priest nods with a sickening smile and you breathe again as your people stand down, blinking in confusion as they face the water.

With your obedience assured, the priest-mage grants you time to rescue those you could not stop. You dive, hauling Samethi up, half drowned. You grab another drowner and wrap yourselves around a lowered rope to be pulled to the safety of wood and the skills of those able to pump water from the lungs of those being rescued.

You wait just long enough for your chief mate to begin

coughing and vomiting before you leap in again to save as many as you can.

Those who did not hit the water and can offer no medical aid take the Yannish weapons. Those bows are far better than your own, and their previous owners no longer need them. Others raid the hold for supplies, but there is little of use.

The third time you clamber back on deck the surgeon, Klaudai, traps you in a corner and sees to your wounds, preventing you from entering the water again. You must trust to your crew to save the rest. She tuts as she cleans and wraps and stitches, but declares that, as long as they remain uninfected, these wounds will not kill you.

Samethi comes next, before you can get away. He is wrapped in a blanket and looks sick. He trembles as he grabs your shoulder. The man who once stood beside your father knows that look in your eye. Even after everything the mage has done, all the things she has taken from you today alone, he still tells you that there are ways to avoid doing what you have promised.

"You are not your father," he says, looking sad. "I would not see you become him, Fiaer."

"No. He enjoyed what he did."

You don't have what it takes. Your father's words echo in your mind and you spit over the side of the ship in lieu of at the mage for bringing his shade to torment you. For letting him out of the cage in your head.

"Not in the beginning," your chief says. He offers aid. Not for the chance to be savage, but because he knows what this will take from you.

You have been party to executions at your father's behest, at the very end, when things were so bad you had to step in and step up, taking control the only way he would let you. You will not put your crew through doing the same in your name. They live with the dirt of survival on their hands. They do not need the stain of baseless cruelty too. You order him to rest and make preparations for after.

As the sun begins to kiss the horizon, you step back onto the Yannish vessel, stitches itching, grimacing against the pain of broken bones in your hands as you take up your sword again, so heavy it adds to the bruising of your heart as you kill the Yannish prisoners.

As with their captain, you beg their forgiveness in a language they do not know and turn them to the sunset as they die. They do not see the tears on your face.

You wish it would become easier, as if you could see them as something inhuman, but it does not. Even when you tell yourself that it was this, or lose your own crew as well.

By the time the moon rises, your work is done and the words of your father are quiet. Silence is the best compliment you could hope for.

You stumble as you clamber back on board *Golden Harvest*, the familiar wood under your feet welcoming you home, bloodstained and weary in heart and body and spirit. There is only so much a man can carry alone and the world goes dark to cries of "Captain down," as you hit the deck, too worn out to make it further.

You wake shortly before dawn. Aching and swollen with bruises and wounds, you haul yourself out of the hammock strung in the hold with your crew. Some are pretending to sleep. Most are lying awake, murmuring to each other in low voices.

The sound of motion on the deck summons you. The

night watch calls out as you move into the fresh air, watching the preparations you asked for. Lined on the deck are the remains of your family who did not survive the things the mage put them through, their limbs bound, their eyes covered so that their shades will neither wander or seek, but move on to whatever lies beyond the veil. Your cabin-hand, Eayr, and her partner are carrying the bodies to the Yannish ship, where your crew has offered the same respects to their fallen enemies.

There are so many of them. You took the lives of seventy-two. As far as you can gather, a similar number again were felled in the battle, the Yannish struggling in close quarter combat they were unprepared for. Eighteen of your own in battle and several more again who sank and did not rise, even in bloated death. Over a third of your crew.

The mage is right in that you do not need many to sail *Golden Harvest* but it is not about logistics. They were your family.

You have been so fixated on watching the bodies move, you failed to notice the way your remaining crew have come to stand behind you, their faces covered for mourning. You do not veil. You do not wish to hide from the death you have caused.

Samethi presses a Yannish bow into your hands and directs you to a bucket of hollow arrows glowing gently in the pre-dawn — their points full of coals.

You nock an arrow, sighting across the water. Your crew do likewise, lining up alongside you, their own pilfered bows drawn.

The Yannish bow is strange; the weight is off, and it requires more strength to draw than you expected. It flexes oddly and it pulls the broken bones in your hands into new and ever more painful positions. You grit your teeth and draw anyway.

With trembling arms, you call for loose and red glows arc through the air until they catch in the sails and rigging of the Yannish vessel. The paper sails go up quickly. The strangely lacquered hull takes time to begin smouldering, but you hold steady until flames engulf the ship and the evidence of your crimes. The smoke lingers, the acrid stench of it seeping into clothes and hair and wood grain.

The winds have abandoned you, but this is a Nionese ship. She knows how to coax the winds, even when they are shy. And if that fails, you have oars. The going will be slow, but you *will* go when you are ready. There is something more important you must do than make for land first. It changes nothing, but it is the *right* thing to do.

You take a deep breath, as far as your aching sides will allow you and begin to hum, then to sing.

Your father banned songs of mourning. *A waste of time*, he would say. *I do not regret what I have done, boy. You must never regret your actions either.*

You sang at his funeral all the same. You sing now. The words of the songs he once whipped you for come unbidden as your voice rises with the sun, growing stronger as it is joined by the crew at your back, their voices of mourning adding to yours until your throat is raw. You keep going.

Not every rebellion has to be loud. But sometimes, volume helps.

The priest does not emerge to pray at noon and the winds stay distant. By mid-afternoon, you take this rare chance of relative privacy to confer with your officers on how best to proceed. As much as you want to be away from this place, you do not want to put the crew to row just yet. They are pained and weary and need rest. You have enough stores to risk waiting for a few days.

You also admit that, despite what the world-breaker says, Isia has no intention of paying their dues. They will take their monster back and then do their best to kill you all rather than risk you speaking out about what happened here.

You intend to get what you have earned. Isian ships will be in the water soon, but they are a laughable design — any Nionese child could do better — and the Isians, having never dared go to war before, are untested in battle. They cannot all be world-breakers.

Golden Harvest will not struggle to exact revenge, but first you have to survive. For that, you need your family by your side. You need to know how the ship lies.

You are met with silence before your officers admit rumours are circulating. The arm-master explains that the crew wonder if you were under the same compulsions they were, or if the Fiaer Dradorn they sail under has the same thirst for violence as his father. Klaudai, the surgeon, tuts as she explains that what you did yesterday you did for great reason, leaving an opening to tell them what that reason might *be*.

You say nothing as your father laughs. *Hopes and dreams, boy. Nothing more than that. But at least those have more use than you do.*

The irritation you have at your father's memories comes out in the tone of your voice. "Keep the peace until we reach shore. Those who wish to will part rich and our paths will cross no more. I will not sail with those who think me like my father."

The cook is the only one willing to raise concerns about the world-breaker directly. He looks uncomfortable as he admits they all worry she will make them think those things again.

You glance towards your quarters. Isia wants the world-breaker back alive, but if not for the backlashes that would come, the mage would be dead at the bottom of the ocean already. She has certainly taken advantage of your hospitality long enough. Your officers call after you, but you are set on this course now. Perhaps you are a little like your father after all.

Of course, it is all bravado. You have not considered how much the humiliation will sting when she freezes you in place, or convinces you to do anything else.

The door bursts under the force of your boot and the priest's strange bird flaps at your face, screeching as it makes for the sky where it begins to circle. The mage sits tucked under your desk, her head moving as through she is following her bird's flight.

She does not resist as you drag her into the sunlight and strap her to the mast, chained a little too high for comfort, her bare feet brushing against the deck. She will be fed and watered and left to the elements she manipulates.

You warn anyone who goes near her for any other reason than to see to her basic needs at the designated times will join her, then you shut yourself in your quarters. You have work you do not wish to be observed doing.

It is hard going. Each strike of knife into wood is a failure: the slaughtered, the drowned, the lost in battle. With each blow, the memory of your father sits in the empty chair behind the desk and mocks you.

You do not know how ashamed you should be, he says when you carve out the mark for the Nionese boy. Your patriotism is second hand, meaningless. You should have saved what was in front of you instead of following this folly of yours. *You are a sham, boy. A disgrace to my name. You are a fraud. A fake. Run back to Esia and let them coddle you. Let the memory of Nion die — choke it out with your pretty lovers and strong wine and the lure of the land.* Choked out the way it was squeezed out of that boy.

The sea does not run in your blood, boy. You are no storm.

On the second day after the massacre, the cabin-hand allows Samethi into your rooms. He is looking better until he runs his hands across the fresh scars you have made in the wooden walls.

That man knows you too well. He knows that gouging the wood of this ship is the same as if you had put them in your own flesh — permanent reminders.

He pulls the knife from the back of the chair where your father's head would have been and hands it back to you.

He does not need to tell you that you have wallowed enough. You know that lecture as well as you know your father's words. There is a job to be done. Plans to be made. The stores have begun to spoil overnight. If the wind does not pick up soon, you and your crew will go hungry. You have to put them to row sooner than you had hoped, or beg the mage for more wind.

You do not relish the thought of hours at the oars, but you fancy a mutiny from starvation less. The mage is entirely out of the question.

You wish you had slept as Samethi encourages you away from the smell of shaved cedar and the lingering scent of the mage and her bird and the shadows of your father's cruel laughter.

No one has felt compelled to approach the priest-mage

since you tied her to the mast. She has remained watching her bird in flight. It is unclear if she has even noticed the change in her circumstances.

You watch her yourself between cleaning and repairs and checking on the injured, avoiding the surgeon before she traps you with them to recuperate. Eventually you reach a compromise. You promise to limit your physical labour. She agrees you do not have to stay holed up in your father's old quarters.

You bring a small desk and the ledgers and files you salvaged from the Yannish ship to the deck, out in the air, and position it close to the mage. If she is to poison anyone's mind, it can continue to be yours rather than your crew's. Instead, she watches the bird fly and you are able to ignore her for the paperwork that brings its own headaches and heartaches.

Promised payouts for those left waiting for the dead, and for those who lost abilities in the fighting. Every name carefully committed, every coin accounted, every kin with a packet for their pain. You draft more payouts for those the surgeon is not sure will survive their injuries, but refuse to add those names yet, hoping they will prove you wrong.

You do the same for the names you can make out of the Yannish logs and manifests. Tracking those kin will take longer, but you will do it. Even for the cook's boy, his name listed as Hawthorn A'Nissa. A princely name. A tribute to a past he would never have known.

Trade receipts show the Yannish vessel's last call had been Ide, Isia. She was returning home when you had caught her.

Working through the Yannish captain's personal logs is a challenge bordering on chore. You know enough of most tongues to get by, but you have little experience with written

Yannish, nor do your crew. With the little you can guess, they uncovered something secret there. You are unsure if they had intended to share what they learned but, from your own story, the Isian government did not wish to take the risk.

You glance at the mage who continues to watch her bird circling the mast. You are more certain than before that they plan the same fate for you.

From the corner of your eye as you toil through the paperwork, you watch Klaudai watching the mage, her thumb running down the handle of the surgeon's knife she wears at her belt. You cannot tell if she disapproves more of your cruelty or of the creature you are inflicting it on. You make a note to ask her when you can spare the time.

On the third day since the massacre, the bird dies.

You look up from logs and ledgers when the world-breaker screams and thrashes against her bindings as the bird falls from the sky and sinks beneath the still waters. Focused on the mage's outburst, it takes you a moment to parse what caused her distress. Your people chase after the bird, too late to do anything for it. Too slow to even fish it from the water.

The mage does not stop screaming, even gagged, and within hours, you do not need the calls of your lookouts to see the dark clouds racing towards you from the north.

A backlash. The world trying to right itself from the misuse of the world-breaker's powers. The price of magic.

If you are lucky, it will only be bad weather.

You do not have much time to prepare. Your best chance is to try and put as much distance between you and the wall of clouds gathering across the sky. The wind is beginning to stir, racing ahead of the pressure. It is enough for *Golden Harvest* under normal circumstances.

You need more than normal now. "Oars!" you yell.

As the job your father only gave those he wished to punish, you use them as little as possible, but you will take your place on the benches below deck, well worn by your backside over the years, once you have seen to everything else.

There are no complaints as the first shift of rowers slip below deck, the long oars extending into the water. Everyone knows what those clouds mean. No one wants to die that way.

Accompanied by the beat of drum and the low thrum of song the oars, in perfect motion, cut the water as you pull west. You take the navigator to one side. With the sun vanishing behind black clouds, you will need his skills to stay true to the course.

For now, you leave the sails full to catch what wind you can to compliment the rowers. They can not stay unreefed for long or you will lose the mast. Or worse.

You sweep across the deck, directing people. Samethi follows your lead with his whistle that cuts through the roaring winds that drown you out. You send people to secure the hold and their belongings too. Crates shifting under force and small projectiles flying through the air at speed will kill as easily as being swept overboard. Your deck-bound desk is stashed away, the logs and journals locked away in your cabin.

It will be a long, dark night and the cook begins his meals early, knowing he will be working until either the storm passes or there are no more mouths to feed.

The surgeon checks her supplies. Not enough after the battle, but it will have to do. Everyone has a job. Yours is to lend hands where they are needed and keep a wary eye on that banking cloud and the narrowing distance. The mage remains screaming through her gag, her eyes darting left and right — sense, gone.

Even if she has the power to combat her own backlash, she cannot help you now.

Trusting your crew, trusting your ship, you take your place on the oar benches, having urged the drummer to speed up the beat. You can only be here for a short time — too much else needs your attention, but you would not have this any other way.

This is your home. What kind of person are you if you do not do all you can to keep her safe? You are not above the other members of your crew, and you will do your part to keep them all safe.

The motion, the push and pull is familiar, and it gives you a short pause where even your thoughts still in the rhythm, your voice joining the chorus around you as you row until Samethi takes your place. The wind has been gathering and the sea has been growing rougher — the weather too fast to outsail, and you are needed back up top.

The storm is almost here, purple-white lightning arcing overhead, the deep rumbles of thunder echo long after they pass.

You signal for those at the pumps in the depths of the ship to make ready. The fate of tonight rests in their strong arms as much as luck. You will be adding what strength you can to ease their burden once they begin to flag.

The deck team are lashed to anchor points, belts tied to the ship, trusting her to keep them safe. You do the same: the leather straps of the harnesses over your shoulders and around your waist safer than rope alone. Abrasive pads strapped to the bottom of your boots add a little extra grip. It is not much, but you have first-hand experience of the slight difference they can make. Cylin himself holds the wheel, tied fast.

Clambering up the rigging, flapping about like laundry, you help bring in the sails, lashing them down before the wind pulls the ship under the churning waves. You order the oars in too, before they are lost or cause damage. From now on, you are at the mercy of the backlash and the sea.

Still, *Golden Harvest* has survived worse things than even a broken world could imagine throwing at you. This is where she shines.

The priest-mage screams in time with the wind, her eyes still searching for her dead bird in the air above her. You could leave her tied to the mast. Mayhap she will be washed overboard and you will be down a problem.

Down one, but gaining many. She stumbles as you cut her down, collapsing on the deck. You hold her close against the way the ship pitches under your feet, already growing rough enough to lead you foul. You throw her in your chambers with the mockery of your father and lock the door behind you as the first rains begin to land.

For an age, you are lost to the wind and the rain and the chores that come with surviving. You bail water and see to ropes, see to people, sending starving men and women to eat what they can stomach, anything they can keep down as *Golden Harvest* pitches and rolls under the constant sluice of the sea.

You brush off concern for your own welfare, shrugging away those who try to usher you towards food or rest. There will be time for that later, or it will not matter. It means you are once again tied to the deck when the mainsail slips loose, catching the wind. The deck shifts under you and everyone flies through the air before you slam into the wet wood, the rain and the waves crashing over the bow trying to drown you in your daze.

Above you, the purple-lit sky shifts to strike green close to your position. Your insides constrict. Wild magic. Uncontrolled. Your shouts do not travel through the storm, but everyone knows what green light means. Where they had been cautious, now they are frantic.

With the wind catching the sail, the ship shifts again and you fight your way to the mast, bringing Khleo and her brother with you. You need steady feet to climb the rigging and enough hands to lash the sail back down. As you climb, the ropes grow hoary with weed and coral. The timbers of the wood age until she barely holds her shape before springing back to the bright wood of her youth. As she cycles between fresh timbers and rot the people below you appear as children barely walking and skeletons tangled in ropes and each other.

A piece of aged rope comes clear away in your hand and you drop the fraying fibres into the storm. Eyes forward, aiming for the loose sail before the visions of sunken doom come true, you pass the decaying bodies of your crow siblings caught in the ropes as they degrade and regress, clinging to each other tightly as they live and die and live and die again.

Tethered to the foot-ropes, arms full of heavy wet sail, there is nothing you can do but watch as a low red mist seeps across the water where the green lightning strikes and rolls across the deck.

This high up, battling against the wind, the screams from those below are oddly distant as the ropes tethering them to the ship begin to writhe like snakes under their own power, against the forces of nature.

The light from flashes alone light up static scenes of men and women fighting the very tethers meant to keep them safe as the ropes and chains wrap around their victims and drag them down or thrash them about, heaving them overboard. You can only witness from your vantage point as ropes strangle those they are meant to protect.

You do not yell. You do not scream. You barely even swear though your heart breaks. Your people fight as well as they are able and without this sail reefed, you are all at risk. The siblings remain tangled in the rigging, tangled together, their own tethers choking them despite them already being dead; half-skeletal, half-childish forms. The red fog creeps upwards, coming for you. Your own tethers begin to move against the wind. You turn back to the knots and pulleys that are your first concern.

The crack of splitting timbers drowns out the sound of the storm. *Golden Harvest* lurches, shuddering, as she drops over the peak of a wave into a deep trough. Towering waves wash over the deck, destabilising those fighting their tethers. Your footing slips and the sail drops again, immediately catching the wind. Your heart pulses at your toes as you dangle from the foot-ropes, unsure if you have the strength to swing yourself up again.

The choice is taken from you as a second crack rocks through the ship. A death knell for your beautiful home. Your heart. The mast — black and rotten through — topples, dragging you with it. People on the deck watch you fly past. The reverberation of the solid wood of the now sturdy, weathered, mast against the hull will claim as many again as have already fallen to drowning and strangulation, but you will not know the full numbers. You will be one of them. Trailing amongst the splintering wood and the tangled lines, your father's legacy ends here in the scream of wind and shriek of timber and a weightless flash of green that moves through you as you hit the dark, dark, water, tangled in ropes and chain and sailcloth.

You are no storm, your father delights as you sink, the sound of his mirthless laughter echoing in your mind.

Chapter Three

The priest stands over you, her face half hidden in shadows. She laughs a masculine laugh that twists around you as you are lifted to a green sky by a swarm of black and white birds that look too like ravens for comfort. *The sea runs in your blood,* she says in that familiar masculine voice with its musical lilt, though she has never sung. Singing is forbidden.

Storm clouds tinged purple and red obscure her from view and something rises in your throat, choking you, pulling you further into the green sky amongst the birds.

The tightness spreads into your chest, down into your abdomen. A tether of living rope writhes around you, through you. It anchors you to an infinite blackness below before it pushes out through your screaming mouth to reach the sky.

You open your eyes to wooden beams and salt in your throat that builds until it fills your mouth. You cough, and sea water dribbles, then pours from your mouth in torrents. You choke on that instead, spluttering as you vomit. Lacking air, you convulse through heavy limbs until you turn yourself over in a low cot built into the wall of the small surgery in the hold of your ship, emptying your stomach onto the floor. Winded and salt-sore, you collapse back into the soiled cot, insides burning, salt fading into the smells of worn cedar, bilge and blood-rot. For the longest time all you can do is lie there, drifting in and out of sleep in the gentle sway of your home, listening to waves lap against the hull and the motion of people.

Days later, when you can at least stand on deck under your own support, you oversee the repairs Samethi started in your absence. Your family stitch sails back together, or work to erect a temporary mast from the remains of the original. Others nail planks over patches of rot and decay. They sit chatting together as they work shortened ropes into longer pieces again, knotting together new rigging and guy-lines. Oars cut through the water, carrying you west.

While far from joyful, there is a palpable peace over the crew. There will be time for mourning those who did not survive, and it will be loud and heart-breaking. There will be tears and stories and songs, but for now there is only relief that they and the ship escaped. She is as battered and bruised as you are, but you will both mend, in time. You will all mend, in time.

You itch to help. When you try, the tools are gently taken from your aching hands as though you are a child again. It galls. While the surgeon has given up chasing after you, she is not shy with the looks she throws your way or the comments she makes. There may be something to be said for rest, but you would rather not hear it.

Being busy quietens your thoughts, as turbulent as the storm that almost killed you. The memories are vague, and the stories you overhear that fill the gaps disturb you: how, caught between the sea and the sky, tethered to the felled mast, a bolt of green lightning lanced through you before you hit the water. It must have been an illusion. A trick of the eyes is easier to live with than the discomfort of knowing anything is possible in a backlash.

Your crew saved the ship, cutting the fallen mast — and you — free before it pulled the hull over, endangering them all. If not for hooking the lost mast safely for salvage, you would have been left behind, sinking to the bottom of the ocean. Instead, you floated on a bed on bloated sailcloth, jetsam caught in the ropes, until you had been dragged back on board once the backlash passed and given to the surgeon until you recovered or died; whichever came first.

Limited in the help you can offer, you again draft up reparations for the too many who did not make it through, like the crow-siblings and even your master rope-maker, strangled by their own ropes. The master carpenter gives orders from his own forced rest, the loss of his arm preventing him from ever taking his trade in his own hands again, his bitter impatience at mistakes echoing across the still air until Samethi takes him to one side. Your master caulker lies in Klaudai's overfull surgery, struggling with the loss of his legs. The mage remains in your quarters lacking the impetus to see to her own basic needs, forced to eat and drink through her continued screaming.

Bringing your desk into the air and the light of the deck helps things feel a little less overwhelming. The rest of your time is spent in idle uselessness, left to enjoy the wind through your hair and salt spray on your skin under the hot sun as if neither are tainted by the memories of your actions and your guilt and grief; everything pretending to be as it should be.

Save for the rations.

Before the storm, you believed Isia had given you short-life food in their disdain of you, but the rot moves too quickly and in ways that defy explanation. No one argues against dumping the lot. With tight rationing it might have been possible to make it back before people begin to starve, but the backlash threw you off course. You follow the setting sun and his best estimates, but Cylin, the navigator, cannot guarantee where you will end up, or when. These open waters are too empty to be sure of anything, though without the mage's influence, weather patterns are becoming more reliable and you throw nets to catch the rare schools of fish you begin to encounter. The fish make the ship reek, but at least they fill some of the gaps the rotten food created.

There had been even less debate about the water barrels, tainted with salt. Unless you are lucky — and luck has been an absent friend of late — your final logs will be the delirium of a dehydrated man, half starved. The ship will sail on, neglected, with her dead crew left unbound, watching the world and aching to return, until she sinks.

Already feeling the cost of fierce rationing and the hot sun and the slog of keeping *Golden Harvest* sailing west at her leisurely pace — to work the crew harder means using your remaining supplies faster — you wonder if the delusions have already arrived. In the haze at the edge of the horizon behind you, you swear you can see the shape of the Yannish ship before it vanishes over the curve of the world. Other members of your crew say the same thing, the unease evident in their hushed voices. It cannot be the same ship. That one burned and sank; you watched it happen. It must be a second.

On the edge of sunset and just before the dawn the Yannish ship trails you. If it were any closer you would consider bartering for supplies, though, with little to offer, you could take her as a prize. She would not expect Yannish bows turned against her, yet you have neither the strength of arms or the strength of mind for a repeat encounter so soon. Despite your great need, it is best if the Yannish ship stays away.

Two weeks after the storm passed, a great bank of fog blankets the ocean, smothering you and your ship and hiding the sun. It is thick, chewy fog and rather than risk being turned around in it, you drop anchor to limit how far you would drift. You hope the fog lasts as you order your crew to set up fog harps — fringes of fine steel rods that force water from low lying clouds, devised in the dry southern deserts around Darr — and to scrape the thin layers of water forming on the sailcloths into barrels. It does not produce much but it buys you a little time.

The fog lasts for three days. On the third night, you can take the building pressure no more. The hold is full of murmuring and snoring, and somewhere in the secret dark, two people are finding comfort in each other. You cannot sleep and find no comfort in the sounds of life around you. You make for the deck and the eerie quiet. The night watch does not hear your approach though the thick air that muffles sound. They jump as you tap them on their shoulders and send them to an early rest. They know better than to argue.

For the first time since you left Ide, the tension in your neck lessens as you lean across the railing at the bow, listening to the creak of wood and rope the lap of water as you gaze out at nothing. The distant noises of people under your feet and the steady drip, drip of collecting water almost lulls you into sleep, so it is with a dreamlike recollection you witness the Yannish ship emerge from through the fog, bearing down on your anchored position.

It moves silently through the water, even allowing for the

way the fog dampens everything. You leap up to brighten the beacons to avoid collision before the Yannish ship comes close enough to board, all without raising the slightest wake. You freeze, unable to explain the terror that pours down your spine, threatening to loose your bladder. On an otherwise empty deck one figure stands looking to the west until they turn and lock eyes with you: theirs grey like the fog, and almost as translucent, a lad a few years younger than you with a pale sheen across his dark skin. He mouths words you cannot hear as his ship sails past. Where wood should strike wood and drag, it leaves nothing but a faint impression of greens and purples and then is gone back into the fog as silently as it arrived.

It will not be back, if it was even there at all; the embodiment of your regrets with only you to witness them. The shade of the boy the mage had killed mouthing words you cannot hear but understand all the same. What you had done had never been the Nionese way. Your father had always decried you were no true son of Nion anyway. Your rule here had always been marred by the blood of those you never got the chance to love. You have never known anything different.

Only once the faint fires of green and purple fade to naught do you let out a breath, feeling the beat of your heart, reassuring, and then you do what no one has witnessed since your father's death.

You weep, sinking to hugging your knees close to your chest, thankful you sent the watch away. You are weeping still when someone pulls you close, pressing your hot face against their chest: Samethi. He holds you like he did when you were a child. He says nothing, and you do not explain. Neither of you need to. Instead, he begins to quietly hum a lullaby, the same one that used to send you to sleep when you were so much younger, so much more innocent. Its power has not faded over the years, and when you have no more tears to shed it carries you away into troubled dreams.

The fog clears by morning, taking the cooler weather with it. You resume your journey west. With any luck, you are a week away from land. You should last that long.

Four days after the fog lifts, the surgeon, Klaudai, approaches you. It is getting harder to feed and water the mage, who still screams without stopping unless she sleeps. You ask if it is possible to drug her — keep her asleep — but Klaudai is hesitant. Even small amounts for too long could kill. All you can do is hold her down and force her rationed share of food and water down her, hoping she does not choke, weighing up the necessity of her care over your crew's — dismissing those thoughts before they take hold. You are not your father.

Three weeks since the storm and more than a week since the heavy fog pinned you down, you spy land to the south-west: the shape of a dark island covered in lush tropical trees, a blip of rich dark green against the unending blue. The relief that washes over you nearly brings you to tears before you realise that you saw no such land on your journey east. Wherever you are now, it is once again new territory. Any hopes you had of a timely return to civilisation are shattered.

Cylin mutters darkly as he pulls out his navigation tools and begins plotting distances as you give the orders to tack towards land. You cannot pass up this opportunity to forage for fresh supplies and undertake real repairs. The crew are eager to obey. They need to stretch their legs and get a little distance from each other before bad tempers win out.

Unfamiliar with the waters around the island, you anchor

Golden Harvest while Cylin and his team of surveyors take the small rowboat to the golden white sand, inspecting the shallower waters for submerged rocks and other dangers — no point bringing the ship to beach for repairs if it would harm her more to make the effort. The navigator's report is favourable as they return with the best course for you to take, inching the old girl closer to land, the anticipation of solid ground running through the crew. As she banks just before the shore, you swing down guy-ropes and land in the water, part of the team to haul her above the high tide mark, anchoring her to the tree line — the wood here proving to be strong and deep rooted. It will make for good repairs.

Then, you grin, wiping the sweat from your face and embrace those around you as they celebrate land: whooping and hollering as they sink to the sand, letting it run under fingers, kicking it up in delight as they race for the shade of trees and the taste of freedom. You step back, closer to the water, to take in the shape of your girl, to see what she needs.

Exposed, it is clear the battering she has taken, her mast half size and patched together from scraps bolted on with little more than wishful thinking, her sails showing scars across the sheets. The damage to her hull is worse than you had hoped, mismatched planks covering the worst of the damage, letting the truth of her condition seep around the edges — a bandage over a growing bruise. At least here is her best chance of recovery, as it may be yours if you can find the water that feeds the trees and if the fruit they drop is edible. There may even be animals for meat.

As the sea washes over your feet there is a tightness in your chest; emotion you do not wish to share yet, and you rub at your sternum to put it back to rest. It does not fade, and as you return to the trees it begins to writhe, threatening to burst out. If anyone notices your discomfort they keep it to themselves as you organise parties to bring back food, water, wood and anything fibrous and tough to replace lost or weak ropes.

The feeling refuses to pass as you join one such group, moving away from the sight of the sea. It tangles through you despite your best attempts to relax, desperate not to take the joy from your group as you hack your way through low growing branches and vines.

The air here is warm and thin, and you cannot get enough. Perhaps Klaudai was right to suggest you wait this out too, but you had to be doing something. You cough, though it brings no relief, wet and salty in the back of your throat. You stop at the trunk of a tall tree — a perfect new mast — and sink to your knees, coughing up water. You are vaguely aware of the commotion around you as you breathe in nothing but salt water. Your vision narrows and darkness overcomes you.

The taste of the ocean is on your tongue, in your mouth — salt between your teeth and coating your throat, burning in your lungs until you force it out in great heaving breaths that leave you bruised from the inside out. You do all this blind, too overcome with pain to realise anything is on your face, or the reason why your hands are not where you need them. You lie back on the uncomfortable cot you rest on and breathe in stale air of warm, damp wood, gulping each desperate breath in as your heart slows to normal.

Only then do you realise your arms and legs are not just constrained, but bound and your blindness comes from the cloth covering your eyes. Bound and blinded to keep your shade from roaming, seeking. Laid out for a funeral.

You call out, but it comes as a whisper, your throat salt-sore, stealing your voice. Your head throbs and nausea writhes in your guts. If you are a shade, it is one with all the unpleasant feelings of the living.

Pushing the cloth from your face with your bound hands spurs another bout of coughing and hacking, though you bring up nothing more than phlegm and bile. For a while you lie back, staring at the ceiling of your quarters and the motes of dust that dance in the late sunshine, listening to shouting from outside. Arguing. Fear.

Distantly, the mage continues to scream through her gag, taken from your quarters to someplace else. The constant background of her distress rings through your head, more pervasive than tinnitus.

Evidently, you are not the only one in desperate need of a good meal and a good night's sleep if Klaudai is making mistakes like this, trussing you up like a corpse. No matter how much nicer it would be to simply lie here and let the world pass you by, you cannot shirk the same work you expect from others. Especially as they argue loud enough to be heard from here, though the nature of their fighting is unclear.

It takes more time and effort than you would like to admit to undo the bindings at your ankles and wrists. Writhing and wriggling around, you are reminded of several enjoyable stays in Keset with people who like to be in charge. They are more pleasant than the memories of why you sought them out in the first place — balms to soothe the harsher memories of dangling over the side of the ship, head towards the sea, bound as you are now. Your father laughing that knowing your knots meant knowing how to slip them as he lowered you on a rope towards the white foam and endless abyss to drown unless you could become free before your hair got wet.

As ever, the thought of your father provides more focus than a dead man warrants, and you laugh to yourself at that, fighting against the bindings of a dead man in more ways than one until you slip one hand free. You leave only the loosened ropes and the scrap of fabric that had blinded you behind as you pass through the office to make for fresh air and warm sun. You pause, still hidden. It is just as well. The shouting is clearer from here.

It is an argument of traditions, of a sort. Whether you should be returned to the sea, the way your father had been, or whether you should be cremated — no nautical burial for a man drowned on dry land. Magicked.

Leaning heavily against the sun-warm wood of *Golden Harvest*, she lends you her strength until your head stops spinning. Magic?

Touching the ship, you can almost handle hearing the voice that argues loudest for cremation: the destruction of your body, no bounty for the sea. Samethi who has become captain in your... absence.

For a moment you consider taking the opportunity provided to run from the pressure and the responsibility a ship like this entails. After all, no captain ought to spend nights crying into his chief's shoulders as if he were three, instead of three and twenty. Samethi taught you everything you needed to know; there would be no one better. If you were truly dead your shade would rest content knowing your family were safe in his care. He would even be welcome to the name and the ready-made reputation he helped to shape.

Yet his words here sour those idle daydreams. He argues your unnatural death necessitates a break from tradition. That you have never particularly held with the ways of Old Nion, and where magic is involved, it is better to be sure. He speaks as if your wishes, as much as you had made any, had been nothing more the appropriation of a culture you could never know. That it did not matter what happened to the flesh; the soul is beyond the veil and can never know. He sounds an awful lot like your father.

A pressure against your kidney, a sharp point digging in through your shirt to your skin is the only warning that someone is behind you. You raise your hands, showing no threat, and turn to find Klaudai, her surgeon's knife now pressing against your gut. A thin line of broken skin through your shirt begins to weep where the point dragged.

She takes your face, turning it into what light there is here. The angle she stands means it halos around her, sharp enough to make you blink as she prods at your body next, that knife steady in place as she checks the inside of your mouth and listens to your chest, counting. Then with a glance towards the exit and the drama, she swears before pulling you away and back into your private quarters, pushing you back down into the cot before you can question what is going on. She blocks the exit with her frame, twisting her surgeon's knife in her hands. She swears again, looking nervous.

So this is what it has come to. A knife, alone. After his relative absence, the laughter of your father in your mind seems especially cruel.

As her hesitation stretches out, you dare to breathe. You dare to whisper just one question, scared that the noise will give her reason to act. "What's going on?"

"You died," she says, wonder and fear fighting each other in her voice, and the darting of her gaze. "Yet — this is no corpse-puppetry. You live again, beyond death."

You swallow salt as she explains how your team had come running to the shore, yelling about your death, too afraid of the magic that had killed you to bring you with them. She and Samethi had retrieved your body.

Klaudai herself had declared it. Samethi had witnessed it. The crew had seen you laid out on the beach until, afraid of the threat of more magic and the disagreements over your... disposal, you had been placed in the ship until an agreement had been reached. You are significantly confusing the matter by no longer *being* dead.

"You deserve better than this," she says into the uncomfortable silence as she lets you come to the only conclusion there is. There is more reason to fear backlashes than for the damage and the instant and unnatural deaths they can cause. Sometimes survivors are changed, altered somehow. Tainted with magic.

"I'm an abomination?" The words are fire against your tongue, burning slow, and they do not feel real as she bows her head. If she is right, there is only one thing she must do. Klaudai is no stranger to inflicting death, never afraid of what must be done. She does not do it. You even stand again, bringing her knife to the soft parts of your neck, knowing it will not take much pressure to destroy something that should not exist. You cannot do it yourself; you have faced a thousand thousand flirtations with death and have never wanted to quit. But Klaudai's hand around the handle stays steady, forcing you to ask her why she has not acted yet.

The heavy silence between you returns. Then she gives an even heavier sigh as she slumps, wrestling with something to large to admit in one piece. "I am many things, but I am no hypocrite," she whispers.

What she says makes its way through your muddled mind. Klaudai will have to kill you now, or you will have to kill her, and you do not share her hesitation. You flip her knife, pressing the blade against her throat.

No abomination, or mage, should live. The one from Isia lives purely on your need to present her back to her people as leverage. Nothing more than a tool, as they used you.

Before you can push the blade home, Klaudai bursts into painful light as the timber walls swell and warp, growing branches that wrap around you, the wood remembering it was once a tree. The knife clatters to the floor as Klaudai pins you to your own ship, her poison seeping through it. A branch forces itself between your teeth, keeping you from making noise. All you can do is follow her with your eyes and try to control your panic as her light fades, once again leaving the woman you thought you had known.

Not purely an abomination, who should be destroyed, though there is no blame for being caught in the accident of wild magic.

She is a mage. The ones who *cause* abominations.

You do not wish to hear her attempts to humanise a monster. You have no interest if she is an earth mage, in tune with life and living things. You do not care if she cannot tear your mind apart the way the air mage from Isia can.

You need to warn the crew, except they will not trust you, the man who should be dead. They will kill you both and, for all it would be the right thing to do, you do not wish to die.

Klaudai offers a compromise: She will still the waters as much as she can, a lie that may sway enough to hold things together long enough to reach civilisation. It will not sway Samethi, but it may scatter his support. All it will cost is your silence: a life for a life, and when next you reach port, if you ask it, she will leave.

It turns your stomach to accept, but you have no choice. She lets you free, the ship returning to the shape it should always have had, the wood no longer remembering sap and growth.

You listen in as she spins half-truths to the waiting crew. She is tired; overworked from the battle and the backlash and the expeditions. Not realising you clung to life was her fault and hers alone. Now, you are recuperating. Not entirely lies. Not entirely truths. The crew do not buy her words easily.

It is hard to hear Samethi's anger and pain — his rare fury at having his grief toyed with. He does not renounce his claim to captaincy, or your ship.

When your father had died, you had offered *Golden Harvest* to Samethi: a child looking for an adult to take the heavy weight of responsibility from your shoulders. You had both known it would be a mistake if he had said yes.

You are not that same child. While you still draw breath — no matter how impossibly — the ship is yours until you surrender her, and that you will not do.

You punch at the wooden walls and swear. It is an impossible situation, to give up all you have ever known or pit yourself against your other father to keep her.

Barely able to stand, with the taste of salt-vomit still in your mouth, you have no doubt you will lose.

The steadiness of your ship holds you up. You have lost Samethi, but you have not lost *Golden Harvest* yet. At least you can meet Samethi's eye as he strikes.

Like your father.

Taking a deep breath, you emerge into daylight, dropping

down a guy-rope onto the sandy beach. Samethi halts mid-sentence, staring at you, the blood leeching from his face as your family pull away, the noise of their whispering shifting across the beach barely louder than the surf as they strive for distance, as if you are contagious. Maybe you are.

You beg Samethi to recant his claim, doing everything you can to keep your voice steady: to stand tall, your hand on the hilt of your sword, ready to draw if you must, hoping for an alternative.

His voice cracks as he refuses, declaring your claim baseless. The Fiaer Dradorn he helped raise is dead. Whatever Nightmare-born abomination you are, you have no rights to his estate, or to the respect due him.

You parry the blades you can see from those who share Samethi's beliefs as they charge, but you are sluggish. Blood blossoms where metal tugs in places it should not be, slicing away at the man, leaving the animal desperate to survive.

You twist and turn, your sword erratic, spittle of panic flying from your mouth with every open breath as you are mobbed, taking blows and slices before grabbing fingers dig in and force you to your knees. Feral, you struggle against those who pry your weapon from your grasp and keep you steady as Samethi approaches, his sword drawn.

His mouth is twisted somewhere between fear and grief and he does not give you the chance to say anything to him before he strikes without apology. No language of the sea to sing you to rest. His sword drives deep into your abdomen and through the other side, the back of your bloody shirt lifting from your skin before it tears. There is only the sound of butchered meat and the pop of organs that perhaps only you can hear. You gasp before the pain even registers — flowering from front to back — and lose control of your limbs, aware of twitches you cannot feel as Samethi pushes you off his sword with the sole of his boot, throwing his weapon to the sand.

You fall against the calloused, exposed hull of *Golden Harvest* as the darkness that must be death overcomes you. Your last visions are of Samethi pushing his new crew aside to stalk further up the beach to be alone with his thoughts and his guilt. He is welcome to them. Who knows? Maybe you will stay dead this time.

The echo of your father scoffs under his breath. *You think this is bad now, boy?*

The pain moves from rear to fore, becoming an unpleasant tingling through your limbs that gains power until it becomes fire in your blood. You are still leaning against the hull of your ship, the sand around you crimson.

You struggle to your feet, teeth near cracking against the pain as the fire dims to a fizz — the wound of your execution now a scar, puckered and fresh. To one side Klaudai looks on with a surgeon's curiosity, or a mage's. Whatever she sees, she makes no comment against the rising chatter at your resurrection.

You share their terror as you poke at the fine line of knitted skin under the blood and sand with trembling hands that do not feel as if they are quite where you expect them to be, but you cannot show it. You breathe again. Samethi has *no* claim to your home.

You spit more blood onto the sand as you pick up your sword again. Exhaustion threatens to overwhelm you, but you have pushed through worse on pain of your father's ire. You will push through this too.

You shift your stance, your legs unsteady — not responding the way they should, and level your weapon at your rival. One last chance to rescind his claims, or to at least regain his own honour by besting you honestly. He cannot refuse both.

He curses you as he takes up his own weapon, waving his cronies back with a shake of his head as he tests his footing in the sand. Despite age weighing heavier on Samethi, you are uncoordinated, slow and sore from your strange revivals. Youth has no benefit here.

As you face each other, the crew create a circle from which to watch, and to keep either of you from turning tail and fleeing. This time, you fight not just for your life. *It is only when a man clings to the last thing he can call his own, that he shows his true nature*. Your father's words, but softer than usual. You have never been sure if you were really meant to hear them.

You and Samethi have been sparring each other since you were big enough to hold a sword without dropping it. Samethi favours the opening overhead strike and will use his entire body as a weapon.

He knows you will counter the first, leaving yourself open long enough to take a blunt force blow. You go back and forth, evenly matched. You take wounds when you are too slow, he takes them when he flounders in the sand, but neither of you score more than shallow gashes or deep bruises that will only truly hurt when they begin to colour. This will continue until one of you surrenders. It cannot be you.

Yet you do not want to be the one to win. Not at this cost. You focus on staying out of his range. Ducking and dodging, parrying and blocking, the shocks ring up through your arms as you bite back the pain, tasting only blood and fear as you hope to exhaust him into surrender.

A blow to your leg threatens to send you to the ground.

You use your new gait to give Samethi pause. It does not work. He pulls a return that drops you as you barely keep him from killing you again. A favourite move of your father's.

You blink away sweat and Samethi presses his advantage against your disorientation with a heavy strike to your head with his hilt. You reel as the horizon bounces, the ring of people spinning. In response, and no small panic, you swing in return, your blade catching Samethi in the waist, grating against hip bone.

He yells, clutching blood with the hand still holding his weapon. It trembles but the old man is not down. He throws another punch. The rings on his fingers catch the sun — golden cresting waves, and the signet seal of an office long since decommissioned — before they hit your nose, bursting it open. They come at you again and the golden glints of sun on metal stained red are different: a different seal, more metal and sharp jewels that cut into your skin as you face your father, his very prestige a weapon against you as you fight, trapped, in a ring on the deck of the ship, the air full of the buzz of cheering and commentary as if it was sport. Eighteen years old and the most piss-scared you have ever been.

Another blow sends you sprawling backwards into sand, not wood. You roll away from Samethi's blade before it lands and throw sand into his eyes. His stumbling gives you only a moment's pause. Any longer and you will die on your back, the way your father always thought you would. *Get up, boy. Face me.*

You and Samethi both stagger now, breath coming hard in the hot air, blood leaking faster than either of you can contain. Everywhere hurts. It throbs and stings and screams, so you do not have to add your voice. The way Samethi wears that particular scowl, he is no better and no worse than you. You stumble towards him while he is still blind.

Samethi has been an exemplary teacher in every regard but one: that to survive, you need more than skill. You need endurance, sheer stubborn pig-headedness and the knowledge that nothing is dishonourable in a fight for your life.

Those lessons had come from your father; and you — bloodied, battered and staggering — had taken them to heart, bringing him to his knees on wooden boards, your hand trembling in a way it does not anymore. Your father did not flinch with the tip of your blade against his throat. He did not even look at you.

I expected better of you.

Samethi's calloused hand had wrapped around yours and driven the point of your weapon home while you had wept, apologies falling thick and fast. He had been a monster, but he had still been your father and, to the end, you had disappointed him. You will not disappoint him again.

Your father kneels not on boards but cowers on sand as Samethi scrabbles away, knowing he is lost. Words of apology dance behind your clenched teeth. He had no words for you, you have none for him. You bring the bloodied point of your sword to his throat and draw a bead of scarlet that dribbles down his neck.

There is no hand to guide you now. Samethi meets your eyes and does not waver. "What am I dying for?"

What is he doing out here on this lost scrap of land after facing magery and a backlash without question? Explain why you could not just follow nature and stay dead.

You had kept it to yourself, not just for your own frail hope but to avoid exactly this, unwilling to risk Samethi's reaction.

Yet here you both are. You let the truth free in a raspy voice loud enough only for him to hear. The promise of the one thing your father could not find. Samethi's face drops further as he holds back a new torment. He pleads against this, as if you could change it now: "Let the dead stay dead."

You chuckle at that. It builds from your stomach and pushes up through your chest where it gathers mirth and out from your ragged throat in guffaws as you double over, sinking to the sand at the absurdity. Tears trickle down your bloody face and you laugh enough to give yourself hiccoughs as, realising what he has said, Samethi does the same. The pair of you — moments away from death — cling to each other, laughing until the tears run thick and fast. Just two men who have been through too much.

Klaudai and her team of surgeons move in before either of you bleed out. Klaudai tuts as she examines you, dressing your wounds. That thoughtful look is back in her eyes, demoting you from human to specimen. You tolerate her touch out of necessity. A life for a life.

You look around at the people on the beach. A life for lives.

When you sailed from Ide, you had a full complement of crew: half a hundred and spare. Now, there are barely more than twenty, including those the surgeon is not sure will pull through their lingering injuries.

Even if you remained nothing more than a man, you would only take volunteers for what you intend next, and you will have no opportunity as good as this to offer an alternative to mutiny.

Access to Isia, and their promised fortunes, rely on two things: your presence at command, and the life of the mage. Those who can stomach their revulsion of you are welcome to join you in spitting in the eye of those who spite them all. After all, some slights can be explained, like the fear of what you are. Others can be forgiven, with time. Isia can be neither.

The cabin-hand, Eayr, her arm splinted and face purple with bruises, is the only one to address you directly, asking what would happen to those who cannot.

In another life, Samethi was one of the best ship builders Nion had known — that decommissioned office he wears on his finger — and the timbers here are good and strong. They will make excellent shelter and ship. None of these people shirk the idea of a few months' hard graft, nor will they do it alone. You are a vengeful man, but not a petty one. You will leave them the tools and equipment they will need and cannot produce here: the spare anchor, reams of chain, barrels and hoops, chests — their personal belongings.

You will remain only as long as it takes for the most essential repairs to *Golden Harvest* and to restock food, water and supplies. You will work alone, if that is the consensus, but they can be free of you sooner if they lend aid.

It is a good offer, yet some still debate killing you and the screaming mage both and taking the ship anyway, trusting you will present no abominable retribution once you are little more than ash on the wind.

The sharp hook then, to the sweet bait: "My father would have killed you all and delighted in the ash of your pyres for today's treachery," you say as loud as you can, despite the pain under your skin, the salty dryness in your throat. "I not only allow you live but to also return to the positions you held and maintain the promise of wealth, or to break clean and make new lives. But make no mistake, do not force my hand another way. I am my father's son enough to do what I must."

A moment to work thick saliva into your ragged mouth. A moment to let the threat settle. You have been generous with Samethi, but further attempts on your life will be met in kind. "*Golden Harvest* is *my* ship. Three deaths or three hundred will not change that."

Then all you can do is wait for the results of the vote with your back against the ship's hull. You can barely keep your eyes open but you cannot rest yet, more from fear you will not be able to wake when you need to, tired enough for a lifetime. Or two. Only Klaudai approaches to see again to your wounds. She does not stay long, and neither of you speak.

It is evening before Samethi sends a runner. She stands at a distance to inform you that your terms are accepted. Anyone who can stomach an abomination will join you when you are ready to leave. The rest will make their own way here.

The news leaves you bitter. Even as you offered them the chance to walk away, you had hoped they would not. You had hoped they knew how much you needed them.

As the night gathers, fires are lit along the beach and under the shelter of the trees but the people are quiet, the sense of celebration long vanished. You stay long enough to eat, more from necessity than hunger, and when you retire, the bar of the door to the captain's quarters falls into place like an anchor into sand. You give in to sleep with the same heaviness. Your nights of safety in the hold are over.

The surgeon wakes you late into the morning, hammering on the barred door. She is here to tend the mage, who resumed her screaming as soon as she woke. She is Husked, Klaudai calls it; burnt out. Powerless.

She tends to your wounds too, changing your dressings. In a low voice, you warn her that if she uses her Nightmare-gifted powers on your ship again, your retribution will be both swift and cruel. When she leaves, she does not look back.

The day is given over to the steady stream of people coming aboard to collect their things and their friends confined to the surgery. You stay out of sight. It hurts less not to witness the evacuation. With each person and chest and pack removed — with every trinket taken down and stowed away — *Golden Harvest* feels more hollow, stirring emotions you do not have the energy to examine.

Instead, you return to sleep, finding it easy despite the noise from the mage huddled in her corner, until hunger wakes you shortly before the dawn. The mage whimpers in her own turbulent rest, looking truly as powerless as the surgeon claims. A pitiable figure, but not one you pity. She has escaped the repercussions of her actions in a way that you cannot: the fault hers, but yours to bear.

With the light, and Samethi's crew taking to work, you follow suit, heading inland for resources. Klaudai joins you; the only one willing to even approach you.

It means she is with you when the tightness in your chest grows again. Nerves: expectation of an ambush, or sabotage while you are away, perhaps retribution taken on the powerless mage. Perhaps Klaudai will lock you inside a tree, or bury you miles beneath the ground to make sure her secret is kept now that you are alone. These are not unreasonable concerns, so you make no comment until the coughing starts. You stumble as water — bitter and salty as the ocean — rises in your mouth. You see yourself reflected in the surgeon's wide, shocked eyes as you crash to the ground, clutching your guts as water pours from your mouth, your nose, dribbling from your ears. Your insides writhe and the world begins to go black. The last thing you see is that the earth mage is as scared of you as the others, despite her own secrets.

The darkness remains incomplete and gives way to light as tree roots find every bruise and create new ones as something drags you face down across the ground by the ankles. The vomiting becomes coughing, then a tightness in your chest that lessens until you can attempt to twist and pull away from Klaudai's grip as she hauls you back towards the shore.

By the time you can see the ship through the thinning trees, you can stumble without support, the feeling in your chest lessening to barely more than a sense of dread, and is gone entirely by the time you pull yourself back aboard, concerned more with the logistics of repair than for yourself. You cannot repair the ship without supplies. If you cannot gather supplies, you cannot repair the ship. Following the circular thoughts push the reasons *why* to the back of your mind to gather dust.

The next day you try to breach the island alone and meet with the same results. You pull yourself back to safety before you drown, barely five hundred feet from shore. Carefully cataloguing the small list of all that *Golden Harvest* can survive without, you realise you are going to have to ask for help. You are going to have to hope it is given.

On the fourth day, you wake to find a pile of materials you need waiting in the sand, more being provided as they become available, the crew prioritising your need if only to be rid of the magic tainting their shore sooner. Volunteers for the repairs remain a wishful dream. Not that you mind. You know every inch of this ship, how every piece of her is meant to fit together. You had never thought you would be thankful for the menial chores your father had used as punishments but, as you become caulker, carpenter, rope-maker, sailmaker and more, you wonder if those had been his way of apprenticing you. It makes it easier now, as you swing from board and suspend from rope and shape new wood and heat pitch. You almost feel as if you are recovering with her.

Already, a small settlement is already taking shape under the trees. Men and women fish and gather and hunt as homes appear. The arm-master has even become something of a bartering merchant. Many of these people had sailed with you because they had no place to call their own. You had promised them that, for as long as they wanted. Needed. Now they have this island. They have tools. They have a competent leader in Samethi. They can, if not prosper, be comfortable.

It is as happy an ending as can be taken, yet you still carve new notches into the walls of your quarters every evening, one for each empty bed space. Those who have died since the battle with the Yannish. Those who have left you now. With the priest and her unending torment beside you as you work, you have fallen behind, finding it harder to take the accustomed comfort from the actions. It does mean you have a knife to hand on the twelfth night when three people come looking to kill you in your sleep.

In the morning, their bodies lie out in the sand, left for the seabirds and the crabs. You make sure to be visible, working away as if nothing had happened. Samethi should have warned them that your threats had not been vainglory. You do not carve their marks into the ship.

Your father had always warned you not to get too close to a crew; that names and faces and loyalties shift and turn more often than the tide. You dismissed him, believing his warnings were fed from growing paranoia. After all, you ate with these people, drank with them. You have laughed and grieved together. You have deliberately worked hard to blur that line between captain and crew. You did not have the connections or appropriations of your father. You had only this ship and whoever sailed with her.

It sours you to learn he had been right.

As the repairs take hold over the following five weeks, and your patchwork ship appears more like herself, there is no denying that you must leave this fledgling colony.

To your surprise, you welcome a crew of six, including Klaudai. She is the only officer, though Cyril, the navigator, presents you with copies of the charts he has been able to make. You pretend you do not understand the swearing in his native Torran language around the borders and thank him sincerely. The cook spits into the sand, but that has always been his habit and you do not take it personally.

What little noise there is falls away as Samethi approaches, limping. It is the first time you have been face to face since your duel, relying on runners to send messages. He does not meet your eye as you hold out your hand and flinches at your touch. He brings no gifts, but also no ill will. It is the best he can do.

Once as close as parent and child, now only acquaintances. Fellows of rank and nothing more. You keep your peace, biting off all the things you wish you could say and know you never can. From the way his cheeks twitch, he does the same.

By moonrise, you are back on the water with a skeleton crew more greedy than fearful and two mages: one insensate, the other... you are not sure what you make of Klaudai. Whichever way you cut it, this is now a ship of abominations, hardly worthy of story. Perhaps not even enough to make it back to civilisation.

With so much to do spread between so few, there is little time for idle thoughts. When they sneak up on you, you play out confrontations for when you return to Ide: the things you will say, the things you expect to hear. The differences between fighting for your life to escape, or a dagger in the night while you sleep. The differences between execution and revenge.

Sometimes you focus instead on the taste of fresh beer and bread and fruits, things unsalted and undried. Those thoughts become more frequent when it becomes clear none of you have your old cook's talent for flavour, texture or, in some cases, temperature. There are a few days of upset stomachs, including your own, that keep Klaudai busy. She prods at you in the throes of your sickness, marvelling that it is not passing sooner, as if it ought to. You remark, dryly, that it is passing fast enough. She tries not to laugh.

After that, she takes responsibility for the galley too. At least things are hot enough, and it keeps her from continuing to hound you for her experiments which you flatly refuse to entertain, though you do not interfere with her secretive communications with the others, save for when it delays something urgent.

Whatever she is plotting, you will deal with it when it becomes an issue. Until then, you have enough to do which is why, when she persists in harassing you, you rise to anger, shouting loud enough to put the noise of the Husked mage into the background. You will *not* die over and over for her curiosity. You would very much like to not think about your abomination at all.

You would very much like to not think about anything: not who you have left behind, and certainly not why. You do not want to invite that pain in.

Your father would have scoffed to see you care after the way they had turned on you, but if your father had seen what you had become, he would have taken your head and burned your body without ceremony, delay or chance to see if you would resurrect from that. He might even have felt remorse at some point, once he realised he had destroyed his favourite example.

Not thinking demands much focus to keep the feelings you cannot name in their little box, tightly lidded: the sharp corners poking at the soft parts of your mind, bringing no relief, not even secret, silent, tears. No matter how many menial chores you take on, forsaking sleep and food — telling yourself you would rather risk starvation than sickness again — that box festers as you cannot help but replay all that has brought you to this point. Especially in the dark of night when you have only the priest's whimpering for company and a heavy door between you and the sea and the sky.

It chews through kinder emotions until all that is left is anger, frustration and terror, leaving a volatile, irate man in your place. It is not long before it spreads through the crew.

There are no songs, not even to break the long silences. Instead there are mutters and grumbles under breaths before they grow brazen, first with vocal barbs and later with fists. First with each other, then with you. You relish the chance to vent the frustration you feel, leaving your paltry crew curled in defeat on the deck or, as the priest-mage had been, strung to the mask for a day and a night, too few of you to keep them there for longer.

Even your victories are not enough to keep your crew in line. You need something stronger than a promise tied to purse strings, something like fear, to truly hold their obedience. For the first time since his death, some of your father's old punishments return to the ship as you become deaf to the sounds of whip cracks, ignorant of the wetness of someone else's blood.

Klaudai implores you to reconsider your actions before you become as you believe yourself to already be, as if you could be anything else. Her pleas have no effect. At least when she vocally wishes your death, it is no longer to satisfy her curiosity.

Four weeks since leaving the island, and with no trace of civilised lands — or of any land — nearby, the only solace you can take is in the rhythm with which you work salt water into the deck. At the heat of the day, with no clouds and barely a breeze, the work had made you sweat, even shirtless. Now the sun has set and the cold, star-filled night stretches on above you. You have already completed this task five times today. You still do not stop. Only the movement of your arms, the pain in the small of your back and the pressure on your knees prove you are still alive through the numbness in your mind.

You ignore the footsteps that approach you, and the warm spice of stew. Klaudai has the night watch tonight, but you do not intend to leave your ship in the hands of a mage, not even for a ship of monsters. She places the stew beside you and steps back. "You're a piece of shit," she tells you.

Suspecting she is going to once again berate you for your crew's suffering, you shift your pail to better get to the deck boards, cutting yourself off from her with a ring of damp wood, aware she is studying you again. You ignore her until she sees to her duties, checking lines and charting alignments from the stars, keeping *Golden Harvest* running true west. You do not let her out of your sight.

The others were lured aboard by their greed, though they were not all names you had expected, but Klaudai is not here for gold and the very sight of her is a reminder that she is the only one of your officers to stand by you. She feeds that darkness built on the knowledge everyone you loved — everyone you fought and killed for — turned their back on you. She is the root of your grief and it angers you that she is here, as much as what she is frightens you. And she brings you comfort that you have not been entirely abandoned. Those feelings war with each other if you let them. Easier to let the void swallow them.

Only when the few and faint sounds below deck fade away as your crew settle down for the night, does your surgeon break the quiet again. "You think you're the only one on this boat who is hurting, Fiaer? We are *all* grieving something we left behind on that island, but only you are lashing out like a child denied his favourite toy, as if your grief is the only one that matters. If you continue to push us, I will not stop the others tossing your body over the side. You can walk home along the seafloor for all I care."

Her tone grinds against you. She a self-confessed world-breaker, capable of atrocities you cannot even fathom and — she is right. She does not deserve your fury. And neither do the others. But to fix this would mean dealing with the box in your mind and all the grotesques inside. You do not have the strength for that. Not yet.

You scrub the deck again, starting from the beginning. It is only when you rise to fill your bucket do you pass where the now cold stew waits for you, and where Klaudai stands staring north, her hand on a line, do you give in to a burst of curiosity: "Why are you here?"

As you chase the strange shape of the word around your mouth, you realise you have not spoken in hours. The surgeon does not immediately answer and you take your full pail to continue scrubbing, believing she will not.

Instead, she ties the line and follows you, leaning against the railing as you go back to work, the swish of the wet brush over boards complementing the sound of water pushing against the hull.

She is indifferent to begin with, maintaining her earlier tone. She was not needed on the island; those she trained were more than qualified, and your promise was to take her to the nearest port where, *if* you ask it, she will leave. As you have not yet reached a port, let alone asked, she has stayed. Semantics you do not have the patience to sift through for the truth. Maybe that shows on your face. Maybe she simply needed to say something out loud, because when she continues you recognise the heaviness that weighs her words down.

"We're all running from something," she says, almost to herself, sinking down beside you, the warmth of her fighting the chill of the night. She is too close. "I've been running so long I don't know if I *can* stop."

You look up and see the way the moonlight reflects in her eyes. Something oppressive settles between the pauses in her words. Your curiosity is gone, having steered too close to caring.

You abandon the swabbing brush to move to the other side of the ship, making as if to check the ropes you know are perfectly held, knocking over the pail in your haste — the water foaming over the boards. The wind rippling over the sails masks her barefoot padding to stand beside you again.

"My very existence causes unspeakable horrors to people like you. I need to help where I can, to balance it out."

There. The confirmation that you are nothing more than

a project to assuage her guilt. You do not need your father's voice to scorn you. Projects born of guilt are hard to let go of, no matter the consequences. A crack forms across the shell you have gathered over a wounded heart. You keep it to yourself. Vulnerability will see you dead.

"I didn't mean to reveal myself to you," she says into the night. "But for the first time in my life, I'm no longer alone with this secret. If I'd stayed on that island, having tasted this freedom, it would have killed me." This time there is the hint of a half-smile as if admitting such a thing was little more than a childish fancy. "And the only person I get to share it with is acting like a shit."

Bombarded by truth, you are overwhelmed and pull away, but Klaudai has the grip of a sailor used to hanging on for dear life.

"What do you want from me, Klaudai?"

She leans in, kissing you. Her tongue parts your lips, her body presses on yours; warm against the cold before she pulls away, embarrassed at the way you freeze at her touch. Revulsion.

Surprise. She is the first to approach you this way since the Isian man who drugged and robbed you, setting you on this path, turning you into a monster. Klaudai apologises, searching for a justification. It is her lifetime of hurts seeking connection in yours. Almost human. It calls to a desperate need for something you did not even know to look for. It is not love. There can be no love between two monsters. Only hunger, and you are starved.

You pull her back, responding in kind — searching for something in her touch — warm hands across your cold back, tongue pressed against yours — to sate you. You take each other there on the deck, grasping and rough, damp wood under bare skin — two abominations together under the stars and the waxing moon with only the pulse of the water to accompany your groans as you move as one. No love, and no emotion beyond the peak, save a hollow catharsis, the void shut away again for a time.

Whether you agree with it or not, you give the crew time to grieve what they have lost to sail with you. Cards and dice, rather than barbed words and fists begin to come out in the evenings, though you do not join in — unwilling to foster relationships where none exists. They are not your family.

When the hunger grows, you sometimes seek, or are sought by the surgeon. Sometimes, afterwards, you lie next to each other, skin to skin, in silence, both still searching for something that cannot be found. Something that cannot be said.

Almost eight weeks from the island, as you are about ready to throw the navigator's charts into the sea for all the good they have done you, you overhear someone, Jacen, humming Samethi's lullaby, her soft voice carrying over the quiet ship.

It takes everything you have not to undo weeks of work in an instant — the roiling rage in your blood at the audacity to remind you of the things you have lost, their razor-sharp edges, almost safely lashed down, once again free. You bite your fury back until your cheeks bleed as you turn away from a simple joy; a complex pain.

Klaudai finds you in your quarters, knees to your chest as you stare at the walls, still unable to let go of the tears building somewhere in that bottomless darkness within you, pressing at the cages you have built around it.

As if sensing that you want neither kind words, or to dwell, she once again approaches the topic of her experiments: not for her curiosity alone, but to arm yourself. Knowing your capabilities and your limits is as powerful a weapon as the blade at your side, or the quickness of your mind. You snort, half laughing. Your thoughts have been thick and dull as the fog the shade-ship had sailed in: the last time you had heard Samethi's lullaby.

This time, you agree, though not with enthusiasm. You did not fight as hard as you did; you did not leave everything you had built behind on an uncharted island simply to risk death by mistake now.

Klaudai cannot guarantee safety, but has never been reckless with life. To soften the blow, she admits you are not the only one she has asked, only the last to agree. In your self-made isolation, you assumed your crew were fuelled purely by coin, never considering that a backlash is indiscriminate.

A ship of abominations indeed.

Of your five other crew members, only two, Lyas and Salva, are here for the money, but they have personal experience with things like you — people they once loved. They can tolerate your strangeness. The three others reveal their own changes. Jacen can no longer feel the heat of fire, but neither does it harm her. She, not realising the food was undercooked, had been the one to poison you all. The second, Toram, is hesitant to share that — unlike you who drowns on dry land — he does not drown at all, as if the admission makes it more real. The last, Kyrel, who was never one for grand speeches before the backlash, does not speak at all. As such, he has managed to avoid most of your wrathful episodes. He nods when you ask him if he will share, and pulls off the boots and thick gloves he wears, revealing suckers on the soles of his feet and the palms of his hands. He astounds you by clambering up the mast without relying on rigging or tethers. When you say so, he smiles. His teeth have become a sharp-looking beak behind thick lips.

That evening, as you sit with your monstrous crew for the first time — surrounded by strangers you dare not trust, plastering on a smile for the sake of peace — Klaudai tells you that you are not so special after all. Her words spark raucous teasing from the others of the thing between you. Let them have this joy, this feeling of humanity. You and Klaudai know better.

The herb mother's tears is well named. In small doses, it eases the passing of miscarriage, Klaudai had said once, her naked body pressed against yours, her hands tracing your scars after you had asked if she really wanted this, given there was no love between you. In larger doses, or without need for its abortifacient properties, the herb becomes addictive, rotting the body from the inside. She does not expect dedication from you as you do not expect it from her.

What you share is medicinal. When you take offence at the notion that the touch of a lover is all it takes to solve your problems she laughs. The medicine is for her. She has no control over how you handle the side effects. As soon as her need to explore the connection she created with her honesty fades, as soon as either of you no longer gain anything from this particular anchor, the treatment ends before it becomes toxic.

That is why you can grit your teeth and take the teasing of the crew, and why you can give it in return, opening yourself to other offers if that is jealousy you detect in their comments. Toram, the loudest, grows quiet.

As the meal ends, the mood shifts as your crew take to sharing their own stories of the backlash, of their own abominations triggering. You listen to the same fear, the same anguish, the same grief that you had thought entirely your own, coming from two voices and one impressive interpretive dance. Even those here for vengeance and profit, Lyas and Salva, share their stories of attempts to stand up for those they could neither change nor save, losing everything in doing so.

In a quiet, contemplative voice once you are alone, Klaudai admits these were only the ones she could find. There may be others among Samethi's people who had not triggered before you left, or who had been better at hiding it. All she, and you, can do is hope those triggers and secrets stay buried. Samethi is a man of principle. If he could strike *you*, others will meet with no extra kindness.

You begin your experiments the following day. The wild, guarded man still licking his wounds who lies behind the forced smiles and jokes for the sake of the ship screams in anguish as you die. Murdered over and over: poison, weapon, suffocation, drowning, until all you know is the pain of death and the agony of recovery. It is hard not to resent the apparent vigour your crew use against you, but you keep your silence. It is a just repayment for your treatment of them and it does not appear permanent.

Then, the deaths spread beyond the ship. Taken out in the rowboat, tied to the ship with measured ropes until you are either killed or begin to drown as you had on the island. As there, you can go little further than five hundred feet.

You are left in the boat to drift, sometimes for days, before you are returned to the ship where you revive and, every time, you hope that your surgeon's theories prove correct: that this

next death is one you can return from. You deny her requests
to leave you dead until significant decomposition occurs. The
rot of days is enough. There are things even you do not want
to know.

When you can no longer deny the times you are
incapacitated by recovery is increasing the strain on the
crew and on the ship itself, already getting by on less than
the minimum attention she needs, Klaudai declares reluctant
satisfaction, confident she knows the main limits of your…
condition.

The ship is more than your home. You are connected
somehow. She has the power to deny you death, no matter
the cause, but stray too far and you drown the way you should
have during the storm. However long you lie in death, it takes
Golden Harvest the same time to bring you back.

That first time on the island, you had been dead almost
half a day. It took almost another half to bring you back.
When you had died against her hull, the resurrection was
instantaneous. That pattern has borne out through all of
Klaudai's experiments since.

You love this ship, but to never set foot on land more than
five hundred feet from her is hard to take. That night sees you
in a fit of despair, and in the morning many things lie broken
and scattered around you in your quarters. The screaming
priest is, for once, not screaming but whimpering gently
against a wall as if it would give her safety from your new
grief, though you have not touched her and despite Klaudai's
conviction she is entirely unaware of her surroundings.

It is a prison sentence. It is an opportunity as Kyrel, acting
as crow, signals the news that makes you truly smile for the
first time in a long time, though not in joy.

After almost five long months, you are back in home waters.

Chapter Four

The priest screams from her place on the deck, lashed to the railing to prevent her from accident or mishap as you once again hoist the repugnant flag of Isia, fixing it into place underneath the Black Shark and Esian purple.

She is gaunt; her once white robes stained and torn, her skin filthy and her hair matted because she will not tolerate attention. Nor do you wish to give her any. As you had reasoned after the Yannish encounter, no mention was ever made of the condition she needed to be in upon her return. Alive is enough. Anything more would be an arduous process, and there is no hiding that the priest has Husked. Not every Husked screams, apparently, and if she had gone some other arcane way you might have had an easier time pretending otherwise, if it would have aided your plans. But she did not, so you have no intention of pretending to be anything other than you are either.

Her screams echo across empty water and an empty ship as you wait, set to anchor outside the narrow entrance of Ide harbour, waiting for permission to enter between the towering cliffs that drop into a natural valley where the Isian city sits. That they have never taken advantage of this feature is a criminal waste. Not even fishing boats sail past as you wait for the Isians to notice you.

Your father would look at these cliffs in envy and twist it to spite. He would give long lectures once he had a few drinks in him about the way storms would destroy foreign ships set against Nion's soft sandbanks — that only true Nionese ships could survive such attacks. A naval nation built from driftwood and sand; somehow able to not only survive the harsh world, but to thrive in it. To spit in its eye and claim defiance against it. That was where true strength lay. Then he would see you and laugh that you would dash apart in anything more than a nine-foot swell. A man convinced you could never be his idealised version of the past.

He was right.

Your grief, minor as it is against the storm that was your father, has stripped you of your softness all the same; abraded by the stains of blood and the ache of betrayal until even the pain means nothing anymore.

It is your own fault. You had grown comfortable around, if not close to, your small crew of abominations, and in a last moment of softness you had given them the choice to turn away from the path you intended to follow. On seeing familiar lands and imagining new opportunities they had, as a mass, taken their leave of you, even Kyrel with his physical changes. All choosing to go places you cannot follow.

The lingering kiss of goodbye Klaudai had given you as you had seen them off the ship had tasted as foul as your mood remained over the two weeks you drifted, fraying like old rope with the work demanded of you. Trusting to your knowledge of the winds and the tides and the places the draught stays deep to get you close enough to Ide in the hope that they will send out tugs so you do not need to navigate the narrow harbour entrance alone.

For that, they need to see your true need. Let them see the matching pair you and the priest make in dishevelment. Torn clothes crusty with salt and blood that will never clean out, hair wild and outgrown, your beard marking the many long months since you had last been a respectable man.

It is impatient work, waiting as glints of glass flash along the harbour, examining you from afar. You do your best to look at ease at the delays, though anxiety and frustration coil inside you with no outlet. Isia intends to kill you, and still you came.

At least it is only you they will kill. You and your ship.

Isia cannot have *Golden Harvest* when you are dead, and the elaborate set-up in the hold will ensure that they will not. There is no risk to you unless you head below, but the warmth of the summer sun makes you nervous all the same.

By the time the tugs — two small boats that lurch through the calm water, their oars working out of time — reach you and bring you slowly in, the sun is not far from setting. If their tardiness was an attempt to intimidate you, they have sorely misunderstood what they were dealing with even before they sent you out to commit their crimes for them.

You may not be intimidated, but you cannot stop the hot burn of humiliation as the Isian tugs pull you through the water in their uncomfortable fashion. Not only for their ineptitude with the boats they already have, but knowing what your father, or even Samethi, would have said to seeing *Golden Harvest* limping along behind them, incapacitated by your own incompetence. Incapacitated by a soft heart.

As you move through the bowl of the harbour towards

the piers used for local barges and the occasional ship like yours, or the Yannish, you see Ide for what it really is: a small city protected by the arms of the cliffs on one side, and the grandiose rhetoric of the priests stationed in their equally grandiose buildings that rise above the rest of the city, erupting from the sprawl — stalling the scientific methods that keep a civilisation growing.

The last time you had sailed past the rudimentary shipyards dotting the shoreline, you and Samethi had laughed at the poor designs of the ships under construction. Determined to do everything themselves, the Isian designers had not taken inspiration from other nations — throwing together little more than the impressions of what oceangoing vessels should be like, the country so repressed that not even ideas had anything to work with. Yet you had expected their shipwrights and builders to be *competent*. Isia has no navy, but it does have light craft for small fishing fleets in some towns and flat barges that travel the rivers, seemingly without incident. Near half a year on, you revise your earlier thoughts.

The frames and half-clad hulls of the ships nearing completion suggest the shipwrights have not even consulted each *other*. You pass three that will keel in any wind above a breeze. Another two have gaps between the boards that even seawater swell will not keep closed. They will sink, slowly but surely, under the strain of their own provisions. One, you are fairly certain will crack in half as soon as it is floated.

They do, however, give the impression that the Isian Navy is growing rapidly. A move to bolster their own population perhaps. It is not as if outsiders will take this secret with them. Isia would not have sent you after the Yannish if they risked word escaping.

The priest-mage had tried to convince you that the Isian people were prosperous and content during many of your early debates. It could be that she lied; the priests acting to maintain a crumbling control.

You shrug those thoughts off as the crews of the tugs help you tie up at your mooring. An important-looking man saunters up to your ship, his ego barely fitting the jaunty coat he wears. You stare at him until he gets close enough to ask you to lower your gangplank and let him retrieve the honourable priest of Nisha. You continue staring: a wild man with no words to spare for this fool. He asks again. This time you spit and inform him that there are no honourable people on this ship, and that you will speak to no one, nor invite anyone on board until you are granted audience with the man who sent you into the east. When you name him, the fool does not just deflate, he steps back into one of the towering minions he has brought with him to impart the respect he does not provide alone, jaunty coat or not. There is whispering; you have invoked a mighty name and the fool only looks over his shoulder at you twice as he hurries back towards the city proper.

The honourable priest continues to scream, no recognition of where she is breaking through whatever torments her. You take to leaning again, watching the sun sink beyond the land, your thoughts very closely guarded. In this place, the priest was never the only one to get inside your head. That will not happen again.

There is more life closer to the shore — banks of light barges shift cargo from moorings similar to yours and carry it towards and up the river. Haulers and warehouse overseers bid each other a fair evening as they leave for their homes, the life of the city winding down as darkness falls.

The second official to approach you is marginally better dressed than the first and carries her superior rank in her bearing, but is still an underling to the one you are waiting for. Her Trade is broken as she calls up from the jetty that she was certain this ship had once looked far more majestic. "Hadn't it a taller mast, and even a secondary vessel?"

You shrug as you light lanterns and beacons. "I used to have a crew too. What of it?"

She offers to listen to the story of your adventures, if you would be willing. You are not, retreating back into your silence. You have expressed your wishes and until they are met, you will wait right here with your prisoner. The official threatens to have you boarded so they may retrieve their priest anyway. You laugh and give a mock bow, as if inviting her to try. She likely does not know the intricacies of your mission, but the one you are waiting for does. If Isia come for their mage, they do so at their own risk.

Her sneer becomes a scowl as you reiterate that you are not here to bandy insults with a lower official. You will speak to who you want, and no one else. He can meet you in the warehouse two hundred feet from your ship — you have seen no one enter or leave it and believe it to be unused — in three hours. Should he refuse, Isia is welcome to fish their honourable priest from the bottom of the bay.

The mage keeps screaming. You bite your tongue to keep from joining her as the night truly takes hold, lanterns winking into life across the city as you continue to wait; ignoring the growing itch of paranoia between your shoulder blades. On these boards, you are safe from anything the Isians may attempt in the dark. But you would rather not reveal that to them. You would rather not think about it at all. Thinking is the most dangerous thing you can do.

Around you the creaking of timbers in water is almost comforting, the lights shifting between warehouses bring a sense of normality you had not realised you had missed. You have had longer voyages than this one, barely stopping to resupply if time was precious, but then you had always known you could take time to sample civilisation once the job in question was complete. Now...

Now, you go two hundred feet and no further, as lights around you twinkle like the stars ahead, brighter for the lack of a moon: the thin sickle still to rise. You bring the mage behind you, pliant enough for all her noise. It is well you are not attempting stealth.

The pressure is already present, that lurking weight in your chest warning you from going much further.

He is late, of course. But what is more waiting to you? Each moment is one more you get to breathe and see the stars and the lights and feel the breeze on your face carrying the smell of salt and seaweed, tar and evening meals and the sounds of distant laughter and chatter from lives you will never touch.

"Those are egotistical thoughts, for such a small and melancholy man," says a melodious voice from behind you. The man from the tavern emerges from the shadows. He is dressed in white robes and he remains as beautiful as he was on the other side of the border. Just the sight of him alone brings out a desire to please him, to be compliant to his wishes. To give him whatever he wants from you. You swallow, heart quickening in your chest as he looks over the stale, dirty state of you. You do not even mind that his lip curls at what he sees. It would not stop either of you, if he willed it again.

"All the lives you touch, you poison or end, Fiaer. That is what you have always thought? Yet here you are, wishing to touch more of them."

You smile, sheepish, before the teeth show the wolf, emboldened by the strings he pulls within you. "Then I am sorry, for I recall you were *very* willing for me to touch you that night in Esia."

Fear passes over the priest's face as the shadows shift again, revealing a second figure that banishes the wish to again serve your once-lover. At least he can hide his monstrosity with a human face and subtle manipulation.

This figure cannot. It towers over you both, humanoid but not human. It also wears white robes that give off an unnatural glow in the dim light of the empty warehouse. It wears a golden circlet around its head, one single white stone set into the front that shines as brightly as the robes. Three birds, the same as the black and white ravens your priest-mage had travelled with, sit on the shoulders of the figure. Those are the only constants. The face of the abomination shifts, feminine, masculine, both — neither. Faces sharing space — too many eyes, not enough noses, lips overlaid with each other as frequently as limbs grow and disappear.

Your once-lover prostates himself before this horror. The pressure in your mind lessens as the priest who once begged to be seduced by you releases his hold.

"You sought to deceive us, Resnah?" It has three voices, all speaking at once as it turns its attention on the man on his knees. "You would have allowed us to take your corruption into our heart?"

Resnah pleads in Isian, words too fast and too strange for you to follow, but by the fear in his expression, and his hesitant clutching of the abomination's robes, he is pleading for something. Perhaps his life.

When he had wanted you to approach him, he had been nervous and eager. You had not stopped to consider why. There are so few places with such strict and strange ideals of what constitutes appropriate relations that you had not thought Isia would be one of them, or what it would mean to be considered deviant in a place where things like this creature are held in high standing.

Perhaps he had thought you would be as ashamed of it as he was, that you would be cowed and keep your silence, taking his barbs — well trained and well broken in by the work of his companion. She has stopped screaming, though that is perhaps more to do with some magery acted on her, as her mouth remains open and she still seems to have no awareness of the things happening around her.

The abomination turns their attention on you, no longer interested in Resnah as he sinks to the floor, clutching his head. It takes all you have not to drop to your knees before them too. They are a fearsome thing, and a blight on the world, but they demand respect for the majesty of their wrongness.

You stand strong, ignoring the weakness in your knees. You have faced worse than this. Where Resnah had pulled at your mind, something pulls at your heart. It is gentle, and perhaps if you had become anyone else, you would not have noticed, but any flicker of emotion pulled from the void you had only ever patched over is something that cannot belong there. Only the coal of fury burns at its centre now. You will not be manipulated that way either.

The abomination demands the priest on your tether. You demand your money. They refuse. The financial reward was for a share of every person on your crew. As you have no crew, you are entitled to nothing. You argue that you *are* your share of the crew, but they hold steady, repeating their demand for your prisoner. You demand the return of your belongings. That too is refused. The priest who accompanied you is no longer able to vouch for your success or your failure. Without that, you get nothing.

Through your exchange and your refusal to cower before this monster, Resnah, the disgraced priest, stares at you, open mouthed in shock. It is almost funny, but not enough to distract you from the abomination and the faces that flicker across where faces should go, never quite falling into place. For all your bravado, your hand twitches to draw your weapon and remove such a twisted thing as this from the world. Instead, you reach for your pocket and produce three pages torn from the Yannish logs, offering them to the swarm of merging people as proof while bells begin to sound in the distance. You mention only that they do your prisoner an injustice to assume she had not succeeded, and it was not your fault that she has lost herself in the doing.

The pages are trade receipts, showing not only the places the Yannish ship had called prior to leaving Ide, which you may have been able to forge if you had a mind to be so duplicitous, but also the items traded within Ide, which you had never known but can be validated here.

The abomination considers the papers and asks once more for your prisoner before they take her by force, promising you such action would be unpleasant. You believe them. With nothing left to bargain with, you surrender your mage.

The creature checks her condition and then, still screaming her silent screams, she begins to smoulder before flames dance across her skin. She remains unaware of her fate as the smell of burning dirty linen, flesh and hair fill the warehouse. You gag, eyes streaming, the smell so much more potent than a traditional pyre, until her seared body lies crumpled at the feet of the abomination.

It is a horrible way to go, but no less than she deserves for the things that she had done. Still, you had expected less cruelty from one of her own people, something swift and painless. Resnah swallows as he glances at you. "She had given herself over to the last true goddess," he says in barely more than a whisper, answering your thoughts. Her spirit had rested in the bosom of Nisha for some time, but the body had been unable to make the same journey. It could feel no other pain, for the separation of body and spirit was too great. The abomination turns back you. The three voices continue to speak as one as they inform you the cruelty was all yours. You should have had more compassion in the face of her suffering.

Perhaps if they had not sent you to slaughter a ship of innocent people, you might have. Perhaps, if your repayment had not hinged on her returning alive, you would have. The cruelty is theirs by design. You will not take responsibility for it.

Yours is of a different nature. The bells grow louder and shouting now accompanies their chimes. The rancid acid of burned flesh has disguised the scent of woodsmoke, but now that too brings the bitter tang of flaming pitch. The abomination's features flicker faster between themselves, and Resnah once again cowers as the abomination grows agitated.

You offer it the chance to leave, if it is needed elsewhere. You desire nothing more than your payment and you will not leave until you see it done. The abomination makes for the door, their varying number of legs and arms giving them the appearance of an unbalanced spider. The birds on their shoulders take flight as they see the sky, glowing orange and red in the darkness.

A city on fire.

They do not look back as smoke, thick and black and oily, roils through the warehouse. The shipyards are burning too, their works destroyed. Under the panic of those trying to fight the fires comes the anger of a people marching, though their words are Isian, and you cannot pick out specifics. Resnah is unsure if he should follow.

He accuses you of causing this, as if you had not been observed from before you even entered the harbour. As if you were some unnatural creature able to summon flame from nothing. Joy in witnessing the confusion of loss from those who do not honour their own agreements is not an admission of responsibility for it.

Resnah snarls, finding no lie. You offer him a new trade. Monster to monster. A hurt for a hurt. You suspected you would be refused your payment. You suspect you will not leave Isia alive; this is a place, and a people, without honour. Still, death at the magery of that blend of people terrifies you.

The priest delights in telling you that you deserve it. "You have undone me, Fiaer," he hisses and indicates the corpse of the mage. "With her dead I was to be the fourth aspect of the God-Child, but they have cut me off from the Divine Link. They will destroy me, all for your loose words."

You offer him your sword; the growing heat is making your head swim, your thoughts already growing dim as the smoke finds its way into you. You have stripped your once-lover of the chance to fulfil his dreams with nothing more than a few misplaced words. Only he has the power to torment your shade in your last moments, condemning it to an eternity of despair. To have come so close to your own goals and, like him, lose them before you could act.

The smoke is suffocating now, and you stagger against the lack of air, sinking to one knee as you cough and gasp. Resnah stands unimpeded, holding your weapon. You are dying anyway. You look up at him. "What am I dying for?"

The mage hesitates, and your time grows shorter. Should you die without knowing the things he could tell you, at least you can rest in ease that neither you nor your father could achieve the impossible after all. You will grant Samethi his last wish. The dead will stay dead.

The priest blinks as you collapse onto the floor, the smoke so thick you no longer even choke. Then he leans in close to tell you the things you will never be able to achieve, wishing you a poisoned eternity after all.

"She is a blasphemy," he tells you, though you do not know that word. "She travels with an old crone who turned her back on us many years ago. They steal those of our order and pervert them. It is a trait you share. More than that, I cannot say. We lost their trail in Torray some months ago and did not care to pick it up. She is your sister, Fiaer — both your essences share the same root. You have failed her as your father always knew you would."

You sag, tears welling, the truth of what he says breaking open the void you had been holding together with your last thin shreds of will. You motion with the last of your strength to the sword in his hands. You promise him that the act is visceral and physical, and cannot be matched by any other means, much like your shared night across the border. He has lost so much — his anger is justified.

You cry out against the pain of approaching death as he strikes over and over and you leave stains of scarlet across your murderer's robes. You grin as you convulse, blood staining your teeth as you fight to hold on just a little longer. "How do you like your first taste of war?"

The last thing you think as you die is that the best rebellions are the ones that are least subtle.

Klaudai sits on a stool, watching you. Her hands are covered in blood and soot, which is all you can smell, though you can feel several of her potent poultices pressing against tender patches of skin, numbing some of the flaring pain running through your nerves: the cost of recovery from the impossible. While your chest aches from smoke at least a death by blade means you will not vomit salt water from your lungs.

The surgeon reaches a hand to touch yours, letting you know she is there. Normally you would wait and recover, but you do not have the time.

"How long?" you ask, your voice raw with smoke and blood.

"A couple of hours," Klaudai says. "The fires outside are almost entirely under control now. A handful of ships survived, fewer still without damage. There was a team nearby to pull you and a priest free when the warehouse collapsed, but you were already dead. The news is spreading. It will not be long before Isia attempts to claim the ship."

Attempts to pull yourself to standing fail and you sink back down, recognising that the poultices cover stitches too, the wounds seeping and cracking with your movement. As if your own feebleness was not enough, Klaudai holds you down before you try again. The wound that killed you has healed, but the damage from the smoke and the collapsing building after you were dead will take longer. She does not recommend you see through the last of your plan in your current state.

You cannot wait. You do your best to explain the abomination out there — the mass of people fighting for the same space. Klaudai will face necrosis, blood and bodily products without concern but, at your description, even your surgeon looks nauseous as you tell her your suspicions that the people were once mages willingly merged together.

Hesitantly, she offers you an alternative. You are wary of the backlash it would cause, but she says for such a small amount, and in a place already so rotten with magery, it would be inconsequential if noticeable at all. You accept.

The touch of her magery is a forbidden thrill, sweet fire through your body as cuts seal and scab and scar, driving infection out first as burns blister and burst and fresh skin regrows in a matter of moments. The threads of connection running between you remind you almost of cold winter wind under crystalline starlight and of something else — maybe green, maybe purple — you cannot quite bring to mind. When she is done you lean towards her, seeking comfort in an afterglow that is already fading. She pushes you away, mocking your stench, as a keening whistle warns that you are out of time.

You fasten your true sword to its place on your hip. You had not wished to risk losing it, offering Resnah nothing more special than a spare from the armoury, and ignore the wash bowl and fresh clothes for now.

Appearing to your audience unharmed, clean and in fresh clothes, would give rise to the idea of a copy or an illusion. They need to know that you are the Fiaer Dradorn who died.

They need to know you will not be so easily controlled. They need to know exactly how much they have lost tonight.

You spring to the deck, feeling more alive than you have in years, and emerge into a world of black soot and orange embers, flames still trying to survive against the odds. *Golden Harvest* — for of course, you could only have returned in her safe embrace — drifts in the middle of the bay, inching towards the open sea. Jacen and Lyam keeping her steady. Jacen is covered in soot, her grin reflecting your own. Lyam gives you a low nod. They both carry Yannish bows ready to use on your command.

A third and a fourth stand ready for you and Klaudai, who comes to stand beside you. She keeps her face emotionless as she presses something small into your palm, a circle of metal, warm from her hand. A signet ring. *Your* signet ring. Pulled from your father's dead hands, it is the only one of his jewels you kept. The embossed Shark riding on waves that are the embellishments of a coronet. Your last link to a family you never knew.

As you slide it into place, covering the exposed skin on your finger, you know, whatever else your crew could find for themselves, you have been paid in full.

Now is not the time for the gratitude in your heart. A grotesque figure in stained white robes awkwardly lunges towards the pier your ship had been moored at. It raises sets of arms and the direction of your drift shifts back towards the shore until one of the birds circling the abomination drops from the sky, as the Husked mage's bird had done. The figure screams as limbs fall still, shifting and changing no more — a frozen face remaining in place as two others twist around it, their own limbs still struggling against the weight of their fallen compatriot. The motion of the water has brought you close enough to be seen, and to be heard.

"How do you like the sound of your families screaming as their home burns?" you shout across the bay. "How do you like the sound of their anger? This is defeat. It is rebellion. War breeds both. Learn to stomach the taste of them. You will know them both again."

The two voices of the God-Child demand to know how you fooled them — how their deviant proxy had not seen your thoughts, as if magery is the only means of manipulation.

They are new to defeat, and so you explain theirs: so used to their own power, they had underestimated you. No more, no less. They turn men into monsters to sate their own need for secrecy and expect to pay no price for it. They are lucky — they will not know what the blood of near two hundred innocent people looks like this night. The city burns, their navy is as good as scuttled, and they have been robbed of anything of value, but there has been enough death. "Slaughter is not the only way to keep a secret."

Around you, the ships who have escaped the blazes unharmed slip into the water with crews too small to man them. The crack of splitting timbers echoes across the water as your earlier observations bear fruit. You signal to your hidden crew who let the sails catch the breeze. *Golden Harvest* surges forward for the freedom of the sea, dancing in the faint wind.

You and the three beside you take your bows and the ember arrows and nock, aiming for the closest ships. The Yannish bows send your small volleys further than can be returned. As you reach the harbour entrance the Isian ships begin to catch, blocking the narrow route out for the others. You leave the three to continue the assault as you slip below to the hold where

Toram waits, soaked and shivering in the night cold now he is free of the water. He embraces you, and you sink into the wet of him for just a moment as he showers kisses soft as spray on your face. You pull away. Not yet; you still have work to do.

The last Isian ships will not give chase for long. Even beyond their incompetent design and build, Toram, with his inability to drown, has sabotaged them all from beneath the waves. They are taking on more water than they can handle. All you need now is time.

The pair of you carry the crates that had given you such cause for concern in the heat of the day — a backup should your crew have deserted you after all. If Isia had managed to board, they would have triggered the rigged torch and the crates of fine dusts and barrels of pitch oil would have taken the ship.

The true secret to manipulating the Isian mages had been to rely on the truth. You *had* given your crew the choice to leave after hearing your plans. They *had* left you weeks ago, taking a smuggler's route into Isia, leaving you to sail to Ide alone and underpowered. You had not known if they would come for you until the bells had started ringing.

You will never tell Klaudai that the pain of revival had hidden the tears of relief when you had seen her face.

You and Toram dump the contents of the crates into your wake; the flours and sacks of sawdust thicken the water before the pitch oil slicks over the top. Once you are clear, another volley of ember arrows sets the slurry alight, blocking the last possible progress of the Isian navy.

With that, you are finally free. It will take time for Isia to rebuild their navy, and now they must also contend with their own civil unrest. That should give you enough time to spread the word of their true threat. Isia wishes to step into the world with a blade to sharpen. You intend to let them find out exactly how civilisation deals with the nightmares they create. You will have to be careful to avoid becoming the example.

In the week before you reach the rest of your crew, you clean up, shave and let your filthy clothes sink to the bottom of the ocean. Almost a respectable man again.

You make plans of the places you will warn, and how to bring such an outlandish story to important people without proof or the ability to leave your ship. You work the others hard to bring *Golden Harvest* back to some small level of repair and through the work they share the stories of how they brought down a country.

The weeks you spent sailing alone, they had told any Isian who would listen — and understand- what their country was doing in their name; describing the battle with the Yannish, the drowning of your own people. The murder of the boy who condemned your actions. The rest of the time they plundered what they could, shipping their treasures out on river barges through the smuggling routes, leaving Klaudai to focus on finding your own stolen goods.

The day you arrived in Ide, Klaudai, Jacen and Lyam had worked quickly. They started fires and used them to rouse the people to rebellion as they spied on the empty warehouse. Keeping an eye on you.

When the priest-mage had not stopped his abuse of your body in his rage, Klaudai had brought the building down. She had not yet experimented your abomination with limb removal and suspected the head would have been a poor place to start.

Some of the time is put to easing the pinings of Toram

and the quieter longings of Klaudai — giving yourself over to the relief their company brings you, allowing their touches to anchor you a little firmer to someone you do not intrinsically hate.

All the while you watch for any Isian vessel determined to give chase. The waters stay clear.

The reunion with Kyrel and Salva and their stolen river barges laden with precious valuables is joyous as you welcome your family home. When you are done, *Golden Harvest* sits heavy and happy in the water. Drinks and the bold confidences of success and celebration flows freely. You still mourn all you have lost, but these people, here and now? They are family.

The morning brings you back to wakefulness in a warm tangle of limbs with a peace of mind you have not felt in a long, long time.

It does not last.

Relieving yourself over the side, you notice you have a tail after all; an Isian river barge out in the choppy waters of the ocean, struggling against the push and pull. You finish your business, then take a closer look with a glass. When you see exactly what follows you, you turn away. Celebrations or no, there is a ship to run and reparations to make.

You intend to honour the promise that each person who sailed out with you will receive their share from the Isian raid. Few had families waiting, but all had something dear to them. You will chase that down in their name and in their honour.

It makes for a long day of cataloguing and appraising what you can; hours in the hold with ink spreading across your fingers. When others come to mention something out on the water, you do not even look. Like the shade of the Yannish ship, it is a mirage and is to be ignored.

Klaudai leans against a support, sucking her teeth at you as you sift through reams of coloured silks. She is not fooled by your act, as if she does not see you as captain.

"Being your lover does not mean I do not see the rank. I will never seek to undermine your authority," she says in response to your accusations. "Whether he lives or dies is of no concern to me, but I have not shut myself away to avoid making the choice, and you are running out of time. The barge will not last the night."

Your surgeon thinks she is right to make you question; she thinks she understands you. Should the man on the barge trailing behind drown it would be a mercy. Hunting you is his game. That he is so poorly prepared is a lesson he will only ever need to learn once.

Klaudai leaves you to your work, seeing to her own matters. If only her words would vanish as easily.

The barge has fallen further behind in the long hours since you had first spied it. It is sinking, its lone crew member struggling to stay afloat. The priest-mage, Resnah. He glows, through the dirt of smoke and blood he still wears, but without enough control to know that wind alone is not enough to sail safely.

He loved you with great passion. Enough that, even now, your new lovers cannot always banish the memory of him. He murdered you, with equal passion. He would do it again, as you would murder him in turn. Letting him drown is the only kind ending. He is not a good person.

"None of us are good people," Toram says, watching the dwindling shape of the mage's craft when you voice your thoughts. "We were all liars and thieves and murderers before you took us in. We will be those things again. Our pasts were not what were important to you, once." He rests a hand on yours.

"Klaudai's been talking to you."

"Or perhaps you are just easy to read, Fiaer," she says, coming to your other side, hand on your other.

"You both advocate for that man?" You shake free and gesture out over the water, unsure where this pity has come from. "After everything he has done to us? Everything he caused?" Have they so easily forgotten the last time one of his kind stepped on board? Perhaps that is it. Perhaps even from here, he controls your crew, seeking to undermine your command from afar.

Klaudai shakes her head and rests her hand on your chest, over your scars. Over your heart. "We're advocating for *this* one."

You look between them and swear, pulling yourself free. They say nothing more of it. It is with you the priest has been bandying hurts; the choices you have are yours alone to make.

He set you on this path, destroying your life. In exchange, you destroyed his. He murdered you. You should leave him to die and call it even. A logic even your father would approve of. You return to your work, calculating and double-checking the values of those who no longer call this place home, and Toram's words haunt you, a headache forming behind your eyes. Taking the ledger back to your quarters, the imprints on the walls of past hurts dig in under your skin as if they were freshly made again. Each one a fresh loss of someone who had nowhere else to go but here.

Kicking at the wall, you swear as you realise why you have been avoiding the problem of the priest-mage. He has nowhere else to go, nowhere else to belong. He told you these things himself before he killed you. Before you asked him to.

Passion born of a path diverted is no crime — and if it is, it is one you are both guilty of. To leave him to the sea would do nothing more than add his shade to the multitudes who haunt you already.

You stalk out, your mood black enough to make the Nightmare himself quake as you order the ship turned about, sailing back to the last place you had seen the barge.

Resnah clings to the last pieces of driftwood, his barge not even making it to full night. He looks up at the beacon you shine down onto him before slumping over his driftwood raft. He dares to beg you for clemency.

He is running for his life. Seeing you stand against the God-Child, for all his anger — for all his despair — had given him a fool's hope; you owe him nothing. He asks that you strike clean. Drowning scares him.

He denies that he is manipulating any of you now, twisting himself into your thoughts. He begs for death, not senselessness. Klaudai gives a small shake of her head from the shadows. She cannot see magery in action any more than you can, but she *can* see his exhaustion. He may be manipulating you, but it is with nothing more than words.

You chew your cheek, disliking your options.

To sail with you is a one-way transaction. He would never be free to walk the lands again. The things he knows, the things he believes — the powers he has — he is a danger, and you will not allow his poison to spread. After all, there are no gods, only abominations.

You intend to warn the world of Isia's intentions, and its threat. He will be a traitor and the work you would put him to is difficult and dangerous. It may kill him, but any use of his magery, trickery, deception or deceit leaves no room for doubt. Unlike you, he would not be returning to life afterwards. If he cannot face those limitations, you will do as he asks. Your aim with a bow is true.

To his credit, he deliberates before agreeing to your limits, making you a hesitant group of eight, well aware of the wild animal in their midst.

You sail first to Yana, offering reparations for the loss of their ship and their people, and to warn them of the danger of sending more trade to Isia. Your messages fall to indifference and mockery. They take the blood money, but your word is worth nothing. The word of an abomination cannot be trusted.

They do not have the details, turning you into a story to your face, but even rumours alarm you. You flee before they take your life and confirm their suspicions.

Even when you journey to the places people know you, they hunt you down. Word is spreading at such impossible speeds. *Golden Harvest* is the fastest ship you know. The news *cannot* move faster than you do.

Resnah has never stopped you speaking about the dangers Isia presents with its rampant use of magery. Equally, he has never volunteered any information until your frustration causes the shadow to the man terrified to trust to rear up, once again working through the bonds that keep him anchored down — the paranoia that defined your father fitting across you like a well tailored jacket.

In doing so, he sides himself against his own people. "As if I could ever go back," he says with a shrug.

Isia may be a secretive country, and proud to many faults, but it has not been disinterested in the world around it. Many countries have Isian spies in prominent positions, all of them connected to the God-Child, able to hear and act on their thoughts and wishes and desires. A link to something divine.

The God-Child will have warned their puppets about you in an attempt to strip your power. After all, what is the word of an abomination worth?

Over the next few months, you do what you can to undermine the spies' efforts, and when that fails, you lean into it. As you travel, your story grows, and some of it is true.

It seems Isia has never discovered the tactics of your raid, and so you use them again to take what you fancy from those who refuse to entertain you until you earn the notoriety to stay wherever you wish, the list of ravaged towns and cities and captured prizes growing longer with every passing month.

There are those few who are interested in you despite your growing reputation, or because of it, who come to you to sate their curiosity, and more. Lovers who come and go like the tides, as Klaudai and Toram do when they take off to the comforts of land before returning to you, always. There is only one who stays with you on those lonely evenings where your family walk where you cannot, but he says nothing, keeping his distance, though you are aware of his hungry eyes.

You miss the land, sometimes, but *Golden Harvest* has always truly been your home, your heart. That you are bound together is natural.

Where the civilised lands send ships to hunt you, they fail, unable to combat your speed, nimbleness or the reach of your plundered Yannish weapons.

When they do, they cannot kill a man who will not stay dead. Those who survive encountering you are sent on with a warning and embarrassment filling their sails.

It makes you a rich man, but you have no need for a retirement fund. You will never leave the water. Instead, it goes to keep *Golden Harvest* in good condition and well supplied. Once your crew are paid, you split what is left for the reparation funds that never seem to end, each encounter leaving more names to chase. It is a small token, but while you are so many things, you have always tried not to be a *bad* man. Driven, ruthless, but one you can face every morning in your own reflection. It is not always simple, but there are ways to ease the difficulty.

You still take on those who have nowhere else to go, mostly those with secrets like yours, to risk sailing with an abomination — the Shark from the East as you are known now. Some become family, while others are just passing faces, much as it always has been.

When you are free from fighting and looting and their aftermaths, you follow whispers on the wind: your sister. The child your father had wanted more than he had ever wanted you. The child that would have healed his grief instead of reminding him of it. A part of you is still afraid to believe she lives and is out there somewhere.

On the first anniversary of Resnah's rescue, you join him on the night watch. A year as prisoner on this ship has been hard. Even you have struggled to adapt. You have not needed the complaints from your small family to know you must now deal with the ex-priest.

He has done well, learning of the world and his demoted place within it, but he still clings to the notion that his attractions make him deviant, unforgivable. His growing acts of self-punishment are causing discomfort you cannot let stand. You have all worked hard to make this a safe place for the unwanted and the unloved to risk on one man's misery.

Besides, you have learned much about magery in the last

year. If that night in the Esian tavern had been nothing more than manipulation, your own thoughts of him would have evaporated with the dawn, or shortly after. You have needed your own time to process that. He is awkward as you watch him work.

"You are a jealous man, Resnah. It needs to stop. I have never belonged to just one person, and I never will. You cannot have me all to yourself."

It is a warning, as well as a boundary. Your ex-priest has the skills to be a formidable warrior, with more training and experience, but your money would always be on Klaudai and Toram if either of them felt they could not have you too. The ex-priest splutters as he tries to find the words. He has not... he does not... "I took your life," he stammers. "You cannot want..."

"And I took yours. Yet here we are, side by side, united in our mission. You have worked hard to pay for your many wrongs against me, but I will not risk this ship, or my own happiness, on your jealousies when they are so easily fixed."

He is confused, hesitant, but does not resist as you bring his head towards yours, fingers tangled in his hair. The taste of salt on his lips matches yours. It is a gentle kiss, a promise of more, should he need it, but with no expectation. You let him go and leave him to his watch. "I will not belong *only* to you, Resnah."

When you next reach a port that will not dare turn you away, your crew take their shore leave with enthusiasm, money to spend and fun to be had. You, as is your way now, remain on board, settling into place with a book to see the evening by when a knock on your door announces a visitor.

You do not belong to any one person, and never will, but

there are quiet evenings now and then when the man who killed you can have you all to himself.

Near two years after venturing east, your reparations are almost paid and your warnings are as spread as far as you manage. You take to Keset in the cold of winter to plant your crew among the city of ships; seeking targets for the upcoming trade season. You are also following a rumour that your sister may be here somewhere. You do not expect to find her amongst all these people, but at least you can say you have tried.

The young guard sent to check your manifest, fodder for the Shark of the East, makes no secret of the deep longing in his posture every time he approaches your ship, and you do not need the request from Klaudai to offer him a place if he wishes one.

The guard does not answer immediately, taking his time to consider over days. It is then that you realise he has another tail: an old woman and a younger. It is the younger that takes your interest.

She is unlike you in almost every way; short, and leaning to fat of a plentiful, life. She smiles often, and her laughter is a bright thing in the cold sharpness of the winter. Your sister. It is in the way she stands, the shape of her face — a softer version of yours. It is in the same dark hair, though yours is outgrown and hers is plaited in the Esian fashion. It is in the way she looks like your father, a shade you had not expected to see. Resnah confirms it, and even Klaudai admits there is a familiarity about her that reminds the surgeon of you. A shared essence — two branches of the same tree.

Without thinking, you risk everything to set foot on the cold cobbled ground, chasing after them, begging a moment of their time as the deep pressure in your chest warns you of your recklessness, gasping out your words as your abomination takes hold, coughing out water as they move out of your way, alarmed by your enthusiasm and your condition. Toram, chasing after you, pulls you back towards the ship before you die on the streets, Klaudai charges forward in your stead but by the time you have recovered, the women are gone, your chance lost.

When Klaudai returns it is with mixed news. She has explained the reason for your chase, to your quarry. Your sister, knowing only your reputation, is hesitant. She knows she is Nionese by birth; she has never been curious about her birth parents, happy in her Esian life. The older woman, the Isian renegade, is more inclined to accept your word, but demands a proof that cannot be forged.

You agree, though you warn her, through Klaudai as proxy, that the safest place you know is your ship. She is welcome aboard, and no harm will come to her, but you cannot come ashore — not more than five hundred feet, which would take you barely past the docks in a place of Keset's size.

And so, it is here in the confines of your father's old study, twenty years after he had thought his daughter lost, amid the gouges of the unforgotten — an imprint of their being on the only place they have ever belonged, the only place you have ever belonged — where Mother Kiera looks into your mind: into your memories. She sees the priest, praying.

She believes you.

I believe you.

Chapter Five

I drop the magery, returning us half-blended back into two distinct people. Enough time has passed that the heavy lamps are now the only source of light. I sink into the chair, exhausted, a venomous headache forming, fuelled by a dangerous nausea.

The child in front of me still leans against the desk, still gripping hard, his head bowed. Tears fall, silent, and he makes no move to either dry them, or dramatise them.

"I thought time and distance had numbed the pain," he says, almost in a whisper. "I did not mean to subject you to that, Mother Kiera."

He wipes his face with the palm of his hand, leaving his eyes red and watery. His jaw twitches as he, even now, tries to hold himself together. This child. This scared boy thrown back into his worst pains as if they were happening now.

I had not meant to torture the boy; I had not known the depths to which I would see into his mind, and the rawness he is experiencing is devastating. The relived hurt and betrayal and the fine line he walks between giving in to the anger he still nurses, giving into the grief the way his father did, or trusting to the heart that gave rise to such pains in the first place. The heart that leads him to paying for his crimes even as he commits them; the heart that made it so easy for his father to abuse him.

The elder Fiaer Dradorn had been a harsh man when I had met him. Anyone who seeks to tame the ocean must be as harsh as it is, but also as forgiving. From the way he treated his son, he lost sight of that after Nion burned.

Mother is an Esian title, and the younger Fiaer means it with respect when he uses it, but I am also a mother, and this boy hurts in so many ways. I pry myself off the chair and bundle him into my arms, humming a soft lullaby we both know he is familiar with.

I can see why he has fed his reputation on these experiences. It forces a gap between him and them. Him and his two sides. A life built on secrets and lies to keep the man inside safe, as if lies are not already the things we tell ourselves to remain human.

When he dries his eyes again, once again boxing his mind up to become the Fiaer Dradorn of legend and title; fearsome predator of the waters, only ever a monstrous abomination, I tell him as much of his sister's story as I have right to.

The rumours of a world-breaker present on the night Nion burned were correct, though I had nothing to do with the fate of the nation. Led there on my own personal path, I had been a passing stranger to the palace estate when the fires broke out. A woman had pressed her infant daughter into my arms and begged me to take her to safety as she took up arms to defend her home. I had done so and she had grown up much loved with my daughter for a mother. I had never known if her true parents had survived.

Granted a wandering spirit, clearly a family trait, she travels with me and seems quite content with her choices.

I am no earth mage, able to see the essence of a person or the ties that bind them to others, but I trust Dradorn's surgeon would not have led him astray, even if the physical resemblances were not so obvious. Enough variation to have different mothers, but close enough to share the looks of their father, once it is pointed out.

I am no fire mage, able to see or experience the shades of the dead, but as I speak, the tension in the room changes as if the lingering shade of his father is finally put to rest. Perhaps it has been.

And I am no water mage, able to ease the emotions that pass through his heart, colouring his thoughts and his expressions as he processes the story of another life he has so long sought.

"Father wanted her to live this life with him," he says. "If she lived at all, I wanted her to be safe and well and happy, out of storms and battles, living the life she chooses to. It is a balm to have that wish fulfilled."

He looks to his bare feet. The things he has done will not endear him to anyone, nor does he expect it. Even if twenty years was not twenty years too long, he does not want to taint her life with the association of abominations like him. But, should she ever need him for any reason, at any time, he will be there.

He sees me out of his chambers, that boyish grin plastered back into place as he emerges into the public sphere of his own cultivated family. A ship of abominations. Outlanders all. And he takes care of his own.

He asks Klaudai, who remains at her post maintaining our privacy, to take a few of the others and escort me back to my lodgings. Keset is dangerous enough in the daylight, and that has long since made way to the long winter nights. He does not doubt my ability to protect myself, but he would rather limit the chances I would need to. A sign of good will. He turns back to his quarters before I have left the ship, seeking privacy — the show to so few already taxing him, those wounds I have opened far from healed.

It is all I can hope that the knowledge his father's quest is over will speed the easing this time around, and whether he knows it or not, he has offered me a means to help him.

Resnah is right. I am a deserter from Isia and the threat it presents is one I take seriously. I can go places Fiaer Dradorn and his crew cannot. I can combat the danger in different ways, and it *does* need fighting.

I beg a moment of time from the earth mage surgeon, looking for a face I know intimately now. I clock the Isian air mage on the head with my staff. "Who are you to call me a crone?" I state, switching to Trade for the benefit of the crew, the words clumsy after so long exchanging familiar Esian with the captain.

The crew laughs as Resnah flushes and give us space for the reaming of an old woman to an insolent youth. As I speak, I offer him a line in his mind to take — a minor magic — in an older language, one I have not spoken since I was younger than this boy here. The language of my childhood still comes easily and, committed to the role of traitor, the boy tells me everything he knows about the God-Child and their movements, even two years out of time.

In exchange, I give him the one thing no one else here can. The knowledge, and the example, that the agony of separation from the Divine Link *will* get easier with time. He nods once as he realises what I am offering and the link between us drops before his thoughts and emotions become uncontrollable. I have had enough of that for one day.

Klaudai thanks me as she escorts me through the dark streets, part of a pack to ward off slight-finger robbers and worse. There are some hurts she can not heal. Whatever comes from this, her captain has a chance to form a scar now. It is hard to take comfort in that; the weight of his mind still lingering in my own. He does not yet believe he deserves to.

My granddaughter waits for me, impatient, at our lodgings. She is full of questions I do not have the energy to answer, and she grumbles as I leave them hanging, finally allowing myself to feel the exhaustion of sharing a life.

Rain spatters. A light shower tainted with traces of magic. There will be inexplicable happenings tonight. A minor backlash for minor magic, as most are.

The windows of our lodging look out over the harbour, and there, on the very edge of the docks, a small ship sits alone, her beacons lit against the night. A dim light shines from the windows of the captain's quarters. Sleep will come easily to me, tinged with nightmares that are not mine. It will not come easily to all of us.

Fiaer Dradorn does not expect his sister in his life. He sees himself in too maligned a light for that, but Shana Illame — Shana Dradorn — has never been one to leave her curiosity unfulfilled. It is why she travels with me; always seeking something, always looking for those she can help. She and her brother have more in common than he expects, and it will be good for both of them to learn of it.

I wish I *had* known before. Twenty years *is* too long, and despite his apparent deathlessness, men like Fiaer Dradorn do not often live long lives. I shall not expose his weakness, but a man can only gather so many enemies before one is likely to stumble on it for themselves.

For now, there is an old shark in the waters around Keset. Long may she stay safe.

Discover Luna Novella in our store:

https://www.lunapresspublishing.com/shop

Lightning Source UK Ltd.
Milton Keynes UK
UKHW041513301222
414628UK00002B/13